Science Educator's Guide to
Laboratory
Assessment

Science Educator's Guide to Laboratory Assessment

By

Rodney Doran

Fred Chan

Pinchas Tamir

Carol Lenhardt

NATIONAL SCIENCE TEACHERS ASSOCIATION

NATIONAL SCIENCE TEACHERS ASSOCIATION

Claire Reinburg, Director
Judy Cusick, Associate Editor
Carol Duval, Associate Editor
Betty Smith, Associate Editor

ART AND DESIGN Linda Olliver, Director
    Cover image, Photodisc
NSTA WEB Tim Weber, Webmaster
PERIODICALS PUBLISHING Shelley Carey, Director
PRINTING AND PRODUCTION Catherine Lorrain-Hale, Director
PUBLICATIONS OPERATIONS Erin Miller, Manager
sciLINKS Tyson Brown, Manager

NATIONAL SCIENCE TEACHERS ASSOCIATION
Gerald F. Wheeler, Executive Director
David Beacom, Publisher

Science Educator's Guide to Laboratory Assessment
    NSTA Stock Number: PB145X2
    ISBN: 0-87355-210-5
    Library of Congress Catalog Card Number: 98-84914
    Printed in the USA by Victor Graphics
    Printed on recycled paper

About the Authors

Rodney Doran has been a professor of science education at the State University of New York at Buffalo's Graduate School of Education since 1969. He previously taught physics, Earth science, and math at a Minnesota high school. He holds degrees from the University of Minnesota (BS, 1961), Cornell University (MST, 1966), and the University of Wisconsin (PhD, 1969). Dr. Doran was U.S. Associate Coordinator for the Second International Science Study, and received the State University of New York Chancellor's Award for Excellence in Teaching in 1998. He has published articles on assessment in *Science and Children*, *Science Scope*, and *The Science Teacher*, and was the author of the National Science Teachers Association 1981 book, *Basic Measurement and Evaluation in Science Instruction*.

Fred Chan is a vice principal with the Toronto, Ontario, District School Board. He previously taught physics, chemistry, and biology in Guyana and the Caribbean. He holds degrees from McMaster University (BS, 1973), the University of Toronto (BEd, 1975), Niagara University (MS in Ed, 1984), and the University of Bridgeport (MS, 1989), and he expects to receive his PhD from the University at Buffalo. He is a 1996 recipient of the Prime Minister of Canada's Award for Excellence in

Science Teaching. He has written articles on assessment for *The Science Teacher* and serves on the manuscript review panel for that journal. He has also served on the National Science Teachers Association's Committee on International Science Education.

Pinchas Tamir is professor emeritus at the School of Education at Hebrew University of Jerusalem in Israel. He was also director of the Israel Science Teacher Center, where he helped introduce BSCS biology to Israel and develop the Israel Matriculation Exam for high school biology. He was Israel's research coordinator for the Second International Science Study and the Third International Science Study, and he is a visiting scholar at dozens of universities around the world. He holds degrees from Hebrew University of Jerusalem (MS, 1966) and Cornell University (PhD, 1968).

Carol Lenhardt is a retired middle school science teacher. She also was an adjunct faculty member at Buffalo State College and the University of Buffalo. She holds degrees from the University of Rochester (BS, 1956), Syracuse University (MS, 1960), and the University of Buffalo (PhD, 1994) She is a past president and fellow of the Science Teachers Association of New York State (STANYS) and coauthor of *Alternative Assessment in Science, Grade 8*.

Contents

Science Educator's Guide to Laboratory Assessment

Preface

Welcome to the second, enlarged edition of *Science Educator's Guide to Laboratory Assessment*. This version contains fifteen new assessment tasks, and like the first edition, it presents multiple assessment formats, strategies, models, and templates appropriate for inquiry activities in the grades 7–12 science classroom and laboratory, as well as outdoors. These assessment formats and strategies are based on the most recent research on assessment, instruction, and learning and include many practical examples you can adapt for use in your classroom.

Background: The Importance of Assessment

As science teachers, we face a continual challenge of assessing what students know, are able to do, and value in learning science. Assessment provides insights into students' rates of progress in conceptual understanding, reinforces productive learning habits, and validates learning activities. Students need recurring, systematic, and regular feedback to understand their own strengths and capabilities in learning and to identify areas for improvement. We now are aware that increased use of formative assessment in science classrooms to modify teaching and to provide feedback to students has powerful positive effects on student learning. A well-designed assessment program, by providing regular and systematic feedback, goes a long way in helping students reflect on their learning. Hence the importance of assessment reform.

The assessment phase of the teaching-learning process is our primary way of "keeping score." Teachers measure how well students learn new concepts and skills, administrators and policymakers measure the effectiveness of teaching strategies and educational and program policies, and parents use grades and marks to monitor their children's progress in school. Also, as a society we use data from assessments to compare our national progress in education with that of other nations.

There is a growing tension between the rich, authentic assessments that the science standards suggest and the increased use of large-scale, high-stakes testing. Science teachers need to come to grips with how much we teach "to the test," and in so doing, how much we narrow the curriculum. We need to balance the requirements of high-stakes testing with designing assessments that provide students with varied opportunities to develop competencies in science and to demonstrate what they know and can do.

Assessment has become increasingly important during the past decade, as educators and policymakers seek reforms to our educational system in response to national and international priorities and challenges. Educators concerned with weak science achievement, low levels of science literacy, and poor international test scores have undertaken major reforms in science instruction. Increased international economic competition has reinforced the importance of excellence in science education as a fundamental priority for every nation to maintain its competitiveness. New insights into how children learn and advances in learning theory, such as constructivism and the identification of alternative and prior conceptions of learning science, have added impetus to assessment reform. As a result, there is a call for widespread use of alternative assessments, and a shift away from textbook- and teacher-centered approaches to instruction.

These reform efforts, embodied in the *National Science Education Standards* (NRC 1996) and in reform documents such as *Project 2061: Benchmarks for Science Literacy* (AAAS 1993), call for widespread reform in science instruction and assessment. Old teaching strategies and assessment formats based on behaviorist theories, such as rote memorization and paper-and-pencil examinations, are being replaced with holistic, constructivist approaches that promote problem solving and higher-level thinking. These sophisticated assessments demand the use of a variety of teaching strategies to help students develop their ability to learn and to solve problems in "real-world" situations and contexts.

The Meaning of Inquiry

Inquiry has been and continues to be a concept near and dear to the hearts of science teachers. Bybee (2000) traces the long history of inquiry at least back to John Dewey in the early 1900s. Inquiry has been in and out of favor since then, depending on the reform efforts popular at a particular time.

One source of confusion about inquiry is that it is both a methodology of how scientists investigate natural phenomena *and* a methodology espoused for facilitating the engagement of students with materials and questions. To add to the confusion, process goals (to include inquiry) have been cited as "content outcomes" since the 1960s (Parker and Rubin 1966). This view is continued with the *National Science Education Standards* (NRC 1996), which uses *inquiry* in two ways: as abilities students should develop to be able to design and conduct scientific investigations and as the understandings they should gain about the nature of professional scientific inquiry.

Although inquiry is a mode of gathering information in many academic/scholarly fields, there are some unique aspects of *scientific* inquiry. In many of the science curriculum projects from the 1960s, inquiry was largely accepted as a collection of science processes (e.g., observing, measuring, predicting, hypothesizing). Currently it is viewed as one set of tools to further the development of scientific explanation. For instance, the *Learning Standards for Mathematics, Science, and Technology* (New York State Education Department 1996) identifies three key ideas of scientific inquiry:

- The central purpose of scientific inquiry is to develop explanations of natural phenomena in a continuing, creative process.

- Beyond the use of reasoning and consensus, scientific inquiry involves the testing of proposed explanations involving the use of conventional techniques and procedures and usually requiring considerable ingenuity.

- The observations made while testing proposed explanations, when analyzed using conventional and invented methods, provide new insights into phenomena.

Other educators have treated inquiry as virtually synonymous with problem solving and/or critical thinking. Although there is much overlap among these concepts, it may be helpful to make the following distinctions: *inquiry* tends to focus on developing new information (relationships, concepts, principles); *problem solving* focuses on finding solutions to problems and is linked with technology; and *critical thinking*, also described as "rational reasoning," can be considered to be a set of cognitive strategies that include, for example, deduction and induction.

In this volume, when we refer to *inquiry* we mean *scientific inquiry*. One of the clearest descriptions of the term is from the *National Science Education Standards*:

> Scientific inquiry refers to the diverse ways in which scientists study the natural world and propose explanations based on the evidence derived from their work. Inquiry also refers to the activities of students in which they develop knowledge and understanding of scientific ideas, as well as an understanding of how scientists study the natural world. (NRC 1996, 23)

Diagnostic, Formative, and Summative Assessment

The current view is that every assessment consists of three interconnected elements—observation, interpolation, and cognition—that form a triangle. Each element is connected to and dependent on the others. Assessment tasks are designed around cognition or theories of learning. Student accomplishments provide observations and evidence for an interpretation of how much they know and can do (NRC 2001).

As we design assessment based on current theories of learning, it is important to clarify the meanings of *diagnostic*, *formative*, and *summative* assessment. The National Research Council's Committee

on Classroom Assessment and the *National Science Education Standards* (NRC 2001) suggest that we ask the following questions to determine what type of assessment we are using:

- Where are we presently? (diagnostic assessment)
- How can we get there? (formative assessment)
- Have we arrived? (summative assessment)

Diagnostic assessment is the use of qualitative and quantitative data and information to determine where students are in terms of their knowledge and skills. The use of this assessment information tells students which areas they are strong in and which areas need academic intervention. This kind of assessment can be informal—for example, interviews, paper-and-pencil tests, and previous academic records. Diagnostic assessment is "low stakes" and answers the question "Where are we presently?"

Formative assessment is also "low stakes" and gives feedback to students about where they are in terms of their knowledge and skills. These assessments are informal and ongoing. The feedback to students should provide a roadmap for "How can we get there?" Using the roadmap, students try new ideas, look at problems differently, and discuss problems with peers and teachers. The roadmap takes us to our destination, which is the standards set forth by your state or school district.

Of our destination, we naturally ask, "Have we arrived?" That is where summative assessments enter the picture. These are culminating assessment tasks that occur at the end of a unit, topic, or course. They are considered "high-stakes" (more about this term below) because decisions regarding further study, jobs, and academic standing are based on them. Summative assessments can be paper-and-pencil format or can be a collection of student work collected over time using a portfolio format. Summative assessments are of the highest stakes when the assessment data are used for credentialing purposes such as the awarding of a high school diploma.

The key distinction among these terms is the use and timing of the assessment data. Diagnostic and formative assessments are intended to support student learning. Summative assessment data are used to certify student accomplishments in terms of their knowledge and skills.

High-Stakes Tests

A few more comments on high-stakes tests are appropriate here. Just what are such tests (or assessments) from the point of view of a classroom science teacher? The key to answer this question is to determine the purpose of the assessment. When assessment results are used to give rewards to those students who obtain high test scores, then such assessments (tests) are "high stakes." (An unwelcome result may be that those students who have low-test scores are denied educational opportunities.) Examples of common high-stakes tests are the SAT and the ACT. A recent trend in high-stakes testing is the use of state tests for graduation decisions, such as the awarding of high school diplomas. It is important that these tests satisfy test measurement principles of reliability, validity, and fairness (National Research Council 1999; AERA, APA, and NCME 1999) and that appropriate accommodations be made for English language learners and students with disabilities.

The classroom science teacher's inclination can be to " teach to the test" in order to maximize students' opportunities to obtain a high test score and prevent any sanctions against the school or the teacher's performance. When the majority of class time is spent practicing and reviewing sections of previous tests, however, the curriculum will tend to narrow. In the context of high-stakes testing, good teachers know they can facilitate student learning in a variety of engaging ways (including through the use of the assessment tasks in this book), while familiarizing students with the item format and cognitive demands of the tests. In this way students are provided with the "opportunity to learn" in preparation for the tests.

It should be noted that high-stakes tests are subject to legal challenges when the test scores are used inappropriately. Test results should not be used for purposes for which the test was not designed. For example, the use of tests designed for program evaluation may be inappropriate for making decisions regarding student accountability. Increasingly, test results are being used for more than one purpose. Such use imposes limits on the consequential validity of the test. In addition, the use of the results of a single test as the sole criterion for a high-stakes decision is problematic (AERA, APA, and NCME 1999).

Professional Development

The authors share the belief that the ongoing professional development of teachers is a priority to bring alive the *National Science Education Standards*. We believe that teachers must be well grounded in their assessment knowledge and be able to use this knowledge in their classroom practice.

In the past, professional development has largely consisted of the one-day workshop where experts use "show and tell" methods to inform teachers about the latest teaching trend. We believe that lasting change in assessment practices will not come about using that disjointed approach. Teachers are professionals; they are active learners who know best what they want to know; and they see their professional development as continuous and ongoing. Our vision for effective assessment-focused professional development for science teachers is that its design must be consistent with appropriate learning theories for adults and must involve the professional's construction of meaning and knowledge (Loucks-Horsley, et al. 1998). School districts and school administrators need to provide support in the form of time and opportunity for science teachers to meet and collaborate in ways to inform and improve classroom assessment practice.

We offer this book, now in its second edition, as a resource to assist science teachers in their ongoing professional development. Many of the ideas will challenge fundamental philosophical beliefs about learning and education. We hope that our colleagues will engage in collaborative discussions to advance their assessment practices. We envisage science teachers working with colleagues in their own schools, school districts, and professional organizations to gain expertise in assessment practices that work with their students.

Organization and Use of This Book

This book has two sections, followed by three appendices. Chapters 1-4 discuss assessment theory, research, and use, and

Chapters 5-8 contain model assessments grouped by science discipline. The following provides a brief description of what you will find in each of the book's chapters.

Chapter 1 discusses the *National Science Education Standards* and recent research suggesting that instruction move from a primarily behaviorist approach toward constructivist models of learning and instruction. Chapter 2 addresses practical issues related to designing performance assessments that are aligned with the *National Standards*. Chapter 3 discusses the benefits and drawbacks of various assessment formats, ranging from short, focused tasks to extended investigations. Chapter 4 provides suggestions for using rubrics to establish reliable and consistent scoring of assessments, and for using data to improve both the overall science program and the performance of students.

Chapters 5–8 are disciplinary chapters that provide model assessment examples from biology, chemistry, Earth science, and physics. Most of these examples are complete tasks with information about measuring the skills appropriate for each task, time requirements, and preparing materials and equipment. There are also directions and answer sheets for students, a list of required materials and equipment, and scoring guidelines for evaluating student responses.

The disciplinary assessment tasks are grouped into three sections:

- Skills Tasks: relatively short, and focus on a few specific process skills.

- Investigations: focus on a wide variety of skills. They typically require one or two 40-45-minute class periods for completion. Students can plan and design an investigation, conduct an experiment, and communicate their findings and conclusions.

- Extended Investigations: last for several 40-45-minute class periods and can require several weeks for completion. Extended investigations are examples of curriculum-embedded assessments that align closely with instruction.

You are invited to use these assessments as is, modify them for specific instructional programs or purposes, or use them as models or templates to design entirely new and innovative assessments.

Although the book's primary focus is on assessing student achievement in the classroom and laboratory, we also include suggestions and examples on using these assessments for program evaluation. Many of the examples also include suggestions for revisions, depending on the uses of the assessment and the availability of materials and equipment.

There are three Appendices: a glossary, the *National Science Education Standards* for assessment, and a complete bibliography consisting of works cited and other relevant assessment resources—especially those that emphasize hands-on inquiry activities.

You can use this book *à la carte* by taking as much or as little as you desire to assist you with your assessments. You may first wish to reacquaint or familiarize yourself with the *National Science Education Standards*, principles of assessment design, and the rationale for new formats of assessment that interface with your evolving instructional pedagogy. Chapters 1-4 and the Appendices are appropriate for these purposes. Once you are comfortable with these concepts, go to Chapters 5-8 and examine the specific assessment ex-

amples that are relevant to the science disciplines you teach.

This book is practical in its approach to assessment reform. The assessments with their scoring rubrics have been field-tested by "real" teachers in "real" science classrooms. We hope you find the book useful as a resource as you continue to implement the assessment standards. We also hope you try the assessments with your students, and suggest you modify and revise the tasks to fit your needs. Involving your students at appropriate times in peer and self-reflection will help to embed your assessments in instructional practices.

Works Cited

American Association for the Advancement of Science (AAAS). 1993. *Project 2061: Benchmarks in Science Literacy*. New York: Oxford University Press.

American Educational Research Association (AERA), American Psychological Association (APA), and National Council on Measurement and Education (NCME). 1999. *Standards for Educational and Psychological Testing*. Washington, DC: American Educational Research Association.

Bybee, R. 2000. Teaching Science as Inquiry. In Minstrell, J. and Van Zee, E., eds. *Inquiring into Inquiry Learning and Teaching in Science*. Washington, DC: American Association for the Advancement of Science.

Loucks-Horsley, S., Hewson, P. W., Love, N., and Stiles, K. E. 1998. *Designing Professional Development for Teachers of Science and Mathematics*. Thousand Oaks, CA: Corwin Press

National Research Council (NRC). 1996. *National Science Education Standards*. Washington, DC: National Academy Press.

———. 1999. *High Stakes Testing for Tracking, Promotion and Graduation*. Board on Testing and Assessment. Commission on Behavioral and Social Sciences and Education. Washington, DC: National Academy Press.

———. 2001. *Classroom Assessment and the National Science Education Standards*. Washington, DC: National Academy Press.

New York State Education Department, University of the State of New York. 1996. *Learning Standards for Mathematics, Science, and Technology*. Albany: New York State Education Department.

Parker, J. C., and Rubin, L. J. 1966. *Process as Content: Curriculum Design and the Application of Knowledge*. Chicago: Rand McNally.

U.S. Department of Education, Office of Civil Rights. 2000. The Use of Tests as Part of High-Stakes Decision-Making for Students: A Resource Guide for Educators and Policy-Makers. (available at *www.ed.gov/offices/OCR*)

sessment. J. Pellegrino, N. Chudowsky, and R. Glaser, eds. Washington, DC: National Academy Press.

National Science Teachers Association. 1992. *Scope, Sequence, and Coordination of Secondary School Science, Volume II: Relevant Research*. Arlington, VA: National Science Teachers Association.

Suggested Readings

American Association for the Advancement of Science (AAAS). 1989. *Project 2061: Science for All Americans*. New York: Oxford University Press.

Black, P., and Wiliam, D. 1998a. Inside the Black Box: Raising Standards through Classroom Assessment. *Phi Delta Kappan* 80 (2): 139–48.

———. 1998b. Assessment and Classroom Learning. *Assessment in Education* 5 (1): 7–74.

National Education Goals Panel. 1996. *The National Education Goals Report: Executive Summary-Commonly Asked Questions About Standards and Assessment*. Washington, DC: National Education Goals Panel.

National Research Council (NRC). 2001. *Knowing What Students Know: The Science and Design of Educational Assessments*. Committee on the Foundations of As-

Acknowledgments

When a project of this scope is completed, it is important to recognize the many people who have contributed to it. Without the support and acceptance of our families, this book would never have happened. The help and encouragement of Shirley Watt Ireton, who was director of NSTA's Special Publications division at the time the first edition was published, was crucial at every stage. Her initial suggestions for the book's focus were both wise and timely, and her continued involvement during all phases was essential. Thanks also to Chris Findlay and the entire Special Publications staff for all their hard work on the first edition and to Judy Cusick, who was the NSTA Press's project manager for the second edition. Linda Olliver designed the cover and drew the illustrations for this later edition. Catherine Lorrain-Hale coordinated production and printing for, and laid out, both the first and second editions.

Two funded projects provided many of the assessment tasks in this book. The University at Buffalo/National Opinion Research Center joint project (UB/NORC) project developed prototype exams for high school science courses. Darrell Bock and Michelle Zimowski of the University of Chicago's National Opinion Research Center developed the multiple-choice and open-ended items, while Rod Doran coordinated the laboratory tests at the University at Buffalo. Joan Boorman, Fred Chan, Nicholas Hejaily, and Diana Anderson focused on assessment tasks in separate fields. The New York Alternative Assessment in Science Project was a joint effort of the New York State Education Department and the University at Buffalo, producing a Teachers Guide and Collection of Tasks for grade 4, grade 8, Earth science, and biology. Douglas Reynolds, Robert Allers, and Susan Agruso were co-investigators. Dozens of teachers from western New York State helped revise and trial test the tasks presented here.

Audrey Champagne, Florence Juillerat, Cornelia Munroe, Mildred Barry, Burt Voss, Mary Kalen Romjue, Angelo Collins, Bill Williams, Lawrence Gilbert, Dwaine Eubanks, and Tony Bartley reviewed the manuscript as it progressed. Gouranga Saha and Jane Anzalone contributed in numerous ways. Special thanks to Lauri Di Matteo for single-handedly entering almost the entire contents of the book onto computer disks.

CHAPTER 1

A Rationale for Assessment

The Present State of Assessment

The roots of our current education system lie in the mass public school programs of the Industrial Revolution. The mechanized assembly lines and standardized processes that dominated that era found their way into education, where they remain deeply embedded today.

> Over most of this century, school has been conceived as a manufacturing process in which raw materials (youngsters) are operated upon by the educational process (machinery), some for a longer period than others, and turned into finished products. Youngsters learn in lockstep or not at all (frequently not at all) in an assembly line of workers (teachers) who run the instructional machinery. A curriculum of mostly factual knowledge is poured into the products to the degree they can absorb it, using mostly expository teaching methods. The bosses (school administrators) tell the workers how to make the products under rigid work rules that give them little or no stake in the process. (Rubba, et al. 1991)

This assembly-line approach relies heavily upon behaviorist learning theory, which is based on three main concepts: that complex learning can be broken into discrete bits of information; that students learn by making associations between different kinds of perceptions and experiences; and that knowledge is an accumulation of discrete facts and basic skills.

Under behaviorist learning, knowledge is "decomposable" and can be broken into its component parts without jeopardizing understanding or applicability. These decomposable skills can be learned separately using stimulus-response associations. In addition, students can learn knowledge out of context. In other words, if students demonstrate a skill in one context, they should be able to then demonstrate it in different contexts or situations. However, behaviorist learning theory does not address how discrete pieces of information are integrated into a coherent whole. Teachers must assume that students integrate this information elsewhere.

The behaviorist approach still plays a dominant role in schools, and results in learning that relies heavily on the memorization of factual information. In science education, the behaviorist legacy takes the form of teaching and learning that relies heavily on using textbooks as curriculum surrogates, and on having students memorize discrete bits of often unrelated science "factoids." Assessments aligned with these approaches use formats made up primarily of multiple-choice, true/false, and short-answer questions. Students focus on identifying the "right" answer, as opposed to developing inquiry skills and conceptual understanding.

As a result, our education system has fallen behind in preparing students to cope successfully with the challenges of an increasingly complex and sophisticated world, a world where scientific and technological skills have become significant avenues to success. Students need opportunities to develop problem-solving and interpersonal skills if they are to succeed in this global yet "smaller" world, where many diverse interest groups compete for increasingly scarce resources.

Science teachers are making these necessary "shifts" by implementing changes suggested by reform documents. We now use current findings from research in learning and research in science education to inform ourselves about exemplary practice. Our shifts are coupled with a move away from stimulus-response learning toward learning that is inquiry based and that focuses on previously learned science concepts, alternative conceptions, and conceptual change. Successful learning is context dependent, and is facilitated by interaction among peers. Our assessment reforms must be aligned with these instructional reforms.

The Constructivist Paradigm

A crucial aspect of this shift is to move toward "constructivist" paradigms in our design of science programs and assessments. The constructivist approach begins with a focus on what students already know about the world around them and on their understanding of this world. Using this as a base, educators work to help students develop methods for further educating themselves about the world. The end result is that students come away not only with scientific information but with an analytical way of thinking that they can apply to any number of situations in life.

Recent work in cognitive psychology suggests that meaningful learning occurs in context, and that some skills used in one context do not necessarily transfer to other contexts. Some cognitive skills are general and are used in a wide variety of academic and "real-world" tasks. On the other hand, other cognitive skills are context dependent, and apply to domain-specific knowledge and skills. There is an interface between the learning of cognitive skills and context. Some cognitive skills are transferable while others are domain specific (Perkins and Salomon 1989).

Constructivism underlies the *National Science Education Standards*, published by the National Research Council in 1996. The result of years of deliberations by educators, scientists, government officials, and a wide range of other participants, the *National Science Education Standards* view science as a process "in which students learn skills, such as observation, inference, and experimentation." Through inquiry-based learning, "students develop under-

Figure 1.1: Assessing the Ability to Inquire or the Ability to do Scientific Inquiry. *National Science Education Standards*, NRC, 1996.

Identify Questions and Concepts That Guide Scientific Investigations
- formulate a testable hypothesis
- demonstrate the logical connections between the scientific concepts guiding a hypothesis and the design of the experiment

Design and Conduct Scientific Investigations
- formulate a question to investigate
- develop a preliminary plan
- choose appropriate equipment
- take appropriate safety precautions
- clarify controls and variables
- organize and display data
- use evidence, apply logic, and construct arguments for proposed explanations

Use Technology and Mathematics to Improve Investigations and Communications
- use a variety of measuring instruments and calculators in scientific investigations
- use formulas, charts, and graphs for communicating results

Formulate and Revise Scientific Explanations and Models Using Logic and Evidence
- formulate models based upon physical, conceptual, and mathematical concepts
- use logic and evidence from investigations to explain arguments

Communicate and Defend Scientific Arguments
- use accurate and effective means of communication, including writing, following procedures, expressing concepts, and summarizing data
- use diagrams and charts to construct reasoned arguments

The *National Science Education Standards* envision change throughout the system.
The assessment standards encompass the following changes in emphases:

Less Emphasis On	More Emphasis On
Assessing what is easily measured	Assessing what is most highly valued
Assessing discrete knowledge	Assessing rich, well-structured knowledge
Assessing scientific knowledge	Assessing scientific understanding and reasoning
Assessing to learn what students do not know	Assessing to learn what students do understand
Assessing only achievement	Assessing achievement and opportunity to learn
End of term assessments by teachers	Students engaged in ongoing assessment of their work and that of others
Development of external assessments by measurement experts alone	Teachers involved in the development of external assessments

standing of scientific concepts; an appreciation of the 'how we know' what we know in science; understanding of the nature of science; skills necessary to become independent inquirers about the natural world; [and] the dispositions to use the skills, abilities, and attitudes associated with science." Figure 1.1 (page 3) provides an outline of standards for assessing a student's ability to inquire or undertake scientific inquiry.

Figure 1.2 shows the changing emphases needed to promote inquiry-based learning. As you can see, the *National Standards* focus on giving students a much greater role in defining problems, designing experiments, and analyzing results. Through this process, students gain the same exhilaration of discovery that practicing scientists experience in their work when they plan and conduct investigations.

Assessment's Changing Nature

As the nature of science education changes, so must our assessments. In general, assessment becomes a more integral part of the learning process, growing both broader and deeper to probe student un-

derstanding. It becomes broader in the sense that it encompasses more varied formats of assessment; it is deeper in terms of measuring more complex skills. As students carry out laboratory investigations that challenge them to increase their conceptual understanding, the distinction between assessment and instruction blurs into a seamless whole, and there is near perfect alignment with standards (outcomes and expectations), programs (instruction), and assessments. As we assess scientific thinking, science inquiry, and problem-solving skills, then we must change our instruction to provide students with opportunities to learn and practice these skills.

Figure 1.3 (page 5) depicts a congruence triangle where standards, instruction, and assessment interact in the planning and implementation of successful science programs. If any of the three dimensions does not clearly link or interface with the other dimensions, then we compromise the fairness, credibility, validity, and utility of the assessment. Figure 1.4 (page 5) provides a checklist that teachers and school administrators can apply to evaluate their assessment programs.

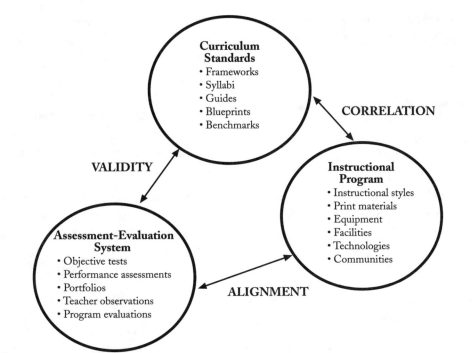

Figure 1.3: Congruence Triangle. Reynolds, et al., 1996.

Figure 1.4: Assessment Checklist.

Question	Yes	No
Do the school, district, or state curriculum guides and assessment frameworks incorporate the *National Science Education Standards*?		
Are the assessment standards relevant to local perspectives and issues?		
Are the assessment standards developmentally appropriate for the age of students?		
Are the assessment standards challenging to the academic capabilities of students?		
Are the instructional activities of teachers aligned with the assessment standards in use by the school or district?		
Can students distinguish between instruction and assessment?		
Are adequate materials available for student use in the laboratory?		
Are students informed of the criteria for success?		
Are students involved in the development of criteria for success?		
Are the science process skills and content outcomes being measured consistent with the standards in use?		
Do the assessment instruments reflect a variety of formats? Is the assessment system multifaceted?		

The Multifaceted Assessment System

Educators have traditionally made wide use of paper-and-pencil examinations, which have typically included multiple-choice, true/false, short-answer, and essay questions. Often these assessments are used primarily at the end of a course or instructional unit as a way of measuring overall student understanding of facts and concepts. The large majority of questions in these examinations or assessment formats tend to measure low-level cognitive skills.

With recent reforms, these assessments are being supplemented with a broad range of assessment tools designed to measure higher-level cognitive skills, such as problem-solving, inquiry, communication, and also interpersonal skills. These multifaceted tools can include a variety of assessment formats, as depicted in Figure 1.5.

These varying assessment formats are discussed in greater depth in Chapter 3. They can be used throughout the instructional process to promote student learning.

Figure 1.5: Multifaceted Assessment System. Adapted from Reynolds et al., 1996.

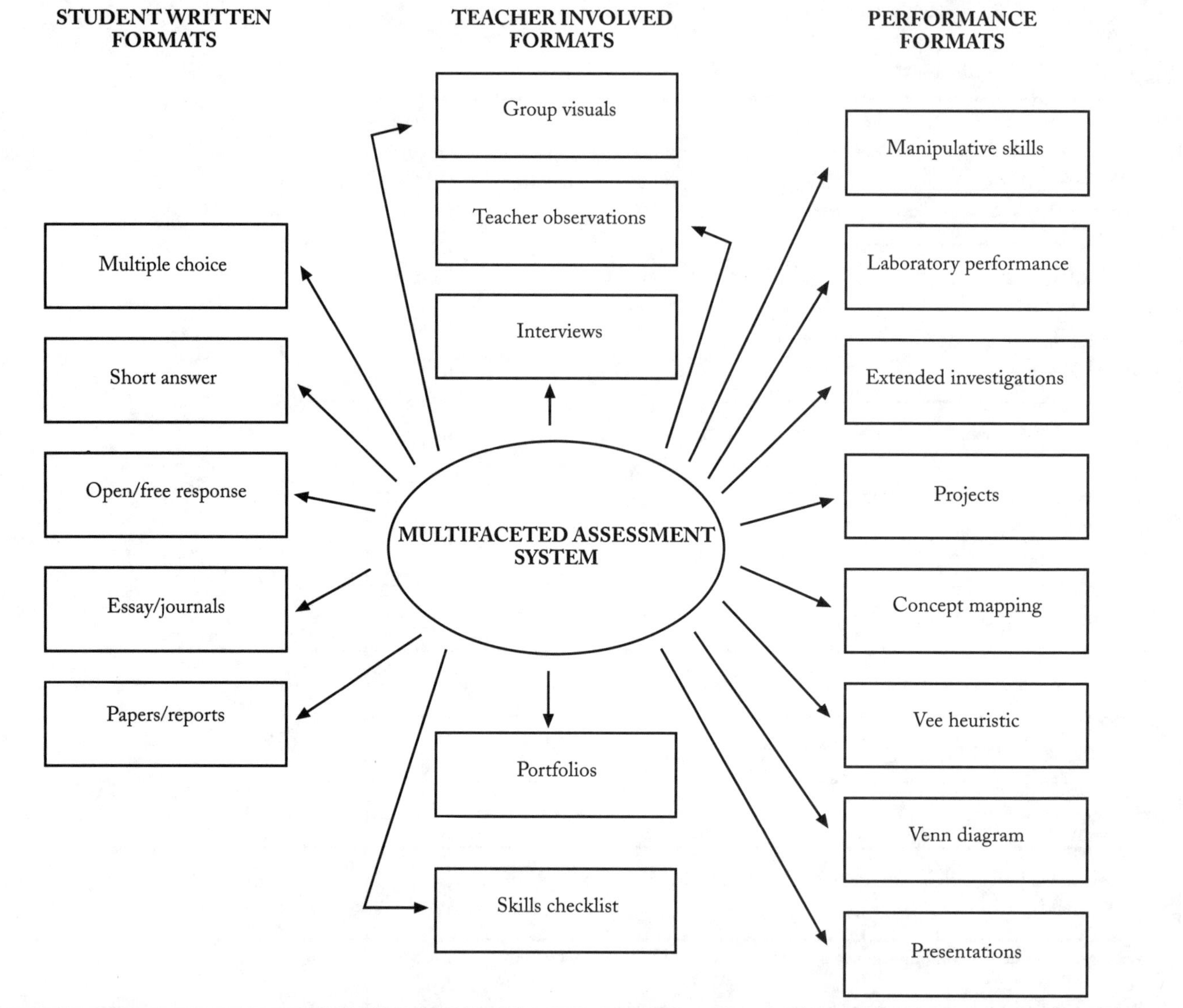

STUDENT WRITTEN FORMATS

- Multiple choice
- Short answer
- Open/free response
- Essay/journals
- Papers/reports

TEACHER INVOLVED FORMATS

- Group visuals
- Teacher observations
- Interviews
- Portfolios
- Skills checklist

MULTIFACETED ASSESSMENT SYSTEM

PERFORMANCE FORMATS

- Manipulative skills
- Laboratory performance
- Extended investigations
- Projects
- Concept mapping
- Vee heuristic
- Venn diagram
- Presentations

Most of these methods share a common benefit. As you measure student progress during implementation of your science program, you can use the data to adjust instruction and provide assistance to individual students as necessary. The data you collect can also help you adjust overall instructional strategies for use in future science classes.

Teachers can select their most appropriate teaching strategies that help students learn new concepts within the confines of their classroom environment. You can also use the most appropriate assessment formats and techniques to determine whether students have mastered new skills and understandings. Just as no one teaching strategy will cover every learning situation, no single assessment format can measure every aspect of student learning.

The assessment formats depicted in Figure 1.5, for example, are contained within neat little cells. While these formats do provide important data about student learning, in reality a given test might fit into more than one category, or even provide information that supports data gathered by several assessment methods.

This book focuses on performance assessments, and how these assessments connect and interface with the *National Science Education Standards*. Its focus is on performance-based assessments that use the science classroom and laboratory as major contexts for inquiry. Performance-based assessment is by definition "authentic" in nature, because it allows students to demonstrate their science inquiry, reasoning, and understanding skills when challenged with relevant, "real-world"

Figure 1.6: Important Aspects of Laboratory Performance-Based Assessment.

The laboratory is an important component of science instruction.

- There are certain features that are common to all models of laboratory performance-based assessment. There is a Planning and Designing phase or step, a Performing or Doing phase, an Analysis and Interpretation of Data phase, and a Conclusions and Making Projections for Future Study phase. The phases are placed in sequence for discussion purposes. In reality, the phases or steps are interrelated, and students can revisit or retrace their thinking at any time to modify their work or investigation.

- The laboratory provides an appropriate context for students to engage in problem-based learning, where they practice and use science process and problem-solving skills.
- Laboratory investigations and tasks by their nature allow students to produce a product and generate, rather than select, responses to questions.
- If appropriately designed, laboratory investigations allow students to generate multiple solutions to novel problems.

- As students produce a product and generate multiple responses to questions, laboratory investigations fit the criteria as being performance based.
- As laboratory performance-based assessment becomes an integral part of science learning, then instruction and the nature of what goes on in science classrooms come closer to the vision of assessment laid out in the *National Standards*. Instruction moves from "a transmission of information" approach to a hands-on, problem-based approach that allows students to integrate new knowledge and skills into their existing cognitive structure.

- The laboratory or practical science is a "holistic activity" (Woolnough 1991) where students do a task rather than write about something. This in essence is a performance-based activity for a limited or extended period of time. This approach is in agreement with the *National Science Education Standards* for assessment.
- Laboratory investigations, while an exemplar of performance-based assessment, are also an excellent approach to problem-based learning. Problem-based learning is where students inquire, debate, and engage in discussion of open-ended problems that have multiple solutions. The entire investigation can focus on a single problem.

problems. The science laboratory, traditionally under-used as a context for assessment, is an ideal setting for teachers to implement many of the reforms suggested by the *National Science Education Standards*, state assessment frameworks, and other standards documents, such as the New Standards Project (1997a, 1997b). Figure 1.6 (page 7) provides an outline of important aspects of performance-based assessment for the science laboratory.

This conceptualization of science inquiry and its interface with laboratory performance-based assessment is consistent with the assessment standards provided in the *National Science Education Standards*, and forms the basic framework for designing performance assessments.

Many traditional assessments have been large-group oriented—that is, a single teacher administering tests to a class. The new assessment formats supplement these formats by focusing on individuals and small groups. Portfolios, interviews, journals, and other assessment formats reinforce individualized instruction, and also accommodate different learning styles, exceptional students, and students with Limited English Proficiency skills.

Presentations, group and peer evaluations, and projects tap into students' creativity and planning and speaking skills by providing them with the opportunity to do the same things adults do every day. Life is not a series of true/false or multiple-choice tests. In most "real-world" decision-making and problem-solving situations, adults gather appropriate information, interpret that information using their own experiences and knowledge, and reach appropriate conclusions. In many cases, their decisions have important consequences. In the process, adults discard irrelevant information, search for additional data, and anticipate the consequences of their actions.

They also communicate their decisions, along with their rationale, to others.

A significant component of our current teaching and assessment is based on words—transmitting information to students verbally and through print, and then requiring students to repeat or replicate that information verbally and through writing. But many students learn best by receiving information through visual tools such as charts, data tables, graphs, and sketches. For such students, these kinds of visual stimuli can produce more effective learning. Several of these student performance-based assessment formats—including concept maps, Venn diagrams, and the Vee heuristic (see pages 35–42 for examples of all three)—emphasize visual stimuli.

Alternative response formats offer significant assistance to learners with Limited English Proficiency skills and other exceptionalities. As teachers, we must be willing to accept many kinds of evidence given by students to demonstrate their understanding of a concept or principle. As there are many ways to demonstrate understanding, we need to go beyond paper-and-pencil assessment formats and embrace alternative assessment formats that reflect a variety of learning styles, cooperative learning in small groups, and the nurturing of multiple intelligences.

Using Assessment Results—The New Paradigm

Science classroom and laboratory assessments are the foundation of a sophisticated process designed to evaluate and improve the science education system. Everyone—from students, teachers, and parents to government officials—uses assessment data to evaluate how well the education system is performing. It's all part of a growing emphasis on making the education system accountable for its progress. According to the *National Science Education Standards*:

Assessment is the primary feedback mechanism in the science education system. For example, assessment data provide students with feedback on how well they are meeting the expectations of their teachers and parents, teachers with feedback on how well their students are learning, districts with feedback on the effectiveness of their teachers and programs, and policymakers with feedback on how

well policies are working. Feedback leads to changes in the science education system by stimulating changes in policy, guiding teacher professional development, and encouraging students to improve their understanding of science.

Figure 1.7 depicts some of the components in the four-part assessment data collection process designated in the *National Standards*, and highlights the complexity of assessment and how different parts all work together to provide a basis for important decisions.

Figure 1.7: Components in the Assessment Data Collection Process. *National Science Education Standards*, NRC, 1996.

The four components can be combined in numerous ways. For example, teachers use student achievement data to plan and modify teaching practices, and business leaders use per capita educational expenditures to locate businesses. The variety of uses, users, methods, and data contributes to the complexity and importance of the assessment process.

Data Use	Data Collection	Collection Methods	Data Users
	To describe and quantify:		
Plan teaching	Student achievement and attitude	Paper-and-pencil testing	Teachers
Guide learning	Teacher preparation and quality	Performance testing	Students
Calculate grades	Program characteristics	Interviews	Parents
Make comparisons	Resource allocation	Portfolios	Public
Credential and license	Policy instruments	Performances	Policymakers
Determine access to special or advanced education		Observing programs, students, and teachers in classroom	Institutions of higher education
Develop education theory		Transcript analysis	Business and industry
Inform policy formulation		Expert reviews of education materials	Government
Monitor effects of policies			
Allocate resources			
Evaluate quality of curricula, programs, and teaching practices			

Conclusion

It is clear that assessment is an important, integral part of science education that promotes learning for all students. Teachers use a variety of assessment instruments of the highest quality for providing feedback to students, parents, administrators, and policymakers. There is no single assessment format that works best for everyone; you must refine your assessments through trial and error to develop a system that works best for your particular situation. Different assessment formats provide different kinds of information used for different purposes. Classroom and laboratory assessments focus on improving student learning by providing feedback to students, while international and national assessments provide data for system accountability.

The next three chapters of this book focus on developing performance assessment tasks, alternative forms of assessment, and the analysis and use of assessment data. These chapters will give you a practical primer on how to improve the assessment process in your classroom or school.

Works Cited

National Research Council (NRC). 1996. *National Science Education Standards*. Washington, DC: National Academy Press.

News Standards Project. 1997a. *Performance Standards. Volume 2: Middle School.* Washington, DC: National Center for Education and the Economy (Tel. 202-783-3668).

—————. 1997b. *Middle School Science Portfolio.* Washington, DC: National Center for Education and the Economy (Tel. 202-783-3668).

Perkins, D., and Salomon, G. 1989. Are Cognitive Skills Context-Bound? *Educational Researcher* 19:16–25.

Reynolds, D., Doran, R., Allers, R., and Agruso, S. 1996. *Alternative Assessment in Science: A Teacher's Guide.* Buffalo: University of Buffalo.

Rubba, P., Miller, E., Schmalz, R., Rosenfeld, L., and Shyamal, K. 1991. Science Education in the United States: Editors Reflections. In *Science Education in the United States: Issues, Crises and Priorities.* Easton, PA: Pennsylvania Academy of Science.

Suggested Readings

Carr, M., Barker, M., Bell, B., Biddulph, F., Jones, A., Kirkwood, V., Pearson, J., and Symington, D. 1994. The Constructivist Paradigm and Some Implications for Science Content and Pedagogy. In *The Content of Science—A Constructivist Approach to Its Teaching and Learning,* Fensham, P., Gunstone, R., and White, R., eds. Bristol, PA: Falmer Press.

Duit, R., and Treagust, D. 1995. Students' Conceptions and Constructivist Teaching Approaches. In *Improving Science Education*, Fraser, B., and Walberg, H. eds. Chicago: National Society for the Study of Education.

National Center on Education and the Economy, University of Pittsburgh. 1997. *Performance Standards, Volumes I, II, and III.* Washington, DC: National Center on Education and the Economy.

National Research Council. 2000. *Inquiry and the National Science Education Standards: A Guide for Teaching and Learning.* Washington, DC: National Academy Press.

New York State Education Department, University of the State of New York. 1996. *Learning Standards for Mathematics, Science, and Technology.* Albany: New York State Education Department.

Woolnough, B. 1991. Practical Science as a Holistic Activity. In *Practical Science,* Woolnough, B. ed. Bristol, PA: Open University Press.

Yager, R. 1995. Constructivism and the
Learning of Science. In *Learning Science
in the Schools: Research Reforming Practice*,
Glynn, S., and Duit, R., eds. Mahwah,
NJ: Lawrence Erlbaum Associates.

CHAPTER 2

Developing New Assessments

Toward Effective Assessment

The design and implementation of an effective assessment program in a school, school district, or state is a formidable challenge faced by teachers and administrators. One essential component of any assessment program is the development of appropriate assessment instruments and tasks, using formats that enable students to demonstrate what they know and can do. These assessment instruments and tasks must collect relevant data and information that are consistent, informative, reliable, and valid for all students. In addition, they must be flexible and adaptable enough to accommodate a variety of learning styles and language proficiencies, enabling students to demonstrate their knowledge and skills in multiple ways. A focus of this chapter is to address the development of alternative assessment tasks where students have the flexibility to create their own answers and solutions to problems.

Some tasks can have a narrow focus linked to the content and skills taught in the classroom. For example, if students are required to measure over specific time intervals the temperature of a liquid as it is heated, then an assessment task can be designed where students use a thermometer to collect temperature data. A paper-and-pencil assessment task asking students to mark temperatures on a graphical scale is inappropriate to measure the knowledge and skills students demonstrate when measuring temperatures of liquids. A more appropriate assessment design is a task where students actually use a thermometer to measure the temperatures of liquids. On the other hand, some investigations have a broader focus, where students face the challenges of designing their own experiments to solve a problem appropriate to their age and grade level. (An example is having students plan and conduct an experiment to determine the effects of temperature on the dissolution of a tablet, such as is described on page 31.)

An Assessment Development Model

Figure 2.1 (page 13) illustrates several steps in developing new assessment tasks. The assessment development process is nonlinear, as you create and trial-test tasks. You need to revise and "fine-tune" assessment tasks based on feedback from students during trial testing. The key is to view the development of alternative assessments as a continuing process rather than as a set, rigid procedure, ever modifying as you learn, and moving toward a seamless interface between instruction and assessment.

Teachers can develop new assessments individually or collaboratively. Collaboration in small groups provides an opportunity to share expertise from diverse viewpoints. Colleagues can also assist in trial testing the tasks with students. This collegial work is productive, and teams can often develop a larger number of high-quality tasks than an individual working alone can.

An easy way to start is for a group of teachers within a school with an interest in alternative assessments to get together,

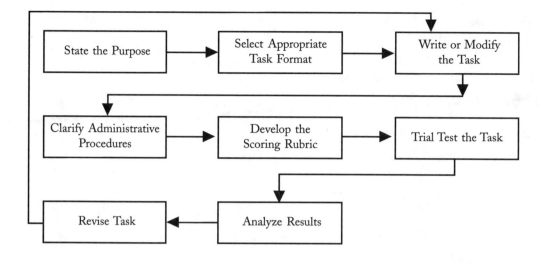

formally or informally, and map out an action plan. "Alternative assessment" is a broad term used to mean any kind of assessment that is not of the paper-and-pencil, true/false, and multiple-choice format. It covers any assessment format that provides students with opportunities to demonstrate their capabilities rather than simply choose an answer. Alternative assessments can include concept mapping, Vee heuristic, planning and designing experiments, and debating controversial topics. You can be as creative as possible. The assessment development model in Figure 2.1 focuses on the development of laboratory performance assessment. However, the model's procedures can be used for any assessment design process.

State the Purpose

The purpose provides the idea for the assessment or the outcomes being assessed, and describes how the information collected will be used to improve instruction and provide feedback to students, as well as to teachers and others. The assessment measures should be clearly delineated by cross-referencing to state curriculum guides, district syllabi, or state standards. The nature of laboratory performance assessment requires that the domain of coverage of content and skills for individual tasks be narrow. However, the domain of content or skills should not be so narrow as to be trivial.

To achieve this balance, try to accomplish two goals. First, determine the purpose and use of the assessment, and its relevance to both classroom instruction and student learning experiences. Second, identify the domain of knowledge and skills the assessment measures.

This is a time for you to be as creative as possible. Ideas for the assessment can come from personal experiences, a magazine or newspaper article, teachers' guides, conference proceedings, and professional journals. Teachers with Internet access may find colleagues willing to share ideas, and many professional organizations—such as the ERIC Clearinghouse for Science, Mathematics, and Environmental Education and the Eisenhower National Clearinghouse—provide important resources and information on their websites. You can also pick up good ideas at professional conferences. Initially, brainstorm with colleagues and consider several concepts or ideas you can potentially use to develop into viable assessments. The *National Assessment of Educational Progress (NAEP)* (O'Sullivan, et al. 1997) and the

Figure 2.2: *TIMSS* Assessment Framework Domain. Robitaille, et al., 1993.

Using tools, routine procedures, and science processes.

Gathering data (observing, measuring, etc.; perceiving characteristics, similarities, differences, and changes through use of the senses; comparing objects or events to standards of length, area, volume, mass, temperature, force, and time).

Figure 2.3 Knowing and Doing Scientific Investigation. *National Assessment of Education Progress (NAEP)*, O'Sullivan, et al., 1997.

"...students should be able to acquire new information, plan appropriate investigations, use a variety of scientific tools, and communicate the results of their investigations.... Practical reasoning subsumes competence in analyzing a problem, planning appropriate approaches, evaluating them, carrying out the required procedures for the approach(es) selected, and evaluating its result(s)."

Figure 2.4: Selecting A Task Format—Questions to Ask.

Third International Mathematics and Science Study (TIMSS) (Harmon, et al. 1997) assessment frameworks are good, informative examples. Figure 2.2 illustrates one outcome from the TIMSS performance assessment framework that you can use to design assessments.

We also illustrate another domain of assessment from the "Science Assessment Framework" of the 1996 *National Assessment of Education Progress (NAEP)* (O'Sullivan, et al. 1997). The domain, described in Figure 2.3, is "Knowing and Doing Science," with the sub-domain of "Scientific Investigation.".This sub-domain focuses on both cognitive and laboratory tools of science within the disciplines of Earth, physical, and life sciences.

Note the similarity between the *TIMSS* assessment domain of "using tools, routine procedures, and science processes" and the *NAEP* sub-domain of "use a variety of scientific tools."

State the Purpose Checklist

❏ Determine the purpose.

❏ Identify domains of knowledge and skills.

❏ Specify intended uses of assessment data.

❏ Be specific.

Select the Appropriate Task Format

So what will it be? Multiple-choice? Short-answer? Laboratory investigation? Laboratory practical examination? Extended investigation lasting several weeks? Portfolio collection? Individual or small group work?

There's no one "right" answer to this question. You can pick and choose from a variety of assessment formats. The choices you make depend on the purpose and use of the assessment, the domain of knowledge and skills the assessment will measure, and how you score student responses and communicate their achievement. Figure 2.4 provides a checklist to guide you in selecting an appropriate task format.

Your choices depend on your classroom situation, the prior science learning of students, their cognitive development, their ability to work in groups and individually, their exceptionalities, and their language proficiency. For example, if a class includes students for whom English is a second language, an appropriate assessment format might be to pair each student with another who has greater English language proficiency when completing an investigation. Pairs of students can communicate their work to both you and the class using a combination of written

- How can I use this assessment in my classroom?
- What information will the assessment provide to students?
- How will this assessment promote student learning?
- How does the task fit into the curriculum?
- What content and skills need to be taught before the assessment task is administered?
- What materials and equipment are needed?
- Will the task require students to work individually, in pairs, or in small groups?
- What kinds of assistance or intervention should I provide to students? What kinds of assistance should I not provide? How should I treat these interventions in scoring the task?
- How will students communicate their achievement?
- What problems or difficulties are likely to occur?

and oral reports. Your challenge is to build individual accountability into assessments when students work in pairs or small groups.

The format(s) you choose should consider whether students will work individually, in pairs, or in groups of three or four in doing the task. If the task is an extended investigation, then students can easily work in pairs or small groups. When students work in small groups, you may wish to first take the time to explain the role demanded of each individual in the group, and what the expectations are regarding individual contributions to the group's effort. The demands of the assessment task should be such that each member of the group must make a contribution for the group to be successful. Vary the approach, as some students prefer to work individually and view competition as an excellent motivator. On the other hand, some students get "turned off" by a competitive approach to learning. Such students will benefit from a less competitive, more supportive and collaborative classroom environment. The task can be a station format, where students go from station to station to demonstrate various science process skills. This format would fit an individual approach. Some students—including those with different cultural backgrounds, many females, and students of Limited English Proficiency—tend to benefit from an approach that is more collaborative. You may wish to ask an English as a Second Language teacher on your faculty to review assessment tasks for suggestions to reduce any ambiguities of language and grammar that might prove confusing to Limited English Proficiency students.

Assessments are constrained by the limits of time, money, and space. Some assessment designs might require equipment that is unavailable or too expensive for purchase by the school. If the task is excellent but requires expensive materials and equipment, then the school district or a number of schools can pool their resources to buy the materials and equipment, which can then be shared by all teachers.

Some assessment tasks may require you to devote more time to teaching students skills they need to complete the assessment task. Also, while some assessment tasks may seem to take up classroom time that could otherwise be devoted to other topics of instruction, if the assessment task really fits with the instruction, then this is time well-spent. This is our vision, where assessment merges with, or becomes "embedded" in, instruction.

Select the Task Format Checklist

❏ Determine the task format: skills, investigation, or extended investigation.

❏ Specify if students will conduct the task as individuals or in pairs or small groups.

❏ Pay attention to the interface of procedural (how-to) knowledge and declarative (content) knowledge.

Write the Task

Once you have settled on the purpose and format of the assessment, then comes the most crucial and challenging part of the process. Your idea needs to be translated into an assessment task for use in the classroom or laboratory. Figure 2.5 (page 16) provides a checklist with points of reference to guide you in writing an assessment task. In our diverse classrooms, where students arrive with different experiences and backgrounds, you must ensure that *all* students have the opportunity to learn the concept, and that no one is at a disadvantage. Use sensitivity in selecting contexts that provide challenges for students, and be certain that students are aware of terminology and what they are required to do.

For an assessment to be useful, it must closely fit the instruction students are experiencing in the classroom. Also, consider practical issues such as the amount of time needed to prepare materials for the assessment, your own professional development, the availability of financial and material

Figure 2.5: A Checklist for Writing an Assessment Task.

Question	Yes	No
Does the idea center on an important concept, skill, or principle in science?		
Does the idea have a meaningful context for students? Does the idea reflect a "real-world" situation? How authentic is it? Is it interesting to students?		
Is the assessment fair and equitable to all students? Does the assessment give an advantage to a group? For example, are boys at an advantage over girls?		
Is the assessment aligned/consistent with instruction?		
Is appropriate time provided for the assessment?		
Does the idea or potential task require students to use and apply science reasoning skills rather than just recall information?		
Does the idea generate interest among students and engage them to reflect on their learning? Does the idea stimulate them to inquire further?		
Does the idea have the potential to allow students to explain it to peers, and allow them to learn with deep understanding?		
Is the language appropriate for all students? Are provisions made to accommodate Limited English Proficiency learners?		
Are provisions made to accommodate exceptional students?		
Does the task assess science content and skills, as opposed to reading ability?		
Can the task be made "multifaceted"? Can it require multiple performances or products around the same theme or experience?		
Will students write reports, give oral presentations, or engage in group discussions?		
Will there be self-assessment and/or peer assessment?		
Can the task be structured to also elicit attitudes and attributes that can be assessed, such as group cooperation, persistence, and resourcefulness?		
Can the task be structured to include small group activity?		

resources, and district and administrative support.

Now it's time to do some writing. You may be able to quickly and easily translate the purpose and format of an assessment into a task. Or it may take more time. A lot depends on how comfortable you feel with your writing skills. Choose a content or skills domain in which you are very familiar and knowledgeable, especially with the first task. The process is easier if you are quite clear about the purpose of the assessment, the format of the assessment, and the potential use of student responses in improving instruction and promoting student learning and achievement. The writing process should flow smoothly. If you run into difficulty, then review the purpose and use of the assessment information. Remember, this is a process, not an end result. The assessment task doesn't have to be perfect on the first draft, or even the second. You probably will need to revise the task a number of times based on suggestions from colleagues and from results collected after trial testing with groups of students. Remember that writing a good assessment task is an iterative process.

A practical first step is to modify an existing paper-and-pencil question using an alternative assessment format. The following section illustrates this process, using as examples three modifications of an existing multiple-choice question.

Write the Task Checklist

Develop a first draft and pay careful attention to:

❏ Equity (for all groups).

❏ Appropriate and clear language.

❏ Opportunity to have learned the outcome.

❏ Promotion of student learning.

❏ Congruence of the task with instruction, and with state and district assessment standards.

❏ Criteria for successful completion of the task.

❏ Alternative conceptions, prior conceptions, misconceptions.

❏ Display of student learning and products from the task.

Modify an Existing Task

Multiple-choice items, or other paper-and-pencil assessments, may be modified to create new or different assessments of student performance. The following three tasks are modified from one original multiple-choice item. The original task in Figure 2.6 is a paper-and-pencil item for assessing an elementary school student's skills at recognizing how someone else has

Figure 2.6: Item 1—Select Property of Grouped Objects. This item was used in the objective test administered to grade 4 students as part of New York State's *Elementary Science Program Evaluation Test* (*ESPET*), 1992a.

The diagrams below show eight objects placed in two different groups.

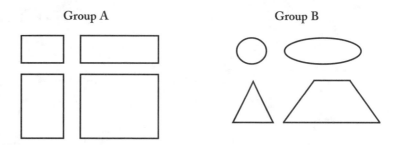

What is a property of each of the objects in Group A, but is *not* a property of the objects in Group B?

A. All group A objects are closed.

B. All group A objects are the same size.

C. All group A objects have the same kind of corners.

D. All group A objects are squares.

Figure 2.7: Item II—
Determine Properties of
Grouped Objects.
Modified from *ESPET*,
1992a.

The diagrams below show eight objects placed in two different groups.

Group A   Group B

What is a property of each of the objects in Group A, but is not a property of the objects in Group B?

classified objects by observable properties. The three modifications follow.

(1) A very simple, but useful, modification of this item is to eliminate the choices and create a constructed response item, such as that shown in Figure 2.7. Students can still determine which property or characteristic is present in Group A, but not present in Group B. In addition

they can write their responses in the space provided. Although this constructed response task will take longer to administer and grade, it helps identify the level of student understanding and identifies any student misconceptions. This format eliminates the "guessing" factor, as there are no choices to select from. The constructed response task gives greater insight

Figure 2.8: Item III—
Determine Property for
Grouping Objects.
Modified from *ESPET*,
1992a.

Sort the objects into two groups so that all of the group A objects share some common property. Similarly, all of the objects in group B must share some common property.

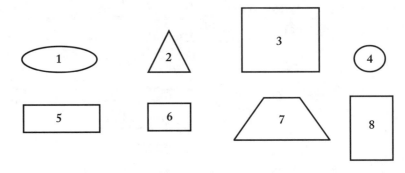

Put the numbers of the objects under the appropriate heading to show your grouping.

Group A   Group B

_____   _____
_____   _____
_____   _____
_____   _____
_____   _____

What is the common property of all the objects in your group A?

into the assessment of student conceptual understanding.

(2) While Items I and II ask the student to interpret an existing system of classification, Items III and IV (Figures 2.8 and 2.9, page 18, 19) challenge the student to create his or her own classification system. Item III includes the same eight objects as in I and II, but students must determine a classification system of their own in order to sort them into two groups. In addition to the grouping criteria shown in Items I and II, students can group these objects using criteria such as those with straight versus curved edges; small versus large objects; square versus not square; or any other grouping criteria.

(3) A further modification is to create a performance task in which students use actual, physical objects for grouping. In this modification, the objects are "authentic" materials that the student would likely encounter outside the classroom. In the task in Figure 2.9, the student sorts different types of seeds into two groups based on some common property. The objects could just as well be rocks, fossils, leaves, screws, nails, or that perennial favorite—buttons.

Use Clear Directions and Questions

One of the most challenging aspects of assessment development is writing directions and questions that are clear and understandable to all the target students. Long reading passages, challenging vocabulary, and complicated directions can quickly transform a good performance task into a reading task. This is true for all formats of assessment. Tasks should be consistent with science standards and written in clear language, easily understandable by the students for whom they were developed. Also, be aware of your students' past and current learning experiences as well as their learning styles and interests. Vocabulary words that students have learned previously, and which they are expected to be able to use and understand, are appropriate to use in assessment tasks. Words that are not an integral part of the assessment should be clear so that some students are not placed at a disadvantage by a limited vocabulary. Again, the writing of understandable questions is dependent on a clearly defined assessment purpose.

Communication skills are important in every field of study and human endeavor. Students, as well as practicing scientists, need to be able to describe to others what they are doing and have done, what they are learning, and what they have learned. You may find it appropriate to read directions aloud to students and record their verbal responses, particularly if specified in their Individualized Education Plans (IEPs). As student reading and writing skills develop, these skills should be integrated with assessment tasks in science. At the high school level, you can expect students to produce clear, articulate written responses using complete sentences, as well as use other writing skills necessary for effective written communication. Trial testing tasks with groups of students who may have limited reading skills or Limited English Proficiency is one way to develop tasks with necessary, but not excessive, reading demands.

Presenting directions and questions for assessments that require students to use equipment—an essential component of manipulative skills and laboratory performance tasks—poses some additional problems. For such assessments, students often have to follow a set of directions to carry out the activity, and then record information and/or respond to questions. Putting all of this together so it is easily

Figure 2.9: Item IV—Actual Objects to Be Grouped. Modified from *ESPET*, 1992b.

In front of you is a plastic bag with seeds. Put the seeds into two groups so that there is something the same about all the seeds in each group. Be sure to use all the seeds.

a. What is the same about all the seeds in your first group?

b. What is the same about all of the seeds in your second group?

- Are any groups at a disadvantage because of unfamiliarity with specific content or the format of the assessment?

- Does the context of the assessment give an advantage to a specific group?

- Have linguistic modifications been made to the assessment to accommodate students of limited English proficiency? Modifications can include changes in vocabulary, visual aids, glossaries in native languages and English, and reading questions aloud in English.

- Are exceptional students provided with additional resources, such as additional time or modifications to print and nonprint materials, to complete the assessment?

understood and manageable by all students presents a challenge.

In addition, students must be informed about the teacher's role during the task administration. Your role may be limited to repeating to the individual student, "Read the directions" and "Do the best you can." Also, in the case of laboratory performance testing, be alert to replacing broken equipment and replenishing consumable supplies. As always, you are constantly making sure that students are following appropriate safety procedures.

Consider Equity

It is important that all assessment tasks be equitable and fair for all students. A bedrock principle of the *National Science Education Standards* (NRC 1996) is that "science is for all students," who, as a result of their learning experiences, achieve the goal of being science literate. This can only occur if each student is given an equal opportunity to learn science. This is a formidable challenge, affecting the nature of both instruction and assessment.

Providing equal opportunity to learn requires that assessments be multifaceted, allowing students to use their individual learning styles and abilities in a variety of assessment formats. In turn, the assessment of student learning must be keyed to the level of achievement you have established for that instructional goal.

As a teacher, you need to understand a variety of learning styles and abilities and modify your instruction and assessment to accommodate them. We know that cultural experiences influence learning styles. Some students are able to work individually with little encouragement from peers or teachers, work well on their own, are task oriented, and do well on tasks requiring abstract and analytical thinking. Other students prefer to work in groups

and do better with encouragement from peers and teachers (Rosenthal 1996).

To be equitable, assessment tasks must be free of gender, ethnic, racial, socioeconomic, geographical, and cultural biases. This is a substantial challenge in the United States and in other countries where students come from many different backgrounds. A student's success on an assessment task should be dependent only on whether the student has the necessary knowledge and skills being assessed. The language used and student background required for a task should be appropriate for all students and must not disenfranchise students because they have not been exposed to a particular social or cultural experience. Figure 2.10 provides questions addressing equity issues that you should consider when designing assessments.

You may wish to ask a colleague who is a specialist in Second Language learning to review the task as to its appropriateness for Limited English Proficiency students. Also, you may wish to ask a colleague or friend familiar with different cultures to review the task for bias in terms of vocabulary, context, and format.

Clarify Administrative Procedures

There are two basic designs for providing directions, questions, and answer sheets for alternative assessment tasks (Reynolds, et al. 1996). You can provide students with the materials they need in either a single, integrated test booklet or in separate ones. Each format has certain advantages and disadvantages, so it is important that the format selected is appropriate for the task and the target population. The format may also be varied throughout the year in order to expose students to different styles. Trying out the formats with a few students may help couple the most efficient format with a specific task.

Separate Test Booklets: In this format, the directions are on a different sheet of paper from the question-and-answer spaces. You can tape the direction sheet directly to the desk or station where the task is to be performed, alongside the necessary equipment for that station. (Laminating the directions protects them from spills and other mishaps.) Each student receives a single sheet of paper containing both the questions and the spaces for his or her answers and carries the sheet to each station setup. If all the question-and-answer spaces are printed on one sheet of paper, the test booklet is easier to handle and less intimidating for students. However, because the task's directions stay at the station, there might be a disadvantage, as students need to go back and forth between the direction sheet on the desk and the question-and-answer sheet in their hands.

Figure 2.11 provides an example of New York State's directions for Station 1 of the Manipulative Skills Test of the Elementary Science Program Evaluation Test, Form X. The directions were taped at the task's location. Figure 2.12 shows the part of the separate answer sheet for that station that provides both the questions to be answered and a place for the student's response.

Integrated Test Booklet Format: In this format, the student directions, questions, and spaces for responses are in one document. While this format is consolidated and sequential, it can be a sizable packet

for younger students to handle. Figure 2.13 (page 22) provides an example of a task using an integrated test booklet that was developed for grade four students.

As always, trying the different formats with a few student volunteers may help you determine the most efficient test booklet format for the specific task to be administered to your classes.

Clarify Administrative Procedures Checklist

❏ Ensure that directions are clear.

❏ Ensure that student and teacher roles are clear.

❏ Pay attention to appropriate safety procedures.

❏ Have available all materials and equipment.

Figure 2.11: Directions for Station Format Assessment. Reynolds, et al., 1996.

Station 1 Measuring Objects
Directions
1. Check the materials:
   - Balance scale   • Ruler   • Measuring cup   • Container of water
   - Thermometer   • Plastic glass   • Pennies
                      (marked A or B)
2. Read the questions on the answer sheet for **Station 1** to find out what to do.
3. Write your answers on the answer sheet in the part labeled "**Station 1.**"
4. Be sure to label your answers with the correct units.
5. When you are done, pour all the water back into the water container.

Figure 2.12: Question-and-Answer Sheet. Reynolds, et al., 1996.

Station 1 Measuring Objects
Answer Sheet

	Amount	Units
1. What is the letter on the glass? _____		
2. How many pennies heavy is the empty glass?	_____	Pennies
3. How tall is the glass?	_____	_____
4. How much water is needed to fill the glass to the line?	_____	_____
5. What is the temperature of the water?	_____	_____

Observing Objects

Materials:

- 2 unsharpened pencils
- duct tape or C clamp
- Pendulum Object (rubber stopper and wire)
- Spring Object (rubber stopper fastened to spring)

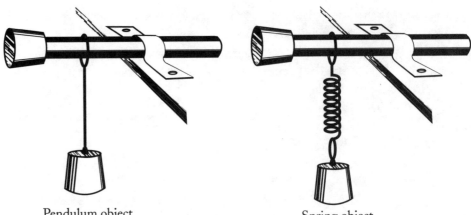

Pendulum object   Spring object

Directions:

1. Try Object A (Pendulum Object) to see how you can make it move. Observe it carefully.

2. In the space below, write two ways that Object A (Pendulum Object) can move.
    1.
    2.

3. Try Object B (Spring Object) to see how you can make it move. Observe it carefully.

4. In the space below, write two ways that Object B (Spring Object) can move.
    1.
    2.

5. Tell one way that Object A (Pendulum Object) and Object B (Spring Object) move the same.

6. Tell one way that Object A (Pendulum Object) and Object B (Spring Object) move differently.

Develop the Scoring Rubric

A reliable scoring rubric to evaluate student performance is crucial to the success of any alternative assessment effort. The scoring rubric details how the student's responses to the task will be scored. Rubrics provide clear standards against which we can judge student achievement. You can use them to provide feedback to students on their areas of strengths and weaknesses and to plan remedial instruction.

Rubrics must match the purpose of the task, and should be clear, concise, and unbiased. You need to consider how these learning outcomes are reflected in the student's responses. Figure 2.14 (page 23) outlines some issues to consider when developing a scoring rubric.

Several teachers should review and use the scoring rubric to be sure that the scoring criteria are clear, appropriate, and correct. Whenever possible, the scoring guide should be shared with students prior to the assessment. More information on scoring procedures will be found in Chapter 4.

Develop the Scoring Rubric Checklist

❏ Use anticipated responses to develop first draft of rubric.

❏ Score a few tests using this first draft.

❏ Work with a colleague if possible and double-score tasks to maintain consistency and reliability and to reduce human judgment errors.

❏ Revise rubric.

❏ Select anchor papers as examples, illustrating a range of proficiencies or levels of performance and achievement.

Trial Test the Task

Try the task out with two or three students, and revise it as necessary prior to administering it to a larger group. This step is crucial to determining whether the task will work with the target audience. Trial testing is like rehearsing a play: you need to make sure everything works well before the curtain goes up. You should focus on evaluating the assessment task, rather than the student's performance on it. Encourage students to freely provide feedback on what components of the task worked well and what improvements might be made to the task. Most students enjoy doing this. Figure 2.15 provides some questions to consider when trial testing an assessment.

During trial testing, you need to determine whether students can accurately interpret the written directions and questions and whether they can complete the

task in the allocated time. You also need to ensure that the materials and equipment are both available and familiar to students, and that the task does indeed measure the content and skills it claims to measure. At this stage of development, review the draft rubric for scoring student responses.

As a result of information from the trial testing, modify and revise the task. It may be that the instructions are not clear or materials need to be changed. This may seem complicated, but it really isn't so daunting. And, it is well worth it.

Trial Test the Task Checklist

❏ Administer task to a few students.

❏ Obtain feedback from students regarding clarity of directions and the purpose of the task.

❏ Analyze student responses.

❏ Ensure the task is measuring what it is designed to measure.

Analyze Results

You can use a scoring rubric to rate the student responses, and analyze the results to evaluate individual and group responses. The results will indicate students' areas of strength and areas where they need improvement. You can use these data to suggest different approaches for students to try to improve their performance. Once they have mastered the skills and content of the assessment, you can move on to

Figure 2.14: Developing a Scoring Rubric.

- Decide whether you are assessing processes or products.

- Identify either dimensions of performance or aspects of the product that reflect the learning outcomes of the task, and what can be observed and rated with reasonable objectivity and consistency.

- Weigh the dimensions in proportion to their importance, using your own judgment and that of colleagues.

- Develop levels of performance that are likely to be present in student performances or products.

- Determine the range of points to be allocated to each level of performance.

- Determine how students will receive criteria for evaluation of their performance, and how students will give and receive feedback.

Figure 2.15: Trial Testing—Questions to Consider.

- Can the target students perform the task?
- Are students challenged by the demands of the task?
- Are the instructions clear?
- What science skills or concepts are involved?
- Are the materials and equipment appropriate for the assessment task?
- Is this a likely learning experience in most school science programs?
- Are safety precautions clear to students?

- Carefully review student written responses for completeness and misconceptions. By noting areas of poor or incomplete information, you can include additional instruction in these areas for future lessons.
- Tally up the number of incorrect responses for each item or task and determine which students made several mistakes. This may indicate that the wording of the assessment is confusing, or that the concept was especially difficult for those students.
- Sort papers according to performance on a specific item. Look at the range of scores and the frequency of high and low scores for indications that the item was too easy or too difficult for students. Review those items most frequently missed.

another topic or lesson. Figure 2.16 provides several relatively simple ways to analyze student responses to alternative assessment tasks.

Analyze Results Checklist

- ❏ Use scoring rubric to score student responses.
- ❏ Provide feedback to students with suggestions for improvement.

Revise Tasks

You need to consider a number of factors or variables as you revise tasks based on analysis of information from trial testing. Paper-and-pencil objective tests can be described in various ways or dimensions. For example, items may be described by their format: multiple-choice, true/false, or matching. Similarly, an item may be described by the content it assesses: life, physical, or Earth science. An assessment item may also be described in terms of its degree of difficulty (easy, moderate, or difficult) or the type of skill (planning, measuring, graphing, and so forth).

Performance tasks may also be described in several additional ways or dimensions. These dimensions include structure, novelty, and sequence, all of which underpin the assessment task (Reynolds, et al. 1996).

Revise Task Checklist

- ❏ Modify instructions or questions.
- ❏ Make changes to materials and/or equipment.
- ❏ Modify task format where appropriate (i.e., structure, sequence, and difficulty).

Structure

The amount of assistance you provide to students for interpreting the directions and questions associated with the task is one of the most important variables in assessment. Structure can be provided in the form of detailed procedures or questions, background materials, labeled data tables and graphs, or diagrams and flowcharts. This dimension can be considered along a continuum from highly structured to open and unstructured, as shown in Figure 2.17.

You need to consider the degree of structure most appropriate for the audience and purpose of the assessment task. A highly structured task consists of well-defined student directions on what to do, how to proceed with the task, the collection and analysis of data, and the questions to be answered. This is the classic "cookbook" task in which students follow prepared directions to complete the task.

At the other end of the continuum, a highly unstructured assessment task requires students to plan and design an experiment to come up with possible

Figure 2.17: Continuum of Structure.

Highly Structured	Moderately Structured	Highly Unstructured
Much Guidance and Detailed Directions	Some Directions	Few Directions
Data Collection Prescribed	Some Help	Multiple Solutions Open Ended
	Some Clues for Data Collection	No Clues for Data Collection

solutions to a problem. In this scenario, no materials/equipment list is provided to students, and students are required to come up with their own. In the middle of the continuum, a moderately structured task provides students with a materials/equipment list and with some instructions or clues on how to proceed. The instructions and materials/equipment list are both factors that determine the degree of structure of the assessment.

Teachers often find it advisable to slowly change the structure of instructional and assessment activities so students are not confused or discouraged. Students adjust much better when they are provided with explanations for shifts in structure and emphasis. Most importantly, students must be comfortable, competent, and confident with a set of skills before the teacher withholds procedural directions. The process of removing instructional crutches or scaffolding should be carefully planned and organized so that students are aware of the changes in the nature of the assessment task. The older the students are, the slower the change process should be as these students have generally experienced traditional instruction and assessment for a longer period of time. The teacher can develop an appropriate initial structure for a specific group of students, and then reduce that structure gradually by eliminating labels, directions, background information, or other elements of the assessment. The goal is to help students develop the skills to handle tasks with less structure. Such assessment tasks are consistent with the *National Science Education Standards* (NRC 1996) in that they move the class toward more learner-centered instruction and assessment.

An assessment task for acid-base testing (page 146) illustrates a rather structured format. By *not* giving students certain information about how one or more indicators behave in the solutions used in the task, teachers can gain important insights about their students' prior science learning by analyzing responses and performances on different assessment versions. Such structural variations are appropriate for use as a summative assessment for a middle school program or as a diagnostic assessment for a high school program where students come from different schools.

The idea of varying levels of structure of instructional and assessment tasks has been around for many years. Some refer to it as scaffolding, others as levels of inquiry, others as teacher- versus student-centered activities. Experienced teachers will frequently modify activities for students by increasing or decreasing the amount of structure. This can be done by varying the directions and procedures (very detailed or minimal), data tables and graphs (prepared and labeled or an empty grid), questions (expecting few words or expecting carefully crafted responses), and so forth.

A RAND report on performance assessment in science (Stecher and Klein 1996) presents "shells" with different levels of inquiry—low, medium, and high. The shells are sets of key questions within the context of the four stages of inquiry (planning and design, performance, analysis and interpretation, and application). Within each of these stages is a series of skills or outcome statements (e.g., "State a hypothesis involving an independent variable," "Explain the relationship"). For each of these skills, the "shell" describes exactly what is provided for/expected of students in a low-, medium-, and high-inquiry approach.

Sequence

Sequence is a characteristic of science inquiry tasks that refers to the flow of skills from the beginning of the task to the end.

Scientists approach problem solving in a variety of ways, depending upon the information available and the prior knowledge and experience they bring to the subject. The sequence in which students conduct investigative tasks can greatly affect the quality of their learning experiences.

Unfortunately, the vast majority of school laboratory activities follow a pre-set sequence beginning with hypothesis and procedure or method, followed by observations and collection of data, and ending with conclusions. Students who experience only this one approach to laboratory work come to believe that there is a singular, linear scientific approach to problem solving: planning, data collection, and conclusions. You can alter the sequence of the components of an inquiry task by having each assessment task begin with a different stage. The standard sequence that is typically presented in most laboratory guides begins with the hypothesis or planning stage. A modified version might begin with a set of procedures for students to follow for data collection and conclusions, and end with the challenge of planning an investigation. Students can be provided with data that have already been collected by another group of students, such as is illustrated in the Physics Extended Investigation Task "Keep It Hot" (page 248), and then be required to analyze the data, form conclusions, and plan and collect data for an investigation that goes beyond their provided data.

These approaches to assessment mirror the problem-solving strategies used by scientists and experts in a field or discipline. Problem solving is nonlinear, and these authentic assessments should provide students with opportunities to experience the nonlinearity of problem solving.

Novelty

An important goal of teaching science is to help students apply their knowledge in new and different situations. This transfer is more difficult than most teachers would expect. Students often experience much difficulty in applying and transferring skills learned in one context to another. Good instruction provides a sequence of activities that helps students move from situations of "near transfer" to "far transfer" (novelty). Three tasks related to density illustrate this novelty dimension by showing examples of near, moderate, and far transfer.

The first task—"Density of a Sinker" (page 221)—is an illustration of "near transfer." It is a small step beyond the normal instructional activity, as the object is irregular in shape and the last question probes the understanding that density is independent of the size of the sample or object.

The second task—"Density of Minerals" (page 179)—applies the concept of density to several mineral samples. The task addresses the differences between geologically similar sedimentary and metamorphic samples. This is an example of "moderate transfer," and illustrates how assessment tasks can involve both inquiry skills and relevant science concepts.

The third task—"Unknown Liquids" (page 233)—is an example of "far transfer." The task does not require standard mass and volume measurements to calculate density values. Students need only to compare the masses of the bottles and use the information provided to solve the problem. Many students find this challenging, as they are confused by the lack of equipment they believe should be provided to obtain measurements for calculating density.

Assessment tasks are based on content and skills that students have been studying. An important element of the assessment design is how novel (different from the instruction) the assessment situation should be. This is an important issue for all test developers, including international committees and classroom teachers. Most educators agree that the equipment used in an assessment (e.g., microscope, stopwatch, balance) should be identical to what students have already been using in class. The car a student takes to a driving test (for a license) is the same vehicle he or she practices with. (For novice learners, it may be useful to repeat the assessment during the same task they experienced to demonstrate a specific skill.) Professional scientists are expected to apply their skills and knowledge to new situations and contexts. However, they have had years of practice to get to that stage. In high school, students only *begin* to practice applying observation, measurement, and classification skills to unfamiliar situations. Many teachers are surprised at just how many practice/learning activities students need before they are confident and competent in new contexts. This goal—transfer of learning—does not magically happen; it is the result of conscious designer instruction.

Works Cited

Harmon, M., Smith, T., Martin, M., Kelly, D., Beaton, A., Mullis, I., Gonzalez, E., and Orpwood, G. 1997. *Performance Assessment in IEA's Third International Mathematics and Science Study (TIMSS)*. Chestnut Hill, MA: TIMSS International Study Center.

National Research Council (NRC). 1996. *National Science Education Standards*. Washington, DC: National Academy Press.

New York State Education Department. 1992a. *Elementary Science Program Evaluation Test (ESPET), Objective Test, Form E*. Albany: New York State Education Department.

———. 1992b. *Elementary Science Program Evaluation Test (ESPET), Manipulative Skills Test, Form X*. Albany: New York State Education Department.

———. 1996. *Alternative Assessment in Science Task Collections*. Albany: New York State Education Department.

O'Sullivan, C., Reese, C., and Mazzeo, J. 1997. *NAEP 1996 Science Report Card for the Nation and the States*. Washington, DC: National Center for Education Statistics.

Reynolds, D., Doran, R., Allers, R., and Agruso, S. 1996. *Alternative Assessment in Science: A Teacher's Guide*. Buffalo: University at Buffalo.

Robitaille, D.R., Schmidt, W.H., Raizen, S., McKnight, C., Britton, E., and Nichol, C. 1993. *Curriculum Frameworks for Mathematics and Science: Third International Mathematics and Science Study; TIMSS Monograph No. 1*. Vancouver: Pacific Educational Press.

Rosenthal, J. 1996. *Teaching Science to Language Minority Students*. Avon, UK: Multi-Lingual Matters, Ltd.

Stecher, B., and Klein, S., eds. 1996. *Performance Assessment in Science—Hands-on Task and Scoring Guide*. Santa Monica, CA: RAND

Suggested Reading

National Assessment Governing Board. 1996. *Science Assessment Framework for the 1996 National Assessment of Educational Progress (NAEP)*. Washington, DC: National Assessment Governing Board.

CHAPTER 3 # Alternative Assessment Formats

What Is "Alternative"?

Alternative assessment means any assessment format that is nontraditional, usually requiring student construction, demonstration, or performance. Alternative assessment formats are more student-focused, student-centered, and authentic. They often provide students with opportunities to generate multiple solutions to problems, rather than merely select "correct" or "right" answers from a predetermined list. While traditional formats—such as multiple-choice, true/false, and so forth—do enable students to demonstrate the acquisition of skills and knowledge, nontraditional, alternative formats provide additional opportunities for students to demonstrate what they have learned, how they have learned, and that they can connect their knowledge to the "real-world."

"Authentic" is an assessment term referring to "real-world" situations or contexts, which generally require a variety of approaches to problem solving and which allow for the possibility that a problem might have more than one solution. Nontraditional, alternative assessment formats provide opportunities for students to demonstrate not only that they have acquired skills and knowledge, but that they are able to apply them to situations and contexts they are likely to encounter beyond the classroom. This chapter focuses on such alternative formats, and discusses how they can be used by both teachers and students to provide additional assessment opportunities.

This chapter's first section illustrates examples of performance-based assessment formats that are student focused. The performance-based formats are skills tasks, investigations, and extended investigations. The second section illustrates other alternative assessment formats that are student focused, including:

- Graphic organizers: concept maps, Venn diagrams, and the Vee heuristic
- Portfolios
- Oral presentations and debate
- Interviews and conferences
- Skills checklists
- Self, pair, and peer evaluations
- Technological applications

The third section includes teacher-directed alternative assessment formats, such as demonstrations and group visuals.

Performance-Based Assessment Formats

Skills Tasks

As the name implies, "skills tasks" focus on a narrow domain of skills. Skills tasks are short assessments (30 minutes or less), usually focused on a small set of skills related to a particular situation or problem. Science teachers refer to these tasks or assessments in various ways: station tasks, where students move from station to station; bell ringer tasks, where a bell or other signal coordinates the movement of students from one task to another; circus tasks, where students move in a circuit or circle; and partial inquiries, where students complete one component of an investigation or laboratory experiment.

Skills tasks often require students to demonstrate and display proficiency in manipulative skills, such as measuring, using apparatus and instruments, reading information from graphs, charts, and tables, graphing, and observing and following specific procedures. Figure 3.1 illustrates a skills task. In this example, eighth grade students are provided with the necessary materials in the form of a science kit, and required to estimate the salt concentration of an unknown salt solution. Detailed instructions allow students to complete a series of tasks in which they place a short pencil in a graduated cylinder containing distilled water, 25 percent salt solution, and an unknown salt solution. Students measure the length of the pencil above the water (when floating), record their mea-

surements on a data table, and graph their results. Students then use the graph to estimate the concentration of the unknown salt solution.

Because skills tasks used in a station, bell ringer, circus, or partial inquiry format focus on a set of narrow domain skills, these assessment formats easily become part of activities within a unit of study. Skills tasks are appropriately used at the conclusion of a unit, semester, or school year.

Many science teachers find skills tasks to be a good way of beginning to use performance assessments because of their similarity to activities used in the classroom. Both students and teachers are familiar and comfortable with this performance-based assessment format. Using skills tasks as an alternative assessment is a safe start.

Floating the Pencil

For this task, you will be estimating the salt concentration of an unknown salt solution. You have been given a kit containing materials you will use to perform an investigation during the next 30 minutes. Now use the following diagram to check that all of the materials in the diagram are included. If any materials are missing, please raise your hand and the instructor will supply you with what you need.

Materials:

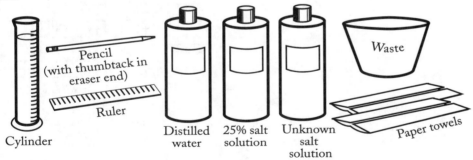

Directions:

1. Place 25 ml of distilled water in the graduated cylinder.

2. Place the pencil in the graduated cylinder.

3. Observe the level of the water on the pencil.

4. Take the pencil out of the water and dry it with a towel. Use the ruler to measure the length of the pencil that was above the water.

5. Record the length in Table 1, below, under Measurement 1.

Figure 3.1 continues on page 30.

Figure 3.1: A Skills Task. *National Assessment of Education Progress (NAEP)*, O'Sullivan, et al. 1997.

Table 1

Types of Solutions	Length of Pencil above Water Surface (cm)		
	Measurement 1	Measurement 2	Average
Distilled Water			
Salt Solution			
Unknown Salt Solution			

6. Place the pencil back in the distilled water and repeat steps 3–4.

7. Record your measurement in Table 1 under Measurement 2.

8. Calculate the average of Measurements 1 and 2, and record your results in the data table under Average.

9. Empty the water from the graduated cylinder into the waste container.

10. Repeat steps 1–9 with the 25% salt solution.

11. On the graph below, label the axes with values appropriate for your data. Plot the average values you obtained for the distilled water and the 25% salt solution. Draw a straight line between the two data points. Assume that this line represents the relationship between the length of the pencil that is above the water surface and the concentration of salt in the water.

Average Length of Pencil
above Water Surface

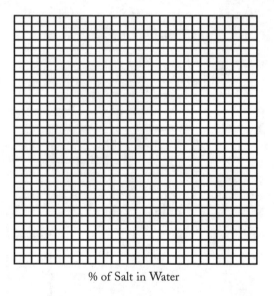

% of Salt in Water

12. Repeat steps 1–9 with the unknown salt solution. Enter data in Table 1.

13. Based on the graph you plotted, what is the salt concentration of the unknown solution?

14. Explain how you determined your answer in the space below.

Investigations

Investigations are the "heart and soul" of an inquiry-oriented science course, especially one that uses the laboratory as a focus for science activities. The *National Science Education Standards* (NRC 1996) stress the need for frequent—such as weekly—inquiry-oriented laboratory activities in order to provide students with direct exposure to experiences that reinforce the investigative nature of science.

In an authentic performance-based activity, students must analyze a problem, plan and conduct experiments, gather data, organize their results, and communicate their findings. Students experience and demonstrate their science inquiry skills and competencies by completing laboratory investigations. Investigations are commonly scheduled for one or two class periods and work particularly well with back-to-back sessions.

In Figure 3.2, we illustrate a laboratory investigation using an assessment task from the performance assessment component of the recent *Third International Mathematics and Science Study (TIMSS)* (Harmon, et al. 1997). The assessment task, "Solutions," requires eighth grade students to investigate the effect of water temperatures on the dissolution rate of tablets. Students are required to plan an experiment for this laboratory investigation, indicating the variables to be measured, the measurements they will take, and how they will record and present the data collected.

In some investigations, teachers can provide "clues" to students if they are "stuck" or experiencing difficulty at a particular step. (This relates to the structure of an assessment, as discussed in Chapter 2; see page 24.) This approach is authentic, paralleling the way scientists seek additional information from reference

Figure 3.2: Laboratory Investigation Performance Assessment. Harmon, et al., 1997.

Solutions

At this station you should have:

- Hot and cold water
- Several beakers
- Some tablets
- A stirrer
- A clock or watch with a second hand
- A thermometer
- A 30 cm ruler

Read all directions carefully.

Your task:

To investigate what effect different water temperatures have on the speed with which the tablet dissolves.

This is what you should do:

Plan an experiment to find out what effect different water temperatures have on the speed with which the tablet dissolves.

1. Write your plan here. Your plan should include:
   - what you will measure
   - how many measurements you will take
   - how you will present your measurements in a table

2. Carry out your tests on the tablets. Make a table and record all your measurements.

3. According to your investigation, what effect do different water temperatures have on the speed with which the tablet dissolves?

4. Explain why you think different water temperatures have this effect.

5. If you had to change your plan, describe any changes you made and why you made them. If you did not have to change your plan, write "No Change."

6. Empty your beakers into the waste container, dry them, and leave everything the way you found it.

materials or colleagues when they reach a roadblock. However, teachers sometimes find it difficult to distribute clues because many students often reach the same points at the same time. Reference materials, Internet sites, and other resources provide additional sources for students to find their own clues.

Another way to provide guidance is to organize investigations into a two-part format, with students completing and handing in the first part for review before continuing with the second part. The TIMSS exemplar, "Solutions," can be modified to form a Part 1, in which students just plan their investigation. Students then submit their plan for review by teachers and peers. Students can proceed with Part 2 of the investigation by following their (possibly) revised plan and completing an experiment they designed themselves. On the other hand, if their Part 1 plan was not viable, the teacher can provide a more workable plan. This ensures that all students are provided with an opportunity for success.

While this approach gives students less flexibility, it can offer a safe, workable procedure enabling students to demonstrate what they are able to do. With successful student experiences using this two-part format, teachers can actually eliminate the middle review step, allowing students to be in control of their own performance at all stages of the investigation. This further simulates the way professionals work.

Extended Investigations

Extended investigations usually take place within a unit or lesson of a science curriculum, and are often linked to student work on specific problems or projects. These assessments are "embedded" in instruction, establishing a seamless fit between assessment and instruction. This assessment format is the most natural and unobtrusive of the teaching-learning interface, because it occurs as part and parcel of the teaching-learning experiences in the science classroom. This format is the "closest to instruction" and is most realistic in terms of its similarity to how problems are commonly encountered and addressed in real life. Student work on extended investigations can be included in their portfolios, as described below (page 42).

You can use this assessment format to measure how well students are learning over an extended period of time, rather than only their performance on an examination at the end of a lesson or unit. A student's ability to develop hypotheses, plan experiments, follow through on a project, solve problems, and persist in reaching solutions can all be observed by using an extended investigation, which can extend for days, weeks, or even months. Students can work individually and/or collaborate with peers on an extended investigation. Assessment results of extended investigations can show students' persistence in ways that traditional testing methods cannot.

Time can be allowed for students to show evidence of their planning and organizational skills. Students can demonstrate their problem-solving skills as they carry out an extended investigation. Also, students can demonstrate their skills at recording information and keeping records in an extended investigation assessment format. Their final product, which may be written, verbal, electronic, or multimedia, provides a mechanism for assessing communications skills.

A further benefit of the extended investigation assessment format is that students can pursue in great depth a particular area of interest. They can apply skills and knowledge learned in the classroom to a similar situation outside the classroom.

Students must always be aware of the intended use of assessment data and, in particular, how this data will be used for high-stakes decisions.

Science teachers informally assess their students' understanding and inquiry skills during lessons and class activities. This informal assessment format is usually anecdotal and intuitive. Extended investigations offer a format that is organized and consistent with the *National Science Education Standards*, where assessment aligns with instruction.

Figure 3.3 illustrates an extended investigation using a performance task that focuses on testing foods for nutrients. In this task, students apply their manipulative and problem-solving skills in testing a variety of common foods for nutrients. Students are provided with a brief background of the chemistry of proteins, carbohydrates, and fats. They are required to perform confirmatory laboratory tests to identify these nutrients before attempting to identify nutrients in unknown food samples. Students complete this extended investigation, and use their data to evaluate nutrient claims on the labels of foods products.

**Food Nutrients
Student Task Sheet**

Task:

In this investigation, you will apply your skills at testing specific food compounds to predict, collect, and analyze data to determine the nutrients present in some common foods.

Background:

Humans obtain energy from nutrients contained in food. This energy is used for growth and the repair of cells. The major classes of nutrients contained in the variety of foods consumed are proteins, carbohydrates, and lipids (fats). Vitamins and minerals, while consumed in smaller amounts, are essential to growth and metabolic maintenance.

Carbohydrates are organic molecules of various sized sugars that form a significant source of nutrients for most organisms. They have a generic formula $(CH_2)n$ and, as the name suggests, they are hydrates of carbon. Carbohydrates are manufactured by green plants from water and CO_2 through a process called photosynthesis. Phototropic organisms contain pigments called chlorophylls (green), carotenoids (yellow), xanthophylls (orange), and phycobilins (red and blue) that trap light energy and convert it into chemical energy via the process of photosynthesis. The primary product of photosynthesis is represented by a deceptively simple equation:

$$6H_2O + 6CO_2 \xrightarrow{\text{light}} C_6H_{12}O_6 + 6H_2O$$

where the primary product is glucose, which is later stored as starch.

Carbohydrates are classified based on the number of carbon atoms in their molecules. Monosaccharides are examples of simple carbohydrates. The most common monosaccharide is glucose $(C_6H_{12}O_6)$. Fructose (corn sugar), mannose, and galactose (found in milk) are other important monosaccharides. Sucrose (table sugar), lactose (milk sugar), and maltose (from starch) are examples of disaccharides (double sugars) being composed of two sugar molecules. Starch is an important member of complex carbohydrates, called polysaccharides, with many sugar (usually glucose) molecules. Starch is made up of two components:

- amylose, which makes up 15–20 percent of the starch molecule and is the soluble part of starch;

- amylopectin, which makes up 80–85 percent of the starch molecule and is the insoluble part, forming a paste with hot water and thickening upon heating.

Proteins, another important nutrient, are compounds of amino acids formed with hydrogen bonds. Meat, fish, and the yolk of eggs from animals and many plant seeds—especially from leguminous plants—are good sources of proteins.

Figure 3.3: Extended Investigation Task on Food Nutrients. Saha and Chan, 1998.

Fats are a type of lipid made up of triglycerides. They possess a high concentration of chemical energy and are used for semi-permanent storage of energy in animals (fats) and plants (oils). Saturated fats are solid, and oils are liquid at room temperature.

Vitamins are organic substances other than carbohydrates, lipids, or proteins and are needed for metabolism. They cannot be synthesized in adequate amounts by the body. Minerals are any inorganic nutrients—such as Ca, Na, Mg, Fe, and P—necessary for the proper functioning of the body.

We need all types of nutrients in our diets to allow our bodies to function normally. Dietary reference intakes and recommended daily allowances are provided as guides for optimum health.

Materials:

- safety goggles
- 250 ml beaker
- test tube rack
- Biuret solution
- iodine solution
- lab aprons
- distilled water
- hot plate
- .005% Indophenol solution
- brown wrapping paper
- plastic gloves
- ten, 18 mm × 150 mm test tubes
- Benedict's solution
- common foods: white flour, rice flour, bean flour, corn flour, soybean flour, pudding mix (without starch), gelatin, glucose, dried coconut, ground almonds, tofu, dried milk powder, corn oil, fruit (i.e., orange, cantalope, apple, banana), and table salt

Procedure:

1. Prepare a table similar to the one provided below.

Food sample	starch	glucose	protein	fat	vitamin C
white flour prediction: results:					
rice flour prediction: results:					
bean flour prediction: results:					
corn flour prediction: results:					
soybean flour prediction: results:					

2. Predict what nutrient you will find in each of the food samples provided. Test your hypothesis through observation of appropriate reaction for each sample with various indicators. Contact your teacher if you need to review how to use some of the indicators.

3. Complete the table with the data obtained from your tests.

Analysis:

1. How did your predictions match with your test outcomes?

2. Which food samples contain more than one nutrient for which you tested?

3. Based on your analysis, which food sample(s) could be used as a source of starch? Of protein? Of glucose? Fat? Vitamin C? Minerals?

On completing the extended investigation, students can orally present their experimental findings and analysis of food labels to the class, or each student or group of students can report their findings by displaying their work in the form of a poster or report. Again, this extended investigation can be included in student portfolios. Chapters 5–8, beginning on page 84, contain many additional examples of skills tasks, investigations, and extended investigations that illustrate these assessment formats.

Student-Focused Assessment Formats

Graphic Organizers

Graphic organizers are maps that represent cognitive structures and thinking processes—they are a "cartography of cognition" (Wandersee 1990). These cognitive maps are consistent with the constructivist view of learning and knowledge acquisition, and hold great potential as alternative assessment formats. They provide additional methods for teachers to find out what students know, and allow students to demonstrate their learning in a variety of ways.

The following sections discuss concept maps, the Vee heuristic, and Venn diagrams as exemplars of graphic organizers that can be used as alternative assessment formats.

Concept Maps

The use of concept maps has been promoted by many science educators and is consistent with instructional approaches that encourage higher-level thinking, conceptual change, and metacognition (Novak 1980, 1981, 1991). While they are often used as advance organizers prior to in-

struction, or as a review or summary after instruction, concept maps can also be used as an alternative assessment format. When used this way, concept maps have several possible characteristics: students construct their response, alternative representations are reinforced, relationships between concepts are highlighted, minimal reading skills are required, and misconceptions can often be detected. This is also an appropriate assessment format to use with pairs or small groups of students.

Concept maps are hierarchical in nature, and focus on one main idea or concept. The main idea or concept branches into more specific concepts in hierarchical levels. Concepts are usually nouns representing objects or events, and are enclosed in ovals or boxes. Concepts are linked with lines, and the relationships between concepts are shown by linking words using verbs, adverbs, or prepositions. Two concepts connected together by linking words form a complete idea. Examples of concepts are placed below the ovals, circles, or boxes used to draw the concept map.

Concept maps can be used in various ways for assessment purposes, and with varying degrees of structure. Teachers must first spend instructional time with students coaching them on how to develop a concept map. Figure 3.4 (page 36) illustrates a highly structured approach to concept mapping using objects in an aquarium.

The concept map in Figure 3.4 is highly structured, with the map already constructed and words provided to choose from for completing the blank cells. The map shows a number of objects in an aquarium. The lines with linking words indicate how some of the objects relate to one another. There are a number of blank spaces in the concept map, and, using the words in the box, students

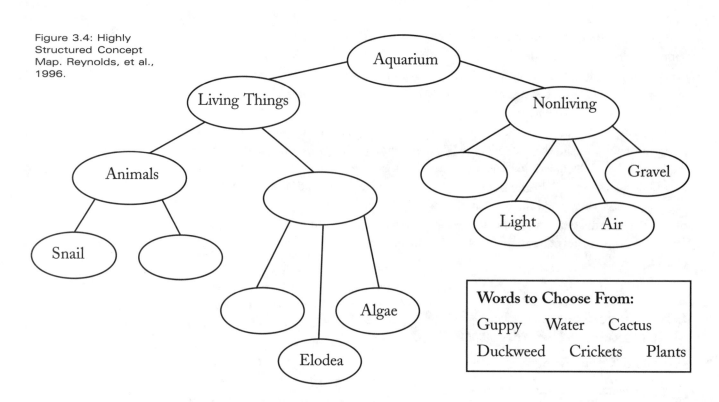

Figure 3.4: Highly Structured Concept Map. Reynolds, et al., 1996.

Words to Choose From:

Guppy   Water   Cactus
Duckweed   Crickets   Plants

select one word for each space and write the word in that space.

A second, less-structured example is provided in Figure 3.5, which uses the concepts from the Figure 3.4 example but with none of the words already printed in an oval. The "Words to Choose From" box includes all the expected responses. One modification could be to place one or more distracters—words that don't fit the map—in the box. A further modification could be to use pictures instead of words. This strategy provides additional support for Limited English Proficiency students

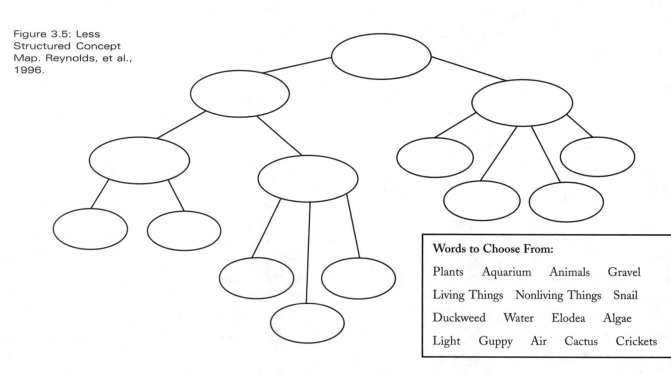

Figure 3.5: Less Structured Concept Map. Reynolds, et al., 1996.

Words to Choose From:

Plants   Aquarium   Animals   Gravel

Living Things   Nonliving Things   Snail

Duckweed   Water   Elodea   Algae

Light   Guppy   Air   Cactus   Crickets

and for students who learn best through visual instruction.

The examples of concept mapping provided in Figures 3.4 and 3.5 are basically matching exercises, and reflect the organization and instruction provided by the teacher. A great strength of the concept map lies in a student's own ability to organize his or her thoughts and to present them in a form that is unique to the student's individual understanding.

Figure 3.6 provides a third modification on the aquarium example. In this example, even less structure is provided than in Figure 3.5, but all the key concepts are listed. Students must construct the map organizing these concepts and presenting appropriate relationships.

A fourth example is provided in Figure 3.7, which requires that the student read a paragraph and construct a concept map showing the major concepts and their interrelationships.

Concept maps can be used for a variety of assessment purposes, such as formative and diagnostic assessment. The nature of concept maps allows for multiple variations. They also tend to be rich and varied, and are appropriate for small-group work and for students working in pairs. Their use is appropriate for discussion, display, and class presentations, and in those ways can be used for summative assessment.

There are no "right" or "wrong" concept maps. It is more important for students to be aware of their skills in processing and interpreting new ideas rather than in eliciting "correct" answers. Maps that display characteristics and relationships tend to be more useful.

To use concept maps as an assessment technique, a scoring system must be available. A number of systems have been suggested, some of which are quantitatively

based while others are more qualitative. The quantitative systems are based on establishing score criteria and assigning points to students' maps as they meet these criteria. The example provided in Figure 3.8 (page 38, top) illustrates a quantitative scoring scheme.

A variation on the quantitative concept map assessment method depicted in Figure 3.8 is illustrated in Figure 3.9 (page 38). This variation uses the same six criteria—number of concepts, relationship of concepts, number of linkages, validity of linkages, branching/cross-linking of concepts, and specific examples—but enables the teacher to rank the student's proficiency in each criteria. This variation allows for a maximum student score of 30 points and a minimum score of six points.

Although the quantitative scoring systems depicted in Figures 3.8 and 3.9 are technically reliable, systems for assessing student concept maps may benefit from and have greater applicability using a holistic, more qualitative approach. In Figure 3.10 (page 39), emphasis is placed on how a student integrates concepts with prior knowledge. The 13 criteria provided in

Figure 3.6: Student Constructed Concept Map. Reynolds, et al., 1996.

Construct a concept map about an aquarium that uses the following words: aquarium, water, guppies, living things, gravel, snails, plants, nonliving things, and duckweed. Organize the words in a pattern that shows how they are related in an aquarium. Label the connecting lines to describe those relations.

Figure 3.7: Student Constructed Concept Map. Reynolds, et al., 1996.

A pond is a shallow body of standing water in which sunlight reaches the bottom, allowing plants to grow. A pond may be a suitable habitat for many different plants and animals, but all ponds share some common characteristics.

Most important is that a pond contains water. This non-living substance provides life-giving oxygen, other gases, and nutrients to the living things in the pond. Life in a pond may include frogs, fish such as minnows or guppies, turtles, insects such as water striders and mosquito larvae, snails, and microscopic plants and animals that drift suspended in the water.

There are many kinds of green plants in a pond as well. Water algae serves as food for many of the small animals in the pond. Some plants' leaves and flowers do not even grow above the surface of the water. Most people call these pond weeds, such as duckweed or water lilies.

Construct a concept map that would help someone understand how the major concepts presented in this paragraph are related.

1. Concept identification (each concept).	1 point per concept
2. Relationship between concepts (i.e., links).	1 point per proposition
3. Coverage	
0–20% of concepts	1 point
21–40% of concepts	2 points
41–60% or concepts	3 points
61–80% of concepts	4 points
81–100% of concepts	5 points
4. Hierarchy (i.e., concepts arranged from general to specific in levels).	5 points per level
5. Branching or cross links (i.e., connections between hierarchical levels).	5 points per connection
6. Specific examples of each concept.	1 point per example

Criteria	Poor	Fair	Good	Very Good	Excellent
	1	2	3	4	5
Number of Concepts					
Concepts Relationship/Hierarchy					
Number of Links					
Validity of Links					
Concept Branching/Cross-Linking					
Specific Examples					

Basis for determining level of excellence:

Number of Concepts: tends to include the major concepts, not too few or too many.

Concepts Relationship/Hierarchy: locates the major concepts logically in the map, from general to specific.

Number of Links: includes important links between concepts.

Validity of Links: uses appropriate linking words.

Concept Branching/Cross-Linking: concepts tend to extend in both directions of map.

Specific Examples: appropriate examples provided.

Figure 3.10 assist the teacher in the qualitative scoring and analysis of concept maps.

Venn Diagrams

In assessment, students can be asked to draw an original, representative sketch, or they may be asked to use an existing diagram, in order to show the relationships they observe among several concepts. Because the completion of such tasks requires only the use of pencil and paper, Venn diagrams can be used quite easily with large groups of students. The diagrams are designed to measure students' understandings of relationships they have observed or discovered among a small number of concepts rather than to measure their comprehension of an entire situation. Venn diagrams are different from many other assessment techniques in that they require the student to make or interpret a nonverbal response—a drawing. Because of this characteristic, a Venn diagram can be used to investigate aspects of concepts not examined by more traditional techniques. Figure 3.11 (page 39) provides an example of how a Venn diagram illustrates the relationships among types of bottled drinks.

Other examples of sets of concepts for which this technique might be used include: animals, insects, mammals, reptiles, and amphibians, as well as elements, compounds, metals, and alloys. Additional examples can be found in Gunstone and White (1986).

Although restricted to only one aspect of understanding—that is, the relation between one concept and others of a similar type—the Venn diagram assessment technique has been found to be both powerful and easy to use. For example, it can be used as a basis for more in-depth interviews with individual students. Questions can be posed as to why students drew their diagram in a particular way and whether the areas and degrees of overlap correspond to cases that actually exist.

Vee Diagramming, or Vee Heuristic

The Vee heuristic is an attempt to help students understand their laboratory work within a constructivist framework. Knowledge acquisition is context dependent, depending on prior concepts, theories, beliefs, and principles the student uses to view and understand the world. The Vee is a graphic organizer, like the one depicted in Figure 3.12 (page 40), that uses prior knowledge and skills by raising the following questions:

- What is the question?

- What are the key concepts that help answer a question?

- What methods of inquiry can provide answers to the question?

- What knowledge is already known that would help answer the question?

	Yes	No
1. Concept map revolves around one idea, topic, or theme.		
2. Each concept represents a simple idea.		
3. Concepts flow from general to specific.		
4. Concepts are *not* repeated.		
5. Different hierarchical levels of concepts are indicated.		
6. Concepts are linked by appropriate words (i.e., verbs, adverbs, prepositions).		
7. Examples are distinguished from concepts.		
8. Concepts are linked to create a logical or complete idea.		
9. Concepts are distinguished from links.		
10. There is some branching of concepts.		
11. Cross-links are shown and indicate logical relationships.		
13. Cross lines are present.		

Figure 3.10: Qualitative Concept Map Scoring and Analysis Criteria. Adapted from Stuart, 1985.

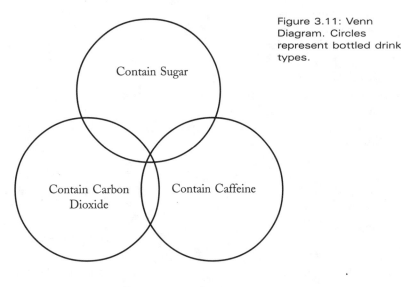

Figure 3.11: Venn Diagram. Circles represent bottled drink types.

Conceptual

(Knowing)

Concepts/Theories

(What do I know?)

1. What do I know about the topic?

2. Which concepts relating to the question do I know?

3. How are the concepts related to each other?

Graphic Organizers

(How are the ideas connected?)

Concept Map

1. How do the concepts and ideas relate to each other?

2. Is the general concept placed at the top of the concept map?

3. Can I build a hierarchy of concepts?

4. What are the possible cross-links?

5. Are the cross-links meaningful? Have I included linking words?

6. Have I included examples of concepts?

Active Interplay

Focus Question

1. What do I need to know?

2. What do I want to find out?

Methodological

(Doing)

Claims

(How can I interpret my findings, observations, and data?)

1. What do my data, observations, and results tell me?

2. What conclusions can I make from my data?

3. Can my data suggest further hypotheses? Further questions? Refute any existing theories?

4. Can I apply this knowledge in real-world, practical situations?

5. Self-reflection: what knowledge and skills did I learn?

Data Collection

(What did I measure and observe?)

1. Did I collect data in the form of tables?

2. Did I graph my data?

3. What do my graphs look like?

4. What are possible errors?

5. Do my data show trends?

6. Are there other ways to report my data?

Events

(How can I find an answer to my question?)

1. What apparatus do I need?

2. What objects and events must I observe?

3. What procedures can I use?

4. What did I use?

• What needs to be done to help answer the question?

The "Vee" shape is useful in laboratory investigations because it focuses on a specific question. Like many graphic organizers, the Vee is appropriate for Limited English Proficiency students, and allows students who prefer to use mapping techniques to demonstrate their knowledge and skills.

As illustrated in Figure 3.12, the focus question is located at the "top" of the Vee. The Vee's left side is the "knowing" side, and provides an opportunity for students to consider how a theory, prior concepts, and skills relate to the focus question. The Vee's right side is the "doing" side, where students record data and observations, interpret data, and draw conclusions. Figure 3.13 illustrates the placement of a focus question at the top of the Vee. (In this example, the investigative or "doing" component is on the left side; the "What am I doing" component can also be placed at the Vee's bottom, as suggested in Figure 3.12.) A concept map can be included on the left side, enabling students to demonstrate their conceptual understanding and to show how concepts connect. This format of alternative assessment aligns closely with instruction that is constructivist in nature, and is appropriate for diagnostic, formative, and summative assessment.

Vee Scoring Criteria

One example of a scoring system for a Vee heuristic is illustrated in Figure 3.14 (page 42). This scoring system focuses on four major components of a Vee: the focus question, a description of the object or event, the principles and concepts identified, and the records/transformations that were included. A score of three or four points is available for each component, varying by the amount of information or detail provided. After a group of teachers

Figure 3.13: Vee Heuristic. Adapted from Shepardson and Jackson, 1987.

Theme
Solutions

Associated Words
calcium chloride
distilled water

Investigative Activity
1. Put 10 ml of distilled water in the beaker.
2. Put 10 drops of soapy water in the beaker. Shake. Record observations.
3. Put 10 drops of soapy water in another beaker along with calcium chloride. Shake. Record observations.

Focus Question
Does the amount of calcium chloride added to the 10 ml of distilled water affect the number of drops of soapy water required to make suds?

Application
If you want more suds in your bath, don't put any calcium chloride in the water.

Conclusion
The beaker without calcium chloride has more suds. So, calcium chloride can affect the amount of suds.

With/Without Calcium Chloride	Suds?
Without	Lots of suds
With	Some suds, but not a lot

Higher number indicates more complete information.

Focus Question	Points
No focus question is identified.	0
A question is identified, but does not focus on the concepts identified on the left side of the Vee.	1
A focus question is identified; includes concepts, but does not suggest objects or the major event; or, the wrong objects and event are identified in relation to the rest of the laboratory investigation.	2
A clear focus question is identified; includes concepts to be used, and suggests the major event and accompanying objects.	3

Object/Event	Points
No objects or events are identified.	0
The major event or the objects are identified and are consistent with the focus question, *or* an event and objects are identified but are inconsistent with the focus question.	1
The major event and the accompanying objects are identified, and are consistent with the focus question.	2
Same as above, but also suggests what observations and data will be collected.	3

Principles and Concepts	Points
No information is presented on conceptual side.	0
A few concepts are identified, but without principles and theory; or, a principle written is the knowledge claim sought in the investigation.	1
Concepts and at least one type of principle (conceptual or methodological) or concepts and a relevant theory are identified.	2
Concepts and two types of principles are identified; or, concepts, one type of principle, and a relevant theory are identified.	3
Concepts, two types of principles, and a relevant theory are identified.	4

Records/Transformations	Points
No records or transformations are identified.	0
Records are identified, but are inconsistent with the focus question of the major event.	1
Either records or transformation are identified, but not both.	2
Records are identified for the major event; transformations are consistent with both the focus question and the abilities and grade level of the student.	3

Figure 3.14: Vee Heuristic Scoring System. Adapted from Novak and Gowin, 1984. See also Gurley-Dilger, 1992.

uses the scoring system, relevant modifications will make it more useful.

Portfolios

Artists, architects, photographers, and many other professionals use portfolios to demonstrate the quality and range of their work. A teacher's credentials file serves a similar purpose of demonstrating a broad range of skills, experiences, and achievements. An increasing number of teachers are using student portfolios to assess progress as curriculum reform efforts take hold.

The Buffalo, New York, Public Schools have instituted a portfolio assessment strategy. Figure 3.15 (page 43) provides items that are included as part of an assessment for a seventh grade life sciences course. Student portfolios must contain eight products from the list. Each element is worth a maximum of 5 points (for a total of 40 points) toward the final course grade. Students are provided more detailed information about each of these products as to time involvement, the number of sources, and other considerations. Many teachers provide class time for students to work on their portfolios and provide a time line/schedule for completing elements of their portfolios to help students organize and pace their work.

Developing a good portfolio is more art than science; there are no "right" answers, but many answers that can be adapted to specific curricula, age groups, and skill levels. The two sets of questions outlined below can guide you on designing a portfolio assessment.

What Does the Portfolio Contain Evidence About?

• Who decided the purpose?

- Is the purpose the same for all students?

- Will the portfolio contain evidence of proficiency or progress?

- To what uses will the portfolio be put?

- When, how often, and by whom will the portfolio be reviewed?

What Will Count as Evidence in the Portfolio?

- Which pieces of evidence are required and which are selected?

- Must evidence be produced alone or can it be collaborative?

- Will the portfolio contain only best work?

- Where will the portfolio be kept?

- How much evidence will be included in the portfolio?

This list of questions, adapted from Collins (1992), is a good starting point for putting together a portfolio. The answers to these questions will be based on the context of the assessment plans and the intent of the teacher or department.

Examples of which pieces of evidence are required and selected are provided in Figure 3.16 (page 44).

Because portfolios are often collected toward the end of the school year when teachers are already overburdened with paperwork, the grading process must be kept simple. One way to facilitate the portfolio assessment task is to encourage students to evaluate their own work using criteria you provide for them. "Counting" the number of satisfactory elements (ones that met the established criteria) is one reasonable way to approach the "grading" of portfolios. Students should know the portfolio requirements throughout the semester, ide-

ally from a rubric posted in the classroom. Teachers should approach portfolios experimentally, changing hypotheses and procedures as needed, and continuing to collect data and form conclusions as to utility.

Portfolio management is a crucial element in the implementation of this alternative assessment format. There is a large amount of clerical work involved in ensuring that student work is both secure and easily accessible. Students must be responsible for their own portfolios, and, if at all possible, a secure file cabinet or container should be made available to students for storing their portfolios. Because portfolios often contain many samples of student work, they can be large and bulky, so careful attention must be paid to providing a storage facility that can accommodate various portfolio sizes and dimensions.

Oral Presentations and Debate

Oral presentations offer an alternative assessment format that has great potential for improving student learning. Oral presentations can be conducted individually, in pairs, or in small groups. Using this format, students have an opportunity to research and present their findings on a particular science topic to their teacher and their peers. Students can include posters and models as part of their oral presentation, effectively combining several assessment formats. This assessment format is interactive by nature, as the audience can ask questions for clarification and challenge the speaker to justify knowledge claims. Teachers and students listen to the quality of the presentation, and draw conclusions about individual and group achievement. This assessment format is truly authentic in nature, as scientists, policymakers, and many other types of

Figure 3:15: Portfolio Assessment Items for Grade 7 Life Sciences Courses. Buffalo Public Schools, 1995.

1. Five journal excerpts.
2. Library research project.
3. Short-term observation record of a nature walk.
4. Dichotomous key reference to a life science collection.
5. Long-term project involving observations or care of living things.
6. Group project requiring experimental design.
7. Persuasive essay written to convince audience to either use or abandon a specific technology related to life science.
8. Interview report.
9. Scientific autobiography.
10. Student authored written request for information from a community resource.

Figure 3.16: Evidence
Required in a Portfolio.
*Middle School Science
Portfolio, New
Standards Project,
1997.*

Purpose

The purpose of this exhibit is to show that you can investigate a question over a long period of time. Your investigation should include:

- **A question** you can study using available resources.

- **Safe, humane, and ethical procedures** that respect privacy and property rights.

- **Data** you collect, record, and represent in ways that others can verify.

- **An analysis of your data** that requires you to use statistical skills.

- **Clearly communicated recommendations, decisions, and conclusions** based on evidence.

- **Acknowledgment** of references, sources, and the contributions of others.

Exhibit Requirements

Prepare one entry for the Scientific Investigation Exhibit. Your investigation must involve research and applications of science over a period of at least three weeks. Entries can include:

Controlled Experiment: An investigation in which you can test if and how a variable will cause a change in another variable, when all other variables are constant.

- Investigate how a variable (i.e., soil, water, fertilizer, etc.) affects plant growth.

- Investigate how a variable (i.e., food, light, toys) affects animal behavior.

- Which de-icer works best, while minimizing cost and environmental harm?

- Which wax is best for skis under certain conditions? Which oil is best for in-line skates or bicycle wheels?

- Does the form of sugar (i.e., crystals, honey, maple syrup) affect yeast growth or the taste of bread?

- Does the shape of a speaker container affect sound quality?

Field Work: Systematic observation of a site to see how its conditions change over a period of time. When doing field work, you don't manipulate the conditions.

- Compare bird distribution near the school with a field guide for your region.

- Determine how the local climate has changed over the last century.

- Adopt a stream and use it to study water and habitat quality over time.

- Study monument deterioration at a local cemetery (or school steps or sidewalk).

- Make recommendations about water quality on and near the school campus.

- Study the distribution of a local species, and determine if it is endangered.

- Study how asthma is related to local weather.

Design: An investigation that solves a design problem or makes something better.

- Design a squirrel-proof bird feeder for a particular bird species.

- Design a greenhouse that will support a particular plant species.

- Redesign the school's fire warning system for students with disabilities.

- Compare different methods of cooking for health and aesthetic effects.

- Compare the functional and aesthetic designs of different sports shoes.

Secondary Research: An investigation that uses data gathered by others.

- Compare the accuracy of local weather information from a variety of sources.

- Use the Internet to get current information on a rapidly changing scientific topic.

- Study the amount of wetlands in your town or county and relate the acreage to the populations of different plant and animal species over the last 50 years.

- Make a geographical history of your area over the last century (to include roads, buildings, ports, etc.).

professionals often share ideas and viewpoints using oral presentations. The quality of the questions that can arise from an oral presentation can stimulate general class discussions, which in turn promotes student learning.

You can take advantage of this assessment format by following some simple guidelines for success. They include:

- Prepare questions and topics in advance.

- Topics can be controversial, requiring students to demonstrate deep understanding of ethical issues, science topics, and other relevant information.

- Involve students in choosing topics, as they may wish to pursue one with personal meaning or connected to their actual experience.

- Provide opportunities for appropriate training and support as students prepare their material.

- Ensure that oral presentations support and enhance concepts being learned. This way, the assessment format is truly part of the instruction, as it is "embedded" in the curriculum.

- Use debate, or other team or small group approaches, to involve as many students as possible. This provides an ideal opportunity for low, medium, and high achievers to work collaboratively toward completing a task. Where time permits, students can reverse positions in the debate to gain insights from opposing perspectives.

- Use this assessment format as an opportunity for Limited English Proficiency students to practice listening and speaking skills. Language acquisition involves a variety of skills, and oral presentations stress listening and speaking over reading and writing.

- Encourage use of visual aids, such as posters, models, and physical demonstrations.

- Encourage use of graphic organizers, such as concept maps and flow charts.

- Use sensitivity with shy and reserved students, as oral presentations involve a sometimes intimidating public display of achievement. Provide encouragement and a safe environment, free of undue criticism, as such students make their initial oral presentation. Subsequent presentations should be easier for them, as they gain confidence in their abilities.

- Develop scoring criteria and, preferably, involve students in its development.

- Allocate adequate time for assessment.

- Encourage students to be appropriately critical of information presented, and to offer alternative and well-supported arguments.

- Use the debate format to critically evaluate opposing viewpoints.

- Encourage self and peer assessment.

- Make students aware of the purpose and use of the assessment.

A variation of this assessment format is to use an interview approach, where students can act as experts on a particular subject or domain of knowledge, and where peers can conduct an interview to probe an expert's knowledge. Both "experts" and "interviewers" should be provided with learning and assessment experiences in integrating new skills and knowledge with previously learned material. Such interviews are authentic, "real-world" experiences because scientists and many others routinely conduct interviews when making important announcements. Professional reputations are enhanced by good interview skills, as audiences use them to form conclusions about an interviewee's expertise.

As part of their oral presentations, students can use posters or models—so-called props—to enhance their presentations. Posters, overheads, and models are tools scientists routinely use to explain their work to professional peers and the public. Television uses simulations and artistic representations to illustrate new developments in science. By assessing these kinds of products, we send a message to students that they are important skills to learn.

For students to improve their design skills, their preparation, and their delivery of oral reports and presentations, they must have the opportunity to learn these skills, as well as the opportunity to receive feedback from assessment. We can use this assessment format to involve students in peer teaching, where "experts" help and assist "novices" in preparing oral reports, and to emphasize interpersonal skills, such as sharing, critiquing, and collaborating. This assessment format encourages students to reflect and think about their learning, and challenges them to solve problems, organize their materials, and synthesize their ideas into a coherent whole.

Interviews and Conferences

In the previous section, we suggested that, as an offshoot to the oral presentation format, students can interview peers who have "expert" knowledge in a particular skill or domain. In the interview assessment format, the teacher interviews students, focusing on conceptual change and misconceptions. We recommend this alternative assessment format for diagnostic and formative purposes. Teachers can follow the suggestions outlined below for conducting successful interviews.

- Prepare questions before the interview or conference with a clear idea of what you wish to discuss about conceptual change and misconceptions.

- Be clear to students about the reason for and use of information from the interview or conference.

- Allocate an appropriate amount of uninterrupted time.

- Be nonjudgmental, and listen carefully to student answers to the interview questions.

- Probe the student's knowledge with additional questions when their responses need clarification.

Interviews and conferences can be a powerful form of alternative assessment, one that provides a window into student achievement. Teachers must be able to clearly articulate the purposes and expectations of the interview or conference, and invite students to participate in their own assessment.

Yet, it may not be appropriate or desirable for every student to participate in an interview or conference format. As interview formats are appropriate for assessing speaking and listening skills, they lend themselves well to both Limited English Proficiency students and students who prefer to explain their ideas and demonstrate their understanding under conditions where they are able to ask questions for clarification. This isn't always possible using paper-and-pencil formats. Apply the old adage "different strokes for different folks" when making decisions about which students would benefit from this alternative (and authentic) assessment format.

Lab Skills Checklists

Checklists are an excellent way to reinforce good laboratory techniques and to embed assessment with instruction. Checklists can be used during related instructional activities by teachers, students, and peers. To keep the management of checklist data as simple as possible, keep the checklists themselves as simple as possible. Checklist forms can be maintained and stored in student portfolios.

For the past several years, demonstrating a set of lab skills has constituted a requirement for New York State science students who are completing Regents biology and physics courses. The first six skills provided in Figure 3.17 must be successfully demonstrated before taking the final exam in biology; the last ten are listed in the biology syllabus as additional key skills.

Student and teacher initial skills when successfully demonstrated.

1. Focus a compound light microscope. (low and high power)
Date _____ Student _____ Teacher _____

2. Prepare wet mounts and apply staining techniques.
Date _____ Student _____ Teacher _____

3. Identify cell parts under the compound light microscope.
Date _____ Student _____ Teacher _____

4. Select and read instruments used for measurement.
Date _____ Student _____ Teacher _____

5. Dissect plant and animal specimens.
Date _____ Student _____ Teacher _____

6. Demonstrate safety skills.
Date _____ Student _____ Teacher _____

7. Formulate a question or define a problem and develop a hypothesis to be tested in an investigation.
Date _____ Student _____ Teacher _____

8. Given a laboratory problem, select suitable lab materials, safety equipment, and appropriate observation methods.
Date _____ Student _____ Teacher _____

9. Distinguish between controls and variables in an experiment.
Date _____ Student _____ Teacher _____

10. Determine the size of microscopic specimens in micrometers (microns).
Date _____ Student _____ Teacher _____

11. Use and interpret indicators such as pH paper, Benedict's reagent, iodine (Lugol's) solution, and bromthymol blue.
Date _____ Student _____ Teacher _____

12. Collect, organize, and graph data.
Date _____ Student _____ Teacher _____

13. Make inferences and predictions based upon data collected and observed.
Date _____ Student _____ Teacher _____

14. Formulate generalizations or conclusions of the investigation.
Date _____ Student _____ Teacher _____

15. Assess the limitations and assumptions of the experiment.
Date _____ Student _____ Teacher _____

16. Determine the accuracy and repeatability of the experimental data and observations.
Date _____ Student _____ Teacher _____

Figure 3.17: High School Biology Laboratory Skills Checklist. New York State Education Department, 1984.

While there are performance tests with the Regents Earth science course and, at grade 4, as part of the *Elementary Science Program Evaluation Test (ESPET)* (NYSED 1992a, 1992b), checklists are also a useful assessment format because they provide an early diagnosis of student achievement. Figure 3.18 includes many of the skills important for laboratory work in Earth science. In contrast with the biology lab skills checklist provided in Figure 3.17, the Earth science lab skills checklist has added space to indicate the level of the skill demonstrated: Needs Improvement, Proficient, and Exemplary. This checklist can be used over a semester or year to monitor a student's improvement in individual skills.

Figure 3.19 (page 49) illustrates a possible checklist that can be used to monitor the development of inquiry skills for K-4 students (the skills are assessed as

Figure 3.18: Earth Science—Checklist for Laboratory Skills. New York State Education Department, 1992.

Earth Science Lab Skills

Enter the date when a new level of skill is demonstrated.

1. Measures angles and distances on flat and curved surfaces.
   Level: Needs Improvement _____   Proficient _____   Exemplary _____

2. Classifies rock samples as being igneous, sedimentary, or metamorphic, and gives evidence to support that classification.
   Level: Needs Improvement _____   Proficient _____   Exemplary _____

3. Uses a key to identify samples of Earth materials based on observed characteristics.
   Level: Needs Improvement _____   Proficient _____   Exemplary _____

4. Determines the density of samples of Earth materials by measuring mass and volume.
   Level: Needs Improvement _____   Proficient _____   Exemplary _____

5. Measures the rate of movement of an object.
   Level: Needs Improvement _____   Proficient _____   Exemplary _____

6. Quantifies observations within the accuracy and precision of measuring devices.
   Level: Needs Improvement _____   Proficient _____   Exemplary _____

7. Constructs an appropriate graph according to accepted conventions.
   Level: Needs Improvement _____   Proficient _____   Exemplary _____

8. Interprets data from a graph including interpolation and extrapolation.
   Level: Needs Improvement _____   Proficient _____   Exemplary _____

9. Gathers original weather data and predicts short-term weather conditions based on those data.
   Level: Needs Improvement _____   Proficient _____   Exemplary _____

10. Creates and interprets models of Earth features and phenomena including drawing an isoline intensity map.
    Level: Needs Improvement _____   Proficient _____   Exemplary _____

11. Demonstrates the application of skills to study change over time in a long-term investigation.
    Level: Needs Improvement _____   Proficient _____   Exemplary _____

12. Orients him- or herself in relationship to land features, the Sun, and other stars.
    Level: Needs Improvement _____   Proficient _____   Exemplary _____

13. Identifies and describes how a current event from the field of the Earth sciences has an economic or social impact on his or her life.
    Level: Needs Improvement _____   Proficient _____   Exemplary _____

---

part of a statewide test administered to all grade 4 students). A teacher might also use the checklist to indicate the topic or context in which each skill was demonstrated.

Since grade 8 is becoming the final grade for many middle school programs, we provide a possible lab skills checklist for that level. Figure 3.20 (page 50) includes some laboratory skills specific to life science, Earth science, and physical science appropriate to the middle school level, and some inquiry skills that apply across all content areas. This middle-level skills checklist illustrates another format for observing and assessing student demonstration of science skills. Here the teacher indicates the date at which the skill is observed in a context, whether it is performed in a standard laboratory or similar situation, or if it has been adapted to a novel situation.

These checklists should be treated as a resource of ideas. They can easily be adapted or modified by including additional skills or tailoring them to fit a specific science assessment task. The kind and method of information collected can be shifted from one checklist to another to reflect the nature of instruction related to these process skills.

Self, Pair, and Peer Evaluations

Over the course of a school semester or year, the overwhelming majority of laboratory and field experiences are conducted by students working as part of a lab team or a group of two or more. The assessment program should match the instructional program for student group work. This provides a particular advantage when a manipulative skills task requires students to use more than two hands or eyes. Dur-

Inquiry Skills—Elementary Science

Enter the date when each level is demonstrated.

1. Measures the mass of objects.
Needs improvement _____   Met the standard _____

2. Measures the volume of objects.
Needs improvement _____   Met the standard _____

3. Measures the length of objects.
Needs improvement _____   Met the standard _____

4. Measures the temperature of objects.
Needs improvement _____   Met the standard _____

5. Observes and describes living and nonliving objects.
Needs improvement _____   Met the standard _____

6. Predicts events based on observations and content background.
Needs improvement _____   Met the standard _____

7. Collects and records data from simple measurements and observations.
Needs improvement _____   Met the standard _____

8. Interprets and creates classification systems.
Needs improvement _____   Met the standard _____

9. States accurate inferences based on observations and content background.
Needs improvement _____   Met the standard _____

10. Applies math skills to science problems.
Needs improvement _____   Met the standard _____

11. Interprets data from graphs, charts, and tables.
Needs improvement _____   Met the standard _____

12. Identifies variables that influence phenomena and organisms.
Needs improvement _____   Met the standard _____

13. Formulates hypothesis/research question.
Needs improvement _____   Met the standard _____

14. States conclusions and generalizations consistent with observations and content background.
Needs improvement _____   Met the standard _____

15. Presents findings and relationships using data tables, graphs, or models.
Needs improvement _____   Met the standard _____

Figure 3.19: Elementary Inquiry Skills Checklist. Reynolds, et al., 1996.

Lab Skills Questions—Middle Level

Place the date in the blank when the skill was observed in a specific context.

1. Measures time, temperature, and linear dimensions (length, area, and volume).
   Developed in Lab _____   Applied in a similar situation _____   Adapted to a novel situation _____

2. Observes changes in objects, organisms, or phenomena, using appropriate tools: hand lens, binoculars, etc.
   Developed in Lab _____   Applied in a similar situation _____   Adapted to a novel situation _____

3. Sorts objects and organisms into groups, with at least three levels of grouping.
   Developed in Lab _____   Applied in a similar situation _____   Adapted to a novel situation _____

4. Uses a dichotomous key to identify organisms.
   Developed in Lab _____   Applied in a similar situation _____   Adapted to a novel situation _____

5. Determines densities of solid objects, by measuring mass and volume.
   Developed in Lab _____   Applied in a similar situation _____   Adapted to a novel situation _____

6. Determines the pH of solutions, using litmus paper and/or phenolphthalein.
   Developed in Lab _____   Applied in a similar situation _____   Adapted to a novel situation _____

7. Determines if material contains sugar, starch, and/or vitamin C, using available simple indicators.
   Developed in Lab _____   Applied in a similar situation _____   Adapted to a novel situation _____

8. Identifyies mineral samples, by observing key physical characteristics.
   Developed in Lab _____   Applied in a similar situation _____   Adapted to a novel situation _____

9. Uses topographic maps and compasses to find and describe physical features.
   Developed in Lab _____   Applied in a similar situation _____   Adapted to a novel situation _____

10. Uses weather maps and information to interpret current conditions and predict future trends.
    Developed in Lab _____   Applied in a similar situation _____   Adapted to a novel situation _____

11. Designs a controlled experiment, to include hypothesis, observation (measurement) procedures, and limitations.
    Developed in Lab _____   Applied in a similar situation _____   Adapted to a novel situation _____

12. Records results and observations in a table or chart that is logically labeled and organized.
    Developed in Lab _____   Applied in a similar situation _____   Adapted to a novel situation _____

13. Presents an accurate summary of data and/or observations.
    Developed in Lab _____   Applied in a similar situation _____   Adapted to a novel situation _____

14. Constructs graphs with appropriate title, scale, labels, and units on the axis.
    Developed in Lab _____   Applied in a similar situation _____   Adapted to a novel situation _____

15. States relationships (qualitative and quantitative), based on data or observations.
    Developed in Lab _____   Applied in a similar situation _____   Adapted to a novel situation _____

16. Interprets data presented in graphs, tables, and diagrams.
    Developed in Lab _____   Applied in a similar situation _____   Adapted to a novel situation _____

17. States conclusions based on experimental results, with appropriate accuracy.
    Developed in Lab _____   Applied in a similar situation _____   Adapted to a novel situation _____

Figure 3.20: Middle
Level Lab Skills
Checklist. Reynolds, et
al., 1996.

ing a lab investigation that is part of an instructional program, we expect students to provide input to the solution of the lab problem as a member of a group, to be receptive to the ideas provided by their partners, and to learn from their partners. These same behaviors can be motivators for students during an assessment task, if the students are provided the opportunity of working together.

There are at least two fundamental questions to be considered and addressed before using this assessment format (Reynolds, et al. 1996). The first deals with the style of the response sheet, and the other addresses how students are to be grouped.

How should student response sheets be constructed? The primary purpose of the assessment, whether it is high stakes or low stakes, will dictate an appropriate style for student responses. High-stakes tests are those that determine if an individual will pass or fail a course of study, if a graduation requirement will be satisfied, or if an honor will be awarded. Low-stakes tests are those in which student results will be used primarily for purposes such as program evaluation, student diagnostics (i.e., pretesting for the prescription of individual or remedial assistance), or as one small part of a much larger grading formula.

There are, basically, four methods that can be used, depending on the purpose for which the assessment has been designed (Reynolds, et al. 1996).

1. Provide the group with a set of directions, or one for each group member, of what is to be accomplished in the assessment task. As a group, the students will conduct the task, discuss it in detail, and complete a single, final group report that includes the necessary data tables, charts, narrative, and conclusions. There should be only one final response sheet or form from the group. The grade on this final report is the grade shared by each group member. This style is useful for low-stakes testing only.

2. Follow the same procedures as described above, but modify the reporting so that each group member can either accept the results of the group report or submit an addendum providing different or alternative analyses or information. This "minority report" can be graded separately from the final, group report. This style is useful for both low- and high-stakes testing.

3. As described above, students conduct the investigation as a group and discuss it in detail. Following their discussion, separate the students and have them develop their own, individual reports without any further assistance from the original groups. Each student's final grade depends solely on his or her individual reports. This style is useful for both low- and high-stakes testing.

4. As described above, students conduct the investigation as a group but keep their own, individual data records. Without the benefit of detailed group discussion of the investigation, separate the students from the group and have them complete their own reports. This style is useful for both low- and high-stakes testing.

How should students be grouped? Several approaches can be used for test partnerships, such as pairs or small groups. One way is to have students stay in their regular lab groups (i.e., those in which they have already been working during instruction). Another way is to rank the students in a hierarchical order, such as from highest to lowest in terms of achievement. Then you can form the student groups by putting similarly ranked students together in groups. This grouping method provides a good indication of how a particular individual would have performed while working alone.

It has been suggested that student pairs or groups should be made up of both high- and low-ranking students. The structure or make-up of small groups is crucial to successful group work and cooperative learning. Small groups can be structured based on interests and ability. Groups tend to work best when teachers do the following (Slavin 1990):

- Ensure group members are heterogeneous. Use prior achievement as a means of groups being made up of high, medium, and low achievers.

- Ensure the task requires individual accountability, where each group member has an assigned task or role.

- Ensure there is a group goal. In assessment tasks, the successful completion of an investigation is an example of a group goal.

- Make group constitutions flexible. Students want to work with friends, so explain that group make-up will change from task to task.

- Teach students how to work in groups and make certain that expectations are clear.

- Establish clear criteria for success. In some cases, small groups can complete an investigation while each group member turns in his or her own report. Or, in some cases,

one report can represent the group's work.

In grouping students for either instructional purposes, such as lab groups, or as assessment partners, care must be taken to ensure that each individual within a group shares equally in each of the steps that make up a learning experience (Reynolds, et al. 1996). Guard against students assuming overly dominant or submissive roles, and structure the groups as equitably as possible to avoid biases, such as might arise from unequal gender distribution. In some situations, initial groupings may need to be reformed if imbalances or inequalities become evident, even if the end result is that some groups are all-male and others are all-female. It is important for the teacher to assess by observing group dynamics and student participation in this style of testing. Assessment by observation should be ongoing during the course of the experience to provide support for a student's final "class participation" grade.

Much can be assessed about students' understanding of a laboratory or field investigation by providing individuals with the opportunity to evaluate other students' work, or peer review. If students have a good understanding of an investigation, they should be able to review other reports and easily critique the strengths and weaknesses in the procedures used, the data gathered and tabulated, and the conclusions drawn.

However, first students need to experience the lab or field investigation, particularly if it is very sophisticated, and learn the underlying content and skills associated with it. This is achieved by having students conduct the investigation, discuss it with their lab partners, write their own lab or field reports, get feedback from their teacher on their report, and discuss the results with their classmates.

About two or three weeks after students have had the above learning experiences, an assessment task can be assigned based on a fictitious student's lab/field report, one that has been carefully developed with specific features the teacher wants to present. It might also take the form of a report by a previous year's anonymous student. The assignment can then be for each student to complete an evaluation of the fictitious lab/field report, identifying its strengths and weaknesses (Reynolds, et al. 1996).

Technological Applications

The application of technologies to science assessment, such as using computer, audio, and video equipment has great potential in the future development of alternative assessment formats. We will focus on the application of using computers in alternative assessment.

Computers are presently used in multiple-choice testing for scoring student responses and analyzing student achievement. In some cases, students complete a multiple-choice assessment on the computer, as opposed to using a paper-and-pencil format. There is very little difference between these two approaches as the assessment is the same, and both formats assess low-level recall of knowledge. Alternative assessment formats demand that our assessments move away from this approach.

An appropriate use of computer technology as an alternative assessment format suggests the use of computer simulations of "real-world" experiences where students can solve problems. Graphic software provides the means for students to construct molecules, rotate molecular structures, and calculate molecular weights of molecules. Also, computers offer the promise of tracking students' responses as they progress through an assessment. This al-

lows teachers and students an additional window into student learning and achievement by monitoring pathways to solution of problems.

While computers are presently used as an information management tool, they also hold promise as an alternative assessment format. Computer software continues to provide more sophisticated, graphic, and interactive programs allowing students to experience simulations of science experiments that could never before be conducted in a high school science laboratory. For example, simulations of dissections can provide an alternative assessment task that could not be done using live specimens in the laboratory.

As our use of computers grows, both in and beyond the classroom, educators need to address issues of gender equity, validity, and fairness. As educators, we must provide all students with the opportunity to learn how to use computer technology, as opposed to merely learning how it works.

Teacher-Directed Assessment Formats

Despite the value of student-directed instruction, there are still times when teacher-directed approaches are useful. Quite often, they place fewer demands on equipment, materials, and other resources. Examples of teacher-directed assessments formats follow.

Demonstrations

In performance testing, it is desirable to have students engage in authentic assessment tasks in which they manipulate equipment and materials to collect their own data. This is consistent with the spirit of having the assessment program match the instructional program as closely as possible. If students are engaged in lab/ field experiences as part of their instructional program, they should be provided with these kinds of opportunities as part of their assessment program as well.

Due to constraints such as time, space, equipment, and safety, however, performance tasks may occasionally be replaced with a paper-and-pencil assessment task in which the teacher provides "canned" data rather than having students collect their own. While this approach does have merit—particularly if students have already had hands-on experiences collecting similar data—it falls far short of the spirit of having the assessment program reflect the complete instructional program.

A compromise is to have the teacher or student conduct/demonstrate an "assessment lab" in front of the whole class, with the actual lab setup located where real data are collected. Those data are then used by the individual students, or lab partners, in completing the assessment task. This technique of using the teacher demonstration as part of the assessment task has advantages and disadvantages when compared to using either the "student hands-on" or "canned data" strategy. Figure 3.21 provides some of these advantages and disadvantages.

Group Visuals

Group visuals that provide large, easily seen images (i.e., slides, videodisks, overhead transparencies, and videotapes) can be a source of useful prompts for assessment tasks. This kind of visual image can be presented to an entire class and used in assessing student observation and analysis skills. Group visuals can also be used to present authentic, "real-world" situations to students, as well as to provide prompts for classroom, group, or individual activities that can then be used to review, refresh, or prepare for further activities. Actual images of locations and situations beyond the classroom give students more of an understanding of reality than do simple line drawings.

Group visuals can provide quick assessment through a guided or unguided practice activity at either the beginning or end of a class period. This is a good way to keep students focused on the topic at hand, and can provide ready input for assessing the effectiveness of your own instruction. Low costs and ease of reproduction make some of these group visual materials readily available. Depending upon your access to technology, some of these media may prove very time and cost effective.

	Data Provided (Canned Data)	Teacher Demonstration	Student Hands-on
Setup time	Least	Modest	Most
Time to conduct	Least	Modest	Most
Safety	Least concern	Modest concern	Most concern
Amount of equipment	Least	Modest	Most
Amount of space	Least	Modest	Most
Scoring	Easiest	Modest	Hardest
Cost	Least	Modest	Most
Standardization	Most	Modest	Least
Reliability	Most	Modest	Least
Student interest	Low	Modest	High

Figure 3.21: Advantages and Disadvantages of Alternative Assessment Techniques. Reynolds, et al., 1996.

Conclusion

This chapter presented a variety of assessment formats that are more student-centered and authentic than most traditional assessments. These formats are significant because they are in keeping with the changes suggested by current science education reform documents. Changes in curricular goals and educational strategies need to be accomplished in tandem with changes in assessment techniques.

The alternative assessment formats are designed to:

- promote student learning and growth,

- make subject matter interesting and relevant, and

- provide a means for students to demonstrate their problem-solving and higher-level thinking skills.

The set of assessments provided in this chapter is by no means exhaustive, but does establish a basis on which teachers may begin the task of developing their own assessment strategies and formats. We consider this very much a "work in progress," and encourage you to revise and modify the assessments presented here as you see fit.

Works Cited

Buffalo Public Schools. 1995. *Portfolio for Grade 7 Science*. Buffalo: Buffalo Public Schools.

Collins, A. 1992. Portfolio for Science Education: Issues in Purpose, Structure, and Authenticity. *Science Education* 76(4).

Gunstone, R., and White, R. 1986. Assessing Understanding by Means of Venn Diagrams. *Science Education* 70(2).

Gurley-Dilger, L. I. 1982. *Use of Gowin's Vee and Concept Mapping Strategies to Teach Responsibility for Learning in High School Biological Sciences*. Doctoral diss., Cornell University.

Harmon, M., Smith, T., Martin, M., Kelly, D., Beaton, A., Mullis, I., Gonzalez, E., and Orpwood, G. 1997. *Performance Assessment in IEA's Third International Math-ematics and Science Study (TIMSS)*. Chestnut Hill, MA: TIMSS International Study Center.

Mason, C. 1992. Concept Mapping: A Tool to Develop Reflective Science Instruction. *Science Education* 76(1).

National Research Council (NRC). 1996. *National Science Education Standards*. Washington, DC: National Academy Press.

New Standards Project. 1997. *Middle School Science Portfolio*. Washington, DC: National Center for Education and the Economy (Tel. 202-783-3668).

New York State Education Department (NYSED). 1984. *Regents Biology Syllabus*. Albany: New York State Education Department.

———. 1992a. *New York State Elementary Science Program Evaluation Test (ESPET) Objective Test, Form E*. Albany: NYSED.

———. 1992b. *New York State Elementary Science Program Evaluation Test (ESPET) Manipulative Sills Test, Form X*. Albany: NYSED.

Novak, J. 1980. Learning Theory Applied to the Biology Classroom. *The American Biology Teacher* 42.

———. 1981. Applying Learning Psychology and Philosophy of Science to Biology Teaching. *The American Biology Teacher* 42.

———. 1991. Clarity with Concept Maps. *The Science Teacher* 59(7).

Novak, J., and Gowin, R. 1984. *Learning How to Learn*. New York: Cambridge University Press.

O'Sullivan, C., Reese, C., and Mazzeo, J. 1997. *NAEP 1996. Science Report Card for the Nation and States*. Washington, DC: National Center for Education Statistics.

Reynolds, D., Doran, R., Allers, R., and Agruso, S. 1996. *Alternative Assessment in Science: A Teacher's Guide*. Buffalo: University at Buffalo.

Roth, W., and Verechaka, G. 1993. Plotting a Course with Vee Maps. *Science and Children* 30(4).

Saha, G., and Chan, A. 1998. Food Nutrient Task. Unpublished document. Buffalo: University at Buffalo.

Shepardson, D., and Jackson, V. 1987. Developing Alternative Assessments Using the Benchmarks. *Science and Children* 35(2).

Slavin, R. 1990. *Cooperative Learning: Theory, Research, and Practice*. Englewood Cliffs, NJ: Prentice Hall.

Stuart, H. 1985. Should Concept Maps Be Scored Numerically? *European Journal of Science Education* 7(1).

Wandersee, J. 1990. Concept Mapping and the Cartography of Cognition. *Journal of Research in Science Teaching* 27(10).

Suggested Readings

Helgeson, S., and Kumar, D. 1993. Applications of Technology in Science Assessment. *Cognosos* 2(3).

Roth, W. 1993. The Unfolding Vee. *Science Scope* 16(5).

CHAPTER 4

Using Performance Assessment Results

Assessment and Evaluation

Many teachers treat assessment and evaluation as the same thing, largely because they are indeed strongly linked. Assessment is the process of collecting qualitative and quantitative information about student achievement and the quality of the science program. On the other hand, evaluation is the process of making judgments about student achievement based on the information collected from the assessments. Assessment data is then compared to established criteria and standards. Figure 4.1 depicts ways in which assessment and evaluation overlap and interface in the implementation of high-quality science programs.

Figure 4.1: Overlap of Assessment and Evaluation.

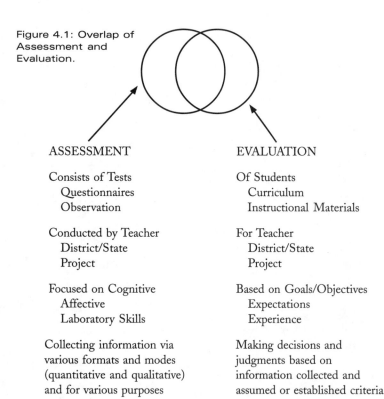

ASSESSMENT	EVALUATION

Consists of Tests
    Questionnaires
    Observation
	Of Students
	    Curriculum
	    Instructional Materials

Conducted by Teacher
    District/State
    Project
	For Teacher
	    District/State
	    Project

Focused on Cognitive
    Affective
    Laboratory Skills
	Based on Goals/Objectives
	    Expectations
	    Experience

Collecting information via various formats and modes (quantitative and qualitative) and for various purposes	Making decisions and judgments based on information collected and assumed or established criteria

Many examples of assessments are illustrated in Chapters 2 and 3, with many more examples in the chapters that focus on particular science disciplines (beginning on page 84). Examples of evaluation statements are:

- Joan was successful on the astronomy unit.

- Frank failed the biology course.

- The chromatography lab improved students' ability to interpret data.

- The chemistry course was ineffective in developing students' ability to design experiments.

- The school's elementary science program improved students' classifying skills.

- The middle school science program was ineffective in improving students' understanding of Earth science concepts.

These statements place a judgment or value on student achievement or program quality.

Norm- and Criterion-Referenced Evaluations

Each of the above statements is based on assessment information, and takes the form of a statement about the expected performance (criteria). These criteria can be based on comparing the performance and achievement of groups of students, courses, or programs with the performance and achievement of a "normed" group. These are quite familiar to most science teachers.

- You've scored in the 90th percentile (meaning you were better than 90 percent of your classmates or some cohort group).

- Your score was "below average" (meaning the number of points you earned on your test was below the average or mean score).

The other primary basis for evaluation is called "criterion-referenced," and examples of these usually include some form of mastery system. A common example defines mastery as correct answers (or successful performance) on 75 percent (or 80 percent) of items or tasks based on some set of concepts or skills. Whether a student is judged to have mastered (or passed) a given course or unit is based on how well the student's performance compares to a pre-established standard, not to some group of cohorts. Such evaluations, or comparisons, are believed to encourage cooperation and group work, rather than individualistic competition.

In other words, in a criterion-referenced system, you measure each student's performance against some previously established standard or criterion. Each student will be "successful" or have "mastered" a particular unit of instruction once he or she demonstrates the skill or knowledge objectives. For effective use, this system requires a clear, understandable description of the content or skill outcome.

Once you have collected a set of assessment data, you can begin to evaluate it in a number of different ways. Criterion-referenced and norm-referenced systems are two dramatically different ways of evaluating data. Assessment and evaluation have traditionally focused on ranking or rating student achievement by comparing their achievement to their peers or a normed group. This approach remains an important technique for monitoring student learning, and for providing information for placing students in academic and employment situations. In norm-referenced assessment, the frame of reference commonly used as a standard is the achievement of a norming group. With standardized tests, a random sample of students is selected from a national or state population to determine the norm. Classroom teachers develop their own tests using a single class or a group of classes under a teacher's direction to obtain a "norm." In addition, school districts use groups of classes from multiple schools to develop norms. The performance of individual students is then compared to the performance or achievement of their peers using the results of the normed group.

The interpretations and decisions based on a "normed" group are based on the traditional construct of intelligence, and use a "normal" or bell-shaped curve. Based on these assumptions, 50 percent of scores fall above the mean score, and 50 percent of scores fall below the mean score. Taking the argument a step further, if a single class is used as the norming group, half of the students in a sample or class will fail and half will pass, using the mean as a cut-off score to indicate success (Gipps 1995).

The *National Science Education Standards* (NRC 1996) call for a shift away from norm-referenced assessment, as is suggested in Figure 4.2 (page 60). The *National Standards* delineate what students must know and be able to do as part of a high-quality instructional program. As a result, student achievement and performance can then be evaluated in relation to established criteria rather than norms. This kind of criterion-referenced assessment (also called domain-referenced) suggests that whenever a student demonstrates mastery of the content and skills being assessed, then that student is judged as successful.

Future assessment should go beyond norm-referenced assessment to provide information on curriculum validity and program effectiveness. One example is New York State's *Elementary Science Program Evaluation Test* (*ESPET*), which is comprised of several tests for students to both demonstrate their competencies and provide information on improving the science programs.

As part of *ESPET*, students respond to a multiple-choice achievement test, a manipulative skills test, a science attitude questionnaire, and a program environment questionnaire. This set of assessment instruments measures outcomes in the cognitive, affective, and laboratory skills domains. Teachers, administrators, and parents also complete program environment questionnaires.

The design of the program environment questionnaires is based on a model that incorporates various factors that make up and influence New York State's science instruction program. Administrators and others can use data from *ESPET* to make policy decisions about revising the state's science programs, and also to monitor the allocation of resources to implement new school plans or district science programs. Classroom teachers are involved in all stages of writing and piloting the assessment instruments, as well as in scoring the *ESPET* assessments.

Figure 4.2: Beyond Norm-Referenced Assessment. Reynolds, et al., 1996.

This interpretation ensures that all students can succeed once they have met the criteria for success, and is in keeping with the principle that all students can learn.

Using Assessment Data

From the perspective of students and teachers, we are most familiar with using assessments to determine student achievement on a unit or course, and whether we are going to move on to the next unit or course in our sequence of instruction. Such evaluations are called "summative," as they are a summary of student achievement after the completion of a theme or unit of instruction. The vast majority of assessment data is used for making post-instruction summative evaluations or decisions.

However, assessment can also be used before or at the beginning of a unit or course. These assessments usually take the form of a pretest or prior knowledge survey, and serve a diagnostic function. You can use such assessment data to determine students' readiness for a given unit or course. Some students may need some remedial instruction or additional practice on some skills, while others may easily skip this unit and move on to the next unit of study. Such assessments are very useful to both students and teachers for improving instruction and promoting student learning.

Every one of us collects information (assessing) while we are teaching. We do this by listening to students' answers, observing their laboratory performance, observing cooperation and interaction between pairs of students and students in small groups, and noting who is not involved in the classroom. We are literally "walking, talking assessment machines." Much of this assessment happens informally. We use this informal assessment data, plus data from more formal quizzes and checklists, to modify our instruction and improve student learning. These evaluations are called formative, because students' understandings are in the process of being built or formed.

Scoring Performance Assessment

With performance assessments, there is no answer key as there is with true/false, multiple-choice, or matching items. The analogous procedure for scoring performance assessments is the "scoring rubric." A rubric is a detailed description of possible answers and associated point values or ratings. For example, rubrics used for writing tasks are often general, with four or five ratings or point values. Figure 4.3

Figure 4.3: Scoring Rubric for a Written Report.

Complete and well detailed	5 points
Complete, but with errors or omissions	4 points
Accurate procedure and observation, but inaccurate conclusions	3 points
Many inaccuracies in each section	2 points
Minimal description of procedure and observations	1 point

illustrates a general scoring rubric for a written report.

When the major focus of the assessment is conceptual understanding, we develop more detailed scoring rubrics. Figure 4.4 is an example of a scoring rubric for an assessment on the density of a sinker.

Scoring rubrics can be classified as holistic, primary trait, or analytical scoring

Figure 4.4: Density of a Sinker Scoring Rubric.

Maximum Score: 10 points

Question 1. Mass of the Sinker   2 Points Total

Criteria:

- Teacher determined mass: _____ grams
- Allow 1 point for mass within the acceptable ranges.
    — triple-beam or double-pan balance = accuracy of +/- 1.0 grams
    — spring scale = accuracy of +/-3.0 grams
- Allow 1 point for labeling the units as grams.

Question 2. Procedure for Volume   2 Points Total

Criteria:

- Response should include:
    —Put sinker into graduated cylinder.
    —Measure initial and final volumes.
    —Difference is the volume of the sinker.
- Allow 2 points if all three elements are included.
- Allow 1 point if two elements are included *or* if student writes "water displacement method."

*** Points are based on the procedure, not the actual value for the volume of the sinker. ***

Question 3. Volume of the Sinker   2 Points Total

Criteria:

- Teacher determined volume: _____ milliliters
- Allow 1 point for volume within the acceptable range.
    —accurate to +/- 1.0 milliliters
- Allow 1 point for labeling the units as milliliters.

Question 4. Density of the Sinker   3 Points Total

Criteria:

- Density calculation is based upon the *student's* values of mass and volume.
- Allow 1 point for density within the acceptable range.
    —accurate to +/- 1.0 g/ml
- Allow 1 point for labeling units as g/ml.
- Allow 1 point for correct substitution of the student's values into the density formula.

Question 5. Density of Half the Sinker   1 Point Total

Criteria:

- Allow 1 point for a statement indicating that the density of half the sinker is the same as the whole sinker, because density is not related to size of sample.

rubrics. Whichever kind of rubric is used, the focus is on student performance in a series of individual skills or categories of skills. The rubrics can be presented to the class, and even posted in the classroom, so students clearly understand what is expected of them. Such detailed, specific feedback on performance is a crucial step toward encouraging students to self-assess their own performance and achievement.

A holistic rubric is designed to be used with one reading of a report or as a response for a "first impression" of the work. Figure 4.3 is an example of a holistic rubric, which is appropriate for evaluating written lab reports. A holistic rubric provides a quick overall impression of student achievement or performance, but provides little feedback to students for areas of improvement.

Figure 4.5: Primary Trait Scoring Rubrics For Laboratory Reports. Adapted from Tamir, et al., 1982.

I. Planning:

- Able to present a perceptive plan for investigation. Plan is clear, concise, and complete. Able to critically discuss plan for experiment. 5
- Well-presented plan, but needs some modification. Understands overall approach to problems. 4
- Plan is O.K., but some help is needed. Not a very critical approach to problem. 3
- Poor, ineffective plan needing considerable modification. Does not consider important constraints and variables. 2
- Little idea of how to tackle the problem. Much help needed. 1

II. Performance:

- Student consistently and independently makes observations and measurements with correct tools and with appropriate precision and units. 5
- Student often observes and measures accordingly, but seldom relates the appropriate precision for instrument being used. 4
- Student usually observes and measures correctly when provided some directions. 3
- Student is able to observe and measure only when provided explicit directions and guidelines. 2
- Student inconsistently and inaccurately measures, even when given specific instructions. 1

III. Analysis:

- Student consistently and accurately summarizes observations and data. Cites appropriate relationships and generalizations with necessary limitations and assumptions. 5
- Student is able to interpret data collected and present reasonable conclusions, but is unaware of limitations and constraints. 4
- Student is able to summarize and organize observations and data, but is unable to formulate meaningful generalizations. 3
- Student is able to organize data only when provided explicit directions, and can only answer specific, narrow questions about conclusions. 2
- Student is unable to go beyond the data collected. 1

IV. Application:

- Student routinely relates conclusions from present activity to underlying themes or models, suggests appropriate applications, and proposes further related work. 5
- Student connects findings to prior work and cites viable uses or applications, but is not able to extend to new areas. 4
- Student relates conclusions only to very similar work, and proposed applications are closely related to their work. 3
- Student is only able to relate work to other examples and contexts when questioned specifically. 2
- Student is unable to apply, extend, or relate findings to other work or situations. 1

A primary trait rubric focuses only on one or two important characteristics of a report or response. For example, depending on the emphasis of experiments, you can vary the trait assessed over a sample of laboratory reports. Figure 4.5 (page 62) provides sample scoring criteria for assessing a variety of science laboratory skills. It is adapted from the Practical Tests Assessment Inventory (Tamir, et al. 1982) and provides examples of several skills, with key elements of each, to be used as primary trait rubrics. Any one of the parts shown in Figure 4.5 (i.e., I, II, III, or IV) can be used as a source for a primary trait rubric.

An analytical rubric is a comprehensive evaluation examining the relevant content and science process skills, as well as communication skills, of an assessment task. Characteristics of an analytical rubric may be listed in tabular form for ease of scoring. Figure 4.6 (right) depicts an analytical rubric for science laboratory reports.

Figure 4.7 (page 64) depicts a scoring rubric for scientific investigations. The scoring rubric is organized by Part A (with three specific skills) and Part B (with four specific skills). These skills reflect the tasks a student or scientist performs while conducting an investigation. The Part A and Part B labels can be eliminated when students are proficient enough in their planning efforts to produce a safe, workable design of an investigation.

Each of the seven skills on this scoring rubric consists of five specific elements. A student must give an answer that includes all the elements in order to obtain a perfect score on a given skill. For example, a well-phrased hypothesis for the chemistry task, "Reaction Rates," provided in Chapter 6 (page 167), is: "Reaction rates vary directly with increasing temperature." Although this is a brief sentence, it includes each of the five items listed under the Statement of Hypothesis section.

The specific elements are listed in a "bottom-up," pyramid fashion, with the most basic items at the bottom and those required for a complete and excellent answer toward the top. For example, a hypothesis written on a very basic level would be a statement that merely included descriptions of the dependent and inde-

INQUIRY SKILLS	Acceptable	Not Acceptable	Does Not Apply
I. Planning			
1. identifies a problem or question to investigate			
2. formulates hypothesis			
3. explains or refers to experimental design			
4. plans appropriate controls			
II. Performance			
1. demonstrates knowledge of technique			
2. describes and observes accurately and completely			
3. demonstrates quantitative measurement			
4. identifies dependent and independent variables			
III. Analysis			
1. appropriately interprets observed data			
2. correctly interprets observed data			
3. shows qualitative relationships			
4. shows quantitative relationships			
5. analyzes accuracy of data			
6. suggests limitations or assumptions affecting data			
7. proposes a generalization or model			
8. draws conclusions			
IV. Application			
1. integrates prior knowledge			
2. suggests original hypothesis			
3. suggests contemporary application			

Figure 4.6: Analytical Rubric For Revising and Evaluating a Science Laboratory Report— Inquiry and Writing Skills. New York State Education Department, 1984.

Science Lab Assessment Scoring Form

1. Please circle the NA code if a skill is <u>not assessed</u> in a particular area.
2. The NR code is to be circled when <u>no attempt</u> to respond to the question is apparent.
3. You may check each element present and sum up to determine a student's score for each skill.
4. There is <u>no</u> need to determine a total score for a student.

Part A: Experiment Design

1. Statement of Hypothesis   NR   0   1   2   3   4   5   NA
   - Effect linked to variable   ___
   - Directionality of effect   ___
   - Expected effect/change   ___
   - Independent variable   ___
   - Dependent variable   ___

2. Procedure for Investigation   NR   0   1   2   3   4   5   NA
   - Resolved experimental problem/feasible   ___
   - Sequenced and detailed plan   ___
   - General strategy   ___
   - Safety procedures   ___
   - Use of equipment/diagram or set-up   ___

3. Plan to Record and Organize   NR   0   1   2   3   4   5   NA
   Observations/Data
   - Space for measured/calculated area   ___
   - Matched to plan   ___
   - Organized sequentially   ___
   - Labelled fully (units included)   ___
   - Variables identified   ___

Part B: Experiment Report

4. Quality of Observations/Data   NR   0   1   2   3   4   5   NA
   - Consistent data   ___
   - Accurate measurements/observations   ___
   - Completed data table   ___
   - Correct units   ___
   - Qualitative description   ___

5. Graph   NR   0   1   2   3   4   5   NA
   - Curve is appropriate to data trend   ___
   - Points plotted accurately   ___
   - Appropriate scale (units included)   ___
   - Axes labelled with correct variables   ___
   - Has an appropriate title   ___

Figure continues on opposite page.

pendent variables, each earning one point. Working toward the top of the pyramid, a more complete hypothesis would include all five elements. One such complete or model response is illustrated in Figure 4.8 (page 65, bottom). For this chemical kinetics task, students are asked to generate hypotheses that suggest possible relationships among variables that affect reaction rates.

The three hypotheses provided in Figure 4.9 (page 66) were written by students completing the kinetics task. Each example includes the part of the student's response that relates to the hypothesis, and the student's words or phrases as they match the five criteria for a hypothesis.

The first sample (student 001) was judged to earn five points, the maximum for this skill, because each of the criteria was included in the student response. The second sample (student 002) was incomplete, earning three out of five points. Only the dependent variable, independent variable, and the expected change or effect were included in this student response. The third sample (student 003) earned no points, as this student response included some relevant words but completely misunderstood the relationship of variables affecting reaction rates.

Students might not need to demonstrate all the skills listed in each category for some tasks. In these cases, you can use the acronym NA (not applicable). Likewise, not all bulleted elements are required in every task. For skills involving fewer than five nonrequired elements, you can use a "holistic" scoring approach so that the remaining elements receive a total value of five points.

For each skill in each task, we analyzed student responses to these lab assessments to find elements present in exemplary student work. Inclusion of these elements became the benchmarks for the standard of excellence in the planning and reporting of investigations. These elements are the five statements listed on the scoring form (Figure 4.7) under each of the seven skills.

The next level of specificity is called the "Task Specific Scoring Criteria." Figure 4.10 (page 67) provides an example of task specific scoring criteria for the kinetics task.

These are detailed descriptions of the "bulleted" elements of each skill for a specific task. When a science department begins this form of laboratory assessment, teachers need to understand the challenges of analyzing student responses. Some teachers will want to produce even more detailed descriptions for each task. These detailed descriptions are crucial elements of the workshops for preparing rating teams.

Scoring criteria are the descriptions of acceptable answers for each question. These criteria provide a critical guide as the scoring process continues. During the training of the raters, the exemplars (samples of scored student answers) are also very helpful. Graders use these exemplars as "templates" for scoring actual student booklets. Three levels of aid—answer sheets, criteria, and exemplars—work best. The scoring rubric for scientific investigations depicted in Figure 4.7 can be used to collect points earned for each question, along with student names, identifying numbers, dates, and so forth. This form may be stored in a student's folder or portfolio.

To help develop scoring rubrics, one valuable tool is the Practical Tests Assessment Inventory (PTAI) (Tamir, et al. 1982), already mentioned. The PTAI, developed in Israel in the 1980s, describes 21 specific skills students use as they conduct science investigations. Figure 4.11 (page 68) depicts the major categories of

Figure 4.7 continued from previous page.

6. Calculations   NR 0 1 2 3 4 5 NA
   • Calculated accurately   —
   • Substituted correctly into relationship   —
   • Relationship stated or implied   —
   • Units used correctly   —
   • Used all data available   —

7. Forms a Conclusion from the Experiment   NR 0 1 2 3 4 5 NA
   • Consistent with scientific principle   —
   • Sources of error   —
   • Consistent with data   —
   • Relationship among variables stated   —
   • Variables stated in conclusion   —

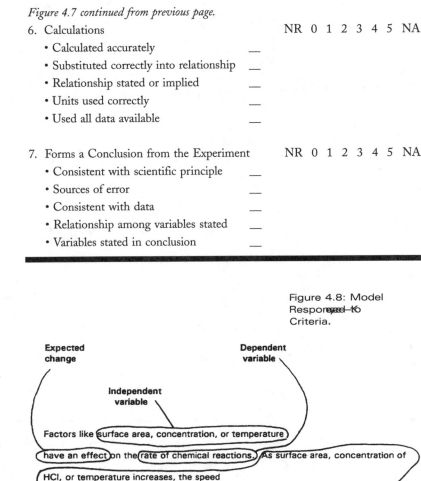

Figure 4.8: Model Response to Criteria.

Figure 4.9 Three
Student Hypotheses.
Doran, et al., 1993.

STUDENT 001:   **Statement of Hypothesis**

Criteria	Matching Student Response	Score
Effect linked to variable	Change in reaction rate linked to variable (i.e., heat → speed up rate)	NR 0 1 2 3 4 ⑤ NA
Directionality of effect	Heat may speed up, dilution may slow down reaction rate	**Student Response**
Expected effect/change	Speed up/slow down	When conducting a chemical reaction, sometimes its rate
Independent variable	Heat and dilution	may need to be changed
Dependent variable	Reaction rate	in order to obtain the desired effect. Heat may speed up a reaction, and dilution may slow down a reaction.

STUDENT 002:   **Statement of Hypothesis**

Criteria	Matching Student Response	Score
Effect linked to variable	Not stated	NR 0 1 2 ③ 4 5 NA
Directionality of effect	Not stated	**Student Response**
Expected effect/change	Speeds up/slows down	To figure a way of
Independent variable	Varying amounts of mass and different setup	speeding up/slowing down a reaction with HCl and Mg ribbon. By varying
Dependent variable	Reaction rate	amounts of each and different setup, you can do it.

STUDENT 003:   **Statement of Hypothesis**

Criteria	Matching Student Response	Score
Effect linked to variable	Not stated	NR ⓪ 1 2 3 4 5 NA
Directionality of effect	Not stated	**Student Response**
Expected effect/change	Not stated	Only an exact amount of heat
Independent variable	Not identified	along with minimal time could
Dependent variable	Not identified	produce a chemical reaction. In other words, try to come up with a reaction in the smallest amount of time.

the PTAI (the four subheadings were added by the current authors).

Each of these 21 science inquiry skills has a rubric you can use as a starting point. As you identify a skill that is needed to address the questions in a task you are assessing, take that skill and rubric from the PTAI. This produces a set of individual skill rubrics that together become a rubric for a test.

Figure 4.12 (page 69) provides an example from the PTAI illustrating a rubric for making graphs, possible student behaviors, and their respective point values. Each category has different specific skills appropriate to that category. The number of possible points varies with the category.

Part A : Experiment Design

1. Statement of hypothesis
   - Effect linked to variable — The relationship between the variables and the expected effect is clearly and correctly defined (i.e., increasing surface area increases reaction rate).

   - Directionality of effect — Rate increases or decreases.
   - Expected effect/change — Indicates that a change in rate will occur (uses words like *effect, change, speeds up, slows down*).
   - Independent variable — Identifies temperature, surface area, or concentration here.
   - Dependent variable — Identifies reaction rate here.

2. Procedure for investigation
   - Detailed procedure/ experimentally feasible — Procedure, sequence, and details (i.e., repeated trials) validate the plan as experimentally feasible.
   - Sequence to plan — Steps are presented sequentially with adequate details (i.e., includes temperatures, volumes, times, or units).
   - General strategy — Strategy manipulates two independent variables (temperature, surface area, or concentration).
   - Safety procedures — Goggles essential, others acceptable.
   - Use of equipment/diagram — Procedure suggests appropriate use of equipment and materials.

3. Plan for recording and organizing observations/data
   - Space for manipulation of data or qualitative description — Space is allowed for manipulation/calculation of measured data or qualitative observation.
   - Matched to plan — Plan records all observations and data necessary to hypothesized experiment (i.e., concentration of HCl).
   - Organized sequentially — Plan is organized so that recording follows as data is generated.
   - Labeled fully (units included) — All columns and rows are identified and correct units of measure used.
   - Variables identified — Time and hypothesized independent variables are identified in table or record.

Part B : Experiment Report

4. Quality of observations/data
   - Consistent data — 3 or 4 trials consistent with expectations (2 points).
     — 2 trials consistent with expectation (1 point).
   - Accurate measurements/ observations — Measurements are within an expected range of time.
   - Completed data table — All trials are performed and data recorded.
   - Correct units — Measurements are in seconds or minutes.
   - Qualitative description — (Not required for this task).

5. Graph
   - Curve is appropriate to data trend — Curve drawn fits data points.
   - Points plotted accurately — Plotted points are equal to data values.
   - Appropriate scale — Value of scale is appropriate to range of data with suitable increments.
   - Axes labeled with variables and units — Temperature in degrees Celsius; Reaction Rate in grams/minute.

Continued on next page.

Continued from previous page.

- Variables placed on correct axes
  - Temperature, the independent variable, is the x axis; Reaction Rate, the dependent variable, is the y axis.

6. Calculations
   - Calculated accurately
     - Calculations are complete and mathematically correct; results are expressed in decimal form.
   - Substituted correctly into relationship
     - Mass (g) and time are correctly substituted into ratio conversion of seconds to minutes
   - Relationship stated or implied
     - Relationship is stated as Reaction Rate = (grams of Mg) ÷ (minutes), or calculations make it evident that relationship is understood.
   - Units used correctly
     - Rate expressed as g/min.
   - Use all data available
     - Calculations are performed on all generated data.

7. Conclusion
   - Consistent with scientific principle
     - Conclusion correctly demonstrates scientific principle.
   - Sources of error
     - Conclusion mentions error with measuring time.
   - Consistent with data
     - Conclusion stated is consistent with experimental results.
   - Relationship among variables stated
     - Statement of change/effect links variables in conclusion.
   - Variables stated in conclusion
     - Reaction rate, temperature, and surface area are named in conclusion.

Figure 4.11: Practical Tests Assessment Inventory (PTAI). Tamir, et al., 1982.

Planning and Designing an Investigation

1. Formulating problems
2. Formulating hypothesis
3. Identifying dependent variable
4. Identifying independent variable
5. Designing control
6. Fitting experimental design to tested hypothesis
7. Completing experimental design
8. Understanding the role of control in experiment

Collecting Data from Observations and Measurements

9. Making and reporting measurements
10. Determining and preparing materials
11. Making observations with equipment

Reporting Results

12. Describing observations and measurements
    12a. Distinguishing between observation and inference
13. Making graphs
14. Making tables
15. Interpreting observed data

Analyzing Findings

16. Drawing conclusions
17. Explaining research findings
18. Examining results critically
19. Applying knowledge
20. Understanding and interpreting data presented in a graph
21. Suggesting ideas and ways to continue investigation

Developing a Scoring Team

Because rubrics don't have the perfect objective and reliable appearance of answer keys for true/false, multiple-choice, and matching test items, a scoring team approach is often used. Two or more teachers experienced with the content and skills being assessed are likely members of such a scoring team. Reliable scoring with rubrics can be achieved if the rubrics are clear and the training workshop is well planned and implemented.

The training of raters should be planned carefully. Have available the equipment, materials, and the test booklet students will use so that the teacher can "verify" how some responses could be obtained. The raters should perform the lab tests just as the students would.

Scorers will better appreciate the benefits and drawbacks of this type of assessment by performing each of the tasks. Because the Part A tasks require the student to plan and design an experimental process to answer a question, there can easily be several "right" answers. Although this step may be time consuming, once the scorers are confronted with the variety of solutions that can result when a number of people attempt to solve a problem, they will value the generalized rubric developed for these items. Each rater scores his or her own responses using the prepared rubric and detailed criteria. This might be a place to "fine tune" the scoring criteria by adding, deleting, or changing the list of criteria.

Undertake this training step soon after beginning to pilot test the tasks and rubrics. Figure 4.13 is an appropriate model for developing scoring teams. The first step—selecting scorers by content areas—works extremely well when participants are scoring performance tasks for the first time.

A. Drawing the Graph	
Complete graph	5
No title or inadequate title	4
Inadequate scaling and relation of x and y axes	3
Inappropriate connection between points of the graph	2
Combination of at least two from above	1
B. Recording of Variables	
Dependent variable on y axis and independent variable on x axis	6
Independent variable on y axis and dependent variable on x axis	5
Inappropriate recording of variable names and units	4
No recording of the variable names and units	3
Confusing the variables on the axes	2
Combination of at least two from above	1

Figure 4.12: Making Graphs. Tamir, et al., 1982.

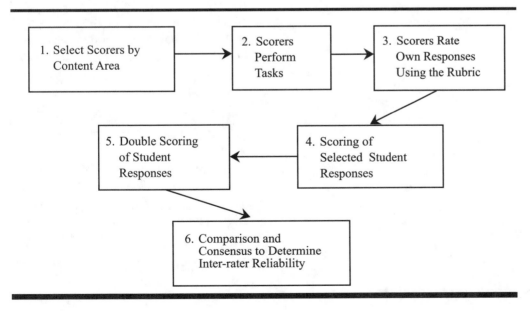

Figure 4.13: Model for Developing a Scoring Team.

Once they gain more experience and confidence, scorers can begin to rate student responses in all science areas, not just their area of specialization.

After each scorer completes the tasks in his or her respective discipline or area, they come together to discuss and analyze their responses. From this process of "social moderation," you arrive at a consensus on benchmark criteria for model or exemplary answers. You obtain a clear sense from this discussion as to what specific steps or criteria are essential to a model answer. You can use examples of students' and teachers' responses to illustrate point values for a range of answers, including excellent, adequate, marginal, and unacceptable. These responses can serve as "anchors," and are useful where assessments include large samples, such as state- and districtwide assessments.

Scorers should practice rating student responses. One excellent strategy is for two raters to score a small group of student papers independently, and then compare the scores they assigned to each paper. If raters are having difficulty with particular skills, they might need more detailed practice in that area.

Scorer Agreement

Raters score packets of approximately 10 student booklets in one session as part of the scoring process. Agreements or discrepancies on the rated booklets are discussed. This process is repeated with additional groups of student booklets until the desired level of agreement is reached (usually 90 percent).

As the raters reach consensus on these samples, the likelihood of good inter-rater reliability increases. Inter-rater reliability means that, if different raters were asked to rate the same set of student responses, they would assign approximately the same grade or score to those responses. Students are very astute at comparing scores received on their work, and expect their teacher to score similar responses the same way every time.

The specific description of each scoring element must be clear to science teachers as they use it as a template for student responses. Detailed scoring procedures provide high inter-rater agreement between independent raters of the same student responses. The easiest procedure to document the level of inter-rater reliability is to determine the "Percent of Agreement" between the scores determined by two independent raters. For the total score for each task, we expect percent agreements in the 90–98 percent range. Another procedure for inter-rater agreement is to use correlation coefficients calculated between these total scores (from two raters), which should be above 0.75. Lastly, an internal consistency value (Coefficient Alpha) on the scoring by one rater of a sample of student booklets should be above 0.75. This calculation is based on correlation coefficients

Figure 4.14: Scoring Consistency. Doran, et al., 1995.

Scores determined by two scorers for a class of students.

Student	Scorer A	Scorer B	Student	Scorer A	Scorer B
1	5	5	16	3	3
2	4	5	17	4	3
3	5	4	18	3	4
4	4	4	19	1	1
5	4	3	20	1	2
6	3	4	21	2	1
7	3	3	22	1	1
8	3	2	23	0	0
9	2	3	24	1	0
10	3	2	25	0	1
11	1	2	26	0	1
12	4	3	27	2	1
13	2	3	28	3	3
14	2	2	29	4	4
15	2	2	30	5	5

Figure 4.15: Graphical Display of Inter-Scorer Agreement.

Scorer B Points Awarded	0	1	2	3	4	5
5					2	1, 30
4				6, 19	4, 29	3
3			9, 13	7, 16, 28	5, 12, 17	
2		11, 20	14, 15	8, 10		
1	25, 26	19, 22	21, 27			
0	23	24				

Scorer A Points Awarded

among a set of randomly selected "halves" of the test. In some formulas, the "halves" are determined by the odd- and even-numbered items.

Figure 4.14 (page 70) provides hypothetical data for 30 students as determined by two scorers on a short test with a maximum of five points. These same scores are presented graphically in Figure 4.15. While there is some variability between the two scorers, the overall agreement is illustrated by the "tight oval" in Figure 4.15. "Perfect" agreement would have created a straight line graph, while "no agreement" would have presented a circular "cloud" of points throughout this square. As a point of comparison, the correlation coefficient between these two sets of scores is 0.86, a value indicating strong agreement by the two scorers (high inter-rater reliability).

Reliability

An assessment is reliable if it consistently provides the same results when given on repeated occasions. Reliability is most important on districtwide or other large-scale, standardized tests. You can calculate reliability after field testing assessments. Reliability is one of several key ideas to testing. It is generally understood as a formula or as some abstract, opaque notion. In reality, reliability is a quantified description of the consistency of a set of scores from an assessment. Reliability can be calculated in different ways, depending on how the scores are produced and how the assessment was administered.

1. *Consistency across time:* When one test is administered twice to one group of students, one can calculate a test/re-test reliability. Often it is a correlation coefficient that can be tested for statistical significance. The time between tests is usually at least two weeks. Reliable tests should have a high correlation of scores (0.90 or higher) for the same set of students from two test administrations.

2. *Consistency across forms:* Commercial test companies produce new forms of tests approximately every 5–10 years. "New" tests measuring the same concepts with the same levels of cognition are considered "parallel" versions of the "older," accepted test.

High correlation coefficients between the parallel versions are used as evidence of the reliability of the new tests.

3. *Consistency within one test:* This is the most common form of reliability, and often is a form of calculating the correlation between "halves" of the one test. Some formulas use the odd numbered items and even numbered items as halves for this calculation. Other calculations are a series of randomly chosen "halves" of a test. Two of the most common methods are the "KR20 formula" and the "Coefficient Alpha" calculation. Reliability coefficients above 0.80 are considered adequate for comparing groups, and above 0.90 for comparing individual students.

4. *Consistency across raters:* This method is used with items not scored by an item key (true/false or multiple-choice). Rubrics often describe the procedures and criteria for rating students' written responses or performances. An assessment (with its scoring procedure) is considered reliable if two (or more) raters produce very similar scores for a set of student responses. Sets of student scores (from two raters) can be compared by "percentage agreement" or by correlation coefficients. The percent agreement calculations are done for "exact same scores" or for "nearly the same score" (plus or minus one score point). One can also plot the student scores with the two raters' scores on the x- and y-axes. The "tightness" of the score "cloud" in Figure 4.15 indicates consistency across the scores. Detailed, clear rubrics and a rater training program

are essential for obtaining reliability among raters.

Reliability of an assessment is based on scores from a sample of students who completed the assessment. The reliability obtained is dependent on several factors.

A. *Size of the student sample:* The calculation of reliability coefficients that are robust and confident requires sample sizes of about 50–250 students taken from the same population. Reliability coefficients calculated from sample sizes of less than 50 students are relatively unstable.

B. *Range of student ability:* A wider representation of student abilities will result in a wider range of scores, which usually means higher reliability. For instance, a test with a sample of all high school students studying biology would have a higher reliability than the same test administered to only the advanced students.

C. *Range of difficulty of items/tasks:* A test with a spectrum of easy, moderate, and difficult tasks is more reliable than a test with only easy (or only difficult) items. A wider range of items will produce a wider range of student scores.

Aggregating Assessment Data and Assigning Grades

The results of tests, quizzes, and other student work are commonly aggregated or collapsed into a single score and reported as a letter grade or percentage. For example, students receive an A or a B (or an 84 or 92) as a class grade on a test or assessment. The problem with this traditional approach is that it primarily measures a student's ability to take an examination. However, it doesn't necessarily tell us much about that student's mastery of skills or overall knowledge of the subject. This is akin to a pilot who scores well on the written examination of flight theory but poorly on take-off and landing skills.

One possible formula for determining student grades in a science course is the following:

Written Tests 30%

Performance Tests   30%

Teacher Observation   20%

Group Projects   10%

Reports   10%

This kind of system is usually applied to data obtained during some marking period, such as a ten-week grading period, a semester, or the entire school year. The amount of information you collect can vary widely, as can the nature of the assessment process used in each of the contributing areas (written tests, projects, etc.). This system enables a teacher to tap into the different skills or channels through which students can demonstrate what they have learned in science. The "formula" becomes a way to combine these separate inputs into a singular evaluation.

Throughout this book, we stress the need to assess students using a variety of formats: written tests, observations, practical tests, and so forth. These varied assessment formats provide a wealth of information for use in describing student achievement and performance in domains of knowledge and skills.

Figure 4.16 provides an example of a criterion-referenced system. This type of assessment is similar to those commonly used in many middle schools. Rather than giving a single grade or assessment to a

Knowing Science Information

1. Responds only in terms of specific examples experienced in class or presented in instructional materials.

2. Responds in terms of generalizations of these experiences, but is unable to show relationship or go beyond that which was experienced.

3. Demonstrates thorough understanding by applying information in a new context or by explaining relationships, implications, or consequences.

Using Science Concepts and Generalizations

1. Rarely connects learning with new situations in which it could be applied unless told what skill or idea is relevant.

2. Uses previous experiences in new situations once the relationship between the new and previous situation has been pointed out.

3. Analyzes what earlier learning could be applied in a new context by using relationships between one situation and another.

Writing Reports and Doing Projects

1. What is written or said is disorganized and difficult to follow; takes time to understand information in books or verbal directions.

2. Seems to have a clear idea of what to express, but does not always find the words to put it precisely or concisely; prefers to seek and receive information orally rather than through printed matter.

3. Expresses and communicates clearly, using words appropriately, economically, and at a level that can be understood by whomever receives the message; expands knowledge through reading.

Experimenting and Investigating

1. Is unable to progress from one point to another in a practical investigation or inquiry without help; fails to grasp the overall plan.

2. Tries things out somewhat unsystematically unless the various steps in a practical inquiry are spelled out, in which case uses materials and collects results satisfactorily.

3. Has a clear idea of the reason for the various steps in an investigation; can work through them systematically, making reasonable decisions with only occasional guidance.

Figure 4.16: Criterion-Referenced System.

student, this assessment uses four categories of science performance, and three levels of performance ranging from a weak understanding of the subject matter (1) to a robust mastery (3). While a few students might be described at the same level in all four skill areas, it is more likely that students will be at different levels for these different skills.

The reporting of student achievement is a challenging and complex undertaking. Employers, teachers, colleges, and universities use a final mark or aggregate grade in making decisions. Consequently, parents and students also place great emphasis on this unitary method of reporting student achievement. Unless there is a viable plan and the political will to come to a shared agreement and understanding of reporting student achievement in different and multiple ways, including clear language, then much of what is suggested in the *National Standards* will be lost. This is a challenge that all teachers must address as part of the assessment reforms suggested in both *Project 2061* (AAAS 1992) and the *National Standards* (NRC 1996).

Assessment Data Management

An effective evaluation system is dependent upon the efficient collection and storage of assessment information. Most teachers have a good system for storing data from tests and quizzes; this process involves letter or number grades that can easily fit into a grade book or spreadsheet. However, many teachers have a more difficult time handling data on assessments that involve performances and behaviors.

The assessment card illustrated in Figure 4.17 (page 75, top) was designed to help teachers compile measures of student performance on various skills using a sampling system. This assessment card can also be placed on a spreadsheet format using software, such as Excel or QuattroPro, for efficient storage and retrieval of information. The numbers entered on the chart are based on a 10-point rating scale developed for each skill area. Although it would be ideal to provide a detailed assessment of each science skill in each activity or report, the time requirements are prohibitive. The system reflected by the card suggests that, for each lab activity, the teacher choose a few skills appropriate to that particular task on which to make a specific observation or assessment. As these are collected over a period of time, the overall assessment obtained is balanced and meaningful.

Using Results of Performance Assessment

You can use the results of performance assessment in a number of valid ways. You have valuable information to probe and interpret student understanding by describing performances with reference to the same laboratory skills across several tasks in various science courses. You can also compare student performance across subject and skills domains to determine which inquiry skills, if any, were transferable from one course to another. These comparisons, however, are only possible if there is a common framework or structure. Figures 4.18 through 4.20 are based on the (hypothetical) data from assessments in which the seven inquiry skill areas were measured in each science course across several years.

You can construct profiles of performance across subject area, such as in Figure 4.18 (page 75) or across years, as in Figure 4.19 (page 76, top) to monitor the impact of the science program on the development of laboratory and other skills. Such performance profiles are very useful

Science Skills Assessment

Course _____   Name _____

Lab Activity	Date completed	A. Planning & Design	B. Manipulative Skills & Conduct of Experiment	C. Observations & Recording Data	D. Interpretations of Data & the Experiment	E. Responsibility/ Initiative/ Work Habits
1	9 / 10		5	4		
2	9 / 20	3	7			2
3	9 / 30		3	4		
4	10 / 10		7			1
5	10 / 20	4		4	6	8
6	10 / 30		5			
7	11 / 10				4	
8	11 / 20	7	8	6		2
9	11 / 30			5	6	3
10	12 / 10		7			5

for a science department's internal program review or for providing reports to the school board or parent groups.

Using the performance profile provided in Figure 4.18, some possible descriptions of student performance within a science program can be:

1. Across all science areas, students are weak on formulating hypotheses and stating conclusions, but very skilled in making observations, graphing, and calculating.

   or

2. Students in chemistry and physics courses are much more skilled than those in biology in all skill areas tested *except* in making observations, in which the biology students perform equally well.

Figure 4.19 shows how a science department can monitor progress on student laboratory skills across consecutive years.

The data in Figure 4.19 can be interpreted as showing consistent improvement in all skill areas over the three-year period.

The individual student performance in the skill of "Hypotheses" portrayed in

Figure 4.17: Science Skills Assessment. Adapted from Hofstein, Lunetta, and Giddings, 1981.

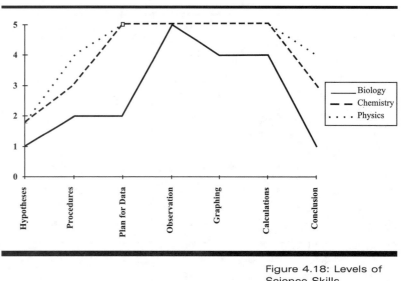

Figure 4.18: Levels of Science Skills Performance by Science Course with Hypothetical Data.

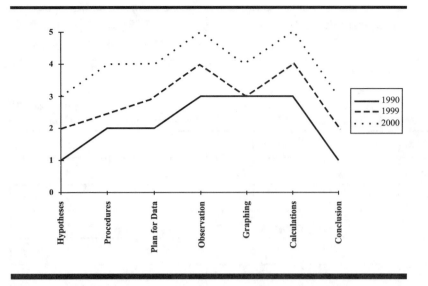

Figure 4.19: Levels of Science Skills Performance Across Years with Hypothetical Data.

Figure 4.20: Levels of Skill Performance for a Student Contrasted with Class and School Performance.

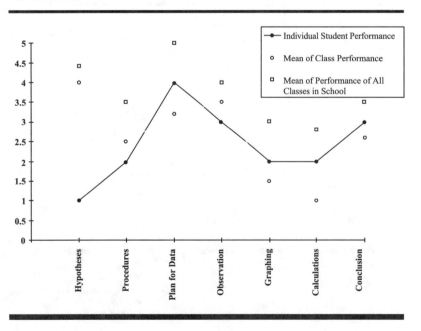

Figure 4.20 is poor compared to that of the class and school mean. The reasons are probably student centered, and suggest a review of attendance and laboratory reports. For the process skill of "Procedures," both individual and class means were low compared with the school/state mean. These results suggest a review of the instructional methodologies used in that science class. The process skill of "Calculations," where individual, class, and school/state means are all low, suggests a review of the state and school curriculum.

Test Validity

Even more important then reliability is the validity of an assessment, which is commonly defined as the degree to which an assessment measures what it is designed to measure for a given population. Content validity is based on what qualified professionals can determine by examining the test itself, its test grid, and the method of development. Generally, no statistics are involved with statements about content validity unless a percent of agreement among experts' opinions is calculated.

By examining a test and its test grid or course outline, the relevance, balance, and specificity of the assessment may be determined. These three characteristics, which are part of the content validity, are defined as follows:

- Relevance—Related to the content and cognition required to respond correctly to a test item and the item's purpose or objective. Each item should be directly related to a course objective and the actual instruction. Relevance must be considered as the primary contributor to validity.

- Balance—Indicated by the degree to which the proportion of the items test particular content outcomes or levels of cognition, often described by a test grid.

- Specificity—Subject matter experts should receive near perfect scores, and test-wise but course-naive students should receive very low scores, indicating that course-specific learnings are being measured.

If a test is deemed to be relevant, balanced, and specific to its expressed purpose and population, it can be described as having content validity. Every test should be scrutinized by its developer(s) and qualified colleagues to ensure that it has clearly established content validity.

Criterion-related validity includes all attempts to compare results from the test in question with results from other tests designed to measure the same objectives. The forms of criterion-related validity include concurrent validity, when tests are administered at the same time, and predictive validity, when the test in question is compared to some future test performance.

If scores from two assessments designed for the same objectives for a population are available, a correlation coefficient can be calculated by hand or by any one of a large number of calculator or computer programs.

The third form of validity—construct validity—assesses the degree to which some related trait or quality (i.e., construct) is reflected in the performance on the test in question. This form is used when there is no criterion measure available. Based on past research and related theory, a variable is selected that can be hypothetically related to student performance on the test being developed. Some relationships that could be hypothesized include spatial-visual ability and performance on a science laboratory exam. Most of these relationships can be described by means of some kind of correlation coefficient.

We use an analogy from target shooting to compare and contrast the ideas of validity and reliability. The reliability of a test is an indication of how consistently a test measures what it measures, and validity is an indication of measuring what it is intended to measure. In target shooting,

reliability is analogous to precision—how close the shots are to one another—while validity is analogous to accuracy—how near the bull's-eye the shots are.

Referring to Figure 4.21, the shots in Group A are both valid and reliable: they are where they're supposed to be (i.e., near the center) and they are tightly grouped. Group B is valid but unreliable: individual shots are near the center but are widely scattered. Group C is invalid but highly reliable: the shots are way off center yet tightly grouped. Group D is invalid and unreliable: the shots are both off-center and scattered. From this analogy, it is clear that test validity is more important that test reliability, though both are valuable characteristics for good tests.

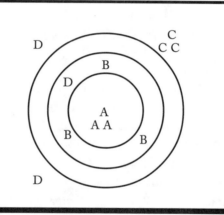

4.21: Target Shooting Analogy for Test Reliability and Validity.

Interpreting and Describing Results

A wealth of information from skills assessments is available for describing and evaluating the quality and effectiveness of a laboratory program. While the details may vary between the different modes of administration, Figure 4.22 (page 78) is illustrative of the various kinds of information that might be available.

If a practical laboratory test is composed of three tasks, the "total test performance" is a weighted average of the mean

Figure 4.22: Information Available for Evaluating Laboratory Programs.

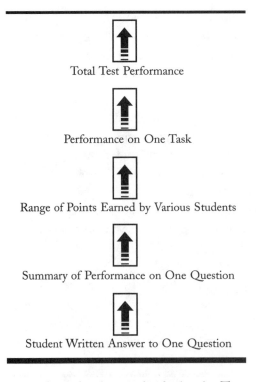

Total Test Performance

Performance on One Task

Range of Points Earned by Various Students

Summary of Performance on One Question

Student Written Answer to One Question

Average Percentage Score

Tasks	Task Score	Total Test (30 points)
Density (10 pts)	40	
Chromatography (10 pts)	90	65
Testing Unknowns (10 pts)	65	

This more detailed information is of considerable importance to teachers, science supervisors, and curriculum coordinators. Such results could reflect the inherent complexity of these tasks, unequal instructional emphasis, teacher professional training, or a host of other factors.

Each task consists of a series of items or questions. Density tasks are commonly composed of three separate questions focusing on the measurement of mass and volume and the calculation of density.

Average Performance Within a Task

Item Task	Density Score (10 pts)	Task
Mass (3 pts)	60	
Volume (4 pts)	40	40
Density (3 pts)	20	

In this example, the data are of great interest to science teachers and supervisors. However, school boards and parent groups may find the data too detailed. Science teachers will have many hypotheses as to the different levels of performance on these items. For example, do the math skills or levels of intellectual development affect students' ability to calculate density? How many instructional activities were involved with the calculation of density?

Additional insights into successful laboratory performance in density tasks can be obtained by examining the detailed skills used in an individual question. In this example, the following three skills

scores from the three individual tasks. Total test performance is commonly reported using a percentage score (proportion of the total points available across all three tasks). Although this single number is hard to interpret in isolation, it can be useful. For example, you can determine changes in school performance when the same test has been used for several years. If several schools or districts have used the same test, educators can make comparisons on the general level of science laboratory performance across schools or districts. Other possible comparisons can be made of students at different grade levels, in different kinds of courses, or by gender. These general results are suitable for presentation to school faculty and administrators, school board members, and parent groups.

A more specific level of assessment includes descriptions (usually average percentage score) on each of the tasks that make up the practical test. The example below shows how individual tasks can have a quite different score when compared to the total test score.

were used to evaluate the adequacy of the answer to the final question on determining/calculating the object's density.

Skills	Density Item (3 pts)	
Formula use (1 pt)	30%	
Calculation (1 pt)	25%	20%
Units (1 pt)	5%	

Students were weak in using the density formula, in calculating the numerical value, and practically unable to list the appropriate unit for density. This finding can lead to many questions, including: Are these students unable to use units with other variables? Did the parallel instructional activity just require a number, not the unit? This is an important issue because, in science, using unit labels with all measurements is essential. Such results would lead to other inquiries.

The most detailed level of information is the collection of students' written responses from their test booklets. This is a rich pool of information that can be used as a source of student errors, misconceptions, and alternative hypotheses. Listed below are the units students used in the density example cited above and the percentage of students (fictitious) using each unit.

Density Units	Percentages Used
g/ml	5%
g	10%
ml	15%
g x ml	5%
density	10%
no units used	55%

These data indicate a wide variety of errors, with the biggest problem being a failure to use any appropriate units. These results suggest further questions: Did these students (55%) not know how to list units? Did they not realize the need for a unit with density?

Program Evaluation

So far, we have focused primarily on student assessments. In this section, we look at the larger challenge of program assessment, which is the task of evaluating how well our curriculum and program assessments are functioning within a school, district, state, or nation. This process involves larger groups of individuals and probing questions to gain insights about the efficacy and overall direction of science teaching. This is our accountability to parents, business, and the larger community regarding teaching and curriculum.

Program assessment has become increasingly important as school districts implement educational reforms. The growing technological nature of our economy, as well as greater economic competition from abroad, has placed pressure on educators at all levels to improve science education. These efforts have resulted in a greater emphasis on developing valid and reliable assessments that can provide information on whether the curriculum and program are appropriate and effective in promoting achievement for all students. Policymakers and administrators use this information for accountability purposes, and for providing administrative support and funding to schools.

Having illustrated several methods for gathering data about the science achievement and performance of elementary school students, the question arises as to how to combine this information for use in a comprehensive assessment program. One must keep in mind the amount of testing that is expected of each student, so as not to cause test anxiety. Further, some of the assessment procedures require extensive teacher and class time.

One technique used to organize the administration of a wide variety of assessment tasks, and to minimize individual student testing burden, is called "matrix" sampling. Figure 4.23 illustrates how matrix sampling could be used in the assessment of science programs. To the left is a list of student names, organized alphabetically or by school and class records. This chart would likely include a given class or the students at one grade level. This student list is necessary so the teacher can allocate randomly different tasks or subtests to individual students. The aim of this procedure is to obtain a balanced and accurate perspective of the performance of the entire class or grade, not of the individual student.

The written test section of the illustrative matrix is composed of five subtests (I–V). If each student responds to just one fifth of the items in the total pool, you can obtain "coverage" of five times as many test items than if each student received all the test items. If a pool of 100 written test items were constructed, each student would be expected to answer just

Figure 4.23: Matrix Sampling. Meng and Doran, 1993.

Students	Written Tests					Group Project		Individual Performance Task				
	I	II	III	IV	V	A	B	1	2	3	4	5
A	X					X		X				
B		X					X		X			
C			X			X				X		
D				X			X				X	
E					X	X						X
F	X						X	X				
G		X				X			X			
H			X				X			X		
I				X		X					X	
J					X		X					X
K	X					X		X				
L		X					X		X			
M			X			X				X		
N				X			X				X	
O					X	X						X

20 of these items. The 20 items assigned to each subtest would need to be chosen so as to represent the content and objectives in as balanced a way as possible. In addition to the "content" items within the written test, several categories of the science processes may be validly assessed by the written format.

Other science performance categories are better assessed using group projects or individual performance tasks. These are more time-consuming to prepare, administer, and score, but are a most appropriate way to assess some skills. If these skills are not assessed, students, administrators, teachers, and parents come to believe that such skills "really are not important." Figure 4.23 depicts a matrix that demonstrates one way to efficiently administer samples of assessment to subgroups of students.

In the example cited, there are two forms of the group project. The two forms (i.e., Form A and Form B) could be composed of different tasks or situations in which students demonstrate certain science skills. The recommended administration is that each student complete just one of these projects.

Many science skills can only be validly assessed by performance tasks. Such skills as the use of apparatus and measuring instruments and the performance of investigations are examples of such skills. The number of those tasks that can be administered in this manner depends on the length of the tasks and the time available for completion. In this matrix, we illustrate a case where each student completes only one of five individual performance tasks. This system can be adapted to a different number of available tasks. You can expand the number of tasks used with each student as their interest, confidence, and enjoyment grow with more experience.

In summary, the sampling matrix illustrates one system for obtaining student responses from a large pool of written and practical tests without overburdening each individual student. As a matter of fact, each student would respond to one-fourth of the total number of subtests or tasks in the pool. Each would respond to one of five subtests of the written test, complete one of two group projects, and complete one of five individual performance tasks for a total of three out of twelve possible assessment tasks. This system has been recommended for several reasons; the main reason, though, is to accomplish the goal of program evaluation without excessive burden on the students. If a teacher or school is interested in assessing individual students, additional testing sessions could be planned that would incorporate some of the remaining testing situations.

Annual Plan

In this book, we have talked about the characteristics and use of tasks we call skills tasks, investigation tasks, and extended investigation tasks. These vary in length of time for administration and scope of outcomes being assessed. Another issue is how to "package" these kinds of tasks into an assessment plan for a particular course. Figure 4.24 (page 82) is one approach to an "annual plan" for assessing laboratory skills. While this chart looks "complete," it does not delineate which task should be used in the cells with an X. All the X means is that during that month the teacher schedules an assessment of one set of skills (or numerous sets of skills in the whole investigation or long-term investigation). To implement the plan, the teacher selects specific tasks for each X in the chart. For instance, if the class represented in the chart is grade 9 science, in

Categories of Skills	Sept.	Oct.	Nov.	Dec.	Jan.	Feb.	Mar.	April	May	June
Planning/Design • hypotheses • variables • control • effect • safety			X				X			
Performing • observation • measurement • recording data • organizing data	X					X	X			
Reasoning • calculation/ graph • relationship/ trends • conclusions • error/limitation		X				X				
Whole Investigation (1-2 Periods)				X					X	
Long-Term Investigation (1-3 Weeks)					X			X		

Figure 4.24 Annual Plan for Laboratory Assessment in Science Class.

September the teacher may assign a set of tasks assessing the students' ability to use some standard science tools: triple beam balance, microscope, meter stick, graduated cylinder, and a thermometer. This set of tasks could be used to diagnose the skills brought by students to their first high school science course.

The annual plan begins with a September assessment of some performance skills, such as observing and measuring. In October, the teacher assesses students' reasoning skills (e.g., using data to describe tasks, developing conclusions, etc.). In November, the teacher assesses planning and design skills. After verifying student proficiency in these sets of skills in isolation, the teacher can begin to assemble those skills into an inquiry or investigation format (suggested for December).

Most research in science, of course, does not occur in 45-minute chunks, but rather over the course of weeks, months, or even years. Assessing students while they are involved in long-term investigations will require several approaches. One approach is a series of "snapshots" along the way, assessing individual skills in the context of an authentic investigation. For instance, early in the investigation, the teacher could assess students on their skills in formulating hypotheses, later in producing data tables and graphs, and still later in formulating conclusions.

The cycle is replicated in the spring semester, with the "pairing" of sets of skills (e.g., performing and reasoning in February) to add more authenticity to the assessment. The month of June is left blank here as there may be district and/or state-wide laboratory assessments scheduled then. Although the details of the annual plan need to reflect the details of individual courses, teachers must not wait until June to begin assessing students' laboratory skills.

Works Cited

American Association for the Advancement of Science (AAAS). 1992. *Project 2061: Benchmarks for Science Literacy.* New York: Oxford University Press.

Doran, R., Anderson, D., Boorman, J., Chan, F., and Hejaily, N. 1995. *Scoring Manual for Laboratory Assessment in Biology, Chemistry, and Physics.* Buffalo: University at Buffalo.

Doran, R., Boorman, J., Chan, F., and Hejaily, N. 1993. Authentic Assessment. *The Science Teacher* 60(6).

Gipps, C. 1995. *Beyond Testing: Toward a Theory of Educational Assessment.* Bristol, PA: Falmer Press.

Hofstein, A., Lunetta, V., and Giddings, G. 1981. Evaluating Science Lab Activities. *The Science Teacher* 48(1).

Meng, E., and Doran, R. 1993. *Improving Instruction and Learning Through Evaluation: Elementary School Science.* Columbus, OH: ERIC Clearinghouse for Science, Mathematics, and Environmental Education.

National Research Council (NRC). 1996. *National Science Education Standards.* Washington, DC: National Academy Press.

New York State Education Department (NYSED). 1984. *Reflections on Writing in Science.* Albany: NYSED.

———. 1992a. *New York State Elementary Science Program Evaluation Test (ESPET) Objective Test, Form E..* Albany: NYSED.

———. 1992b. *New York State Elementary Science Program Evaluation Test (ESPET) Manipulative Skills Test, Form X.* Albany: NYSED.

Reynolds, D., Doran, R., Allers, R., and Agruso, S. 1996. *Alternative Assessment in Science: A Teacher's Guide.* Buffalo: University at Buffalo.

Tamir, P., Nussinovitz, R., and Friedler, Y. 1982. The Design and Use of Practical Tests Assessment Inventory. *Journal of Biological Education* 16.

CHAPTER 5

Illustrative Assessment Tasks for Biology

This chapter is organized in three parts: skills tasks, investigations, and extended investigations. All three parts contain models or templates of biology assessment tasks, many of which are "complete." These models may be used as is, incorporated into existing assessment programs, adapted and modified to address additional educational objectives, or completely redesigned to form entirely new and innovative assessments.

Biology Skills Tasks

The chart below shows the skills tasks in this chapter and the skills they assess. The skills tasks usually focus on one skill, or on a small set of skills assessing a single event or experience. Most skills tasks assessments include student directions, answer sheets,

material preparation guidelines, and scoring rubrics. Suggestions for possible revisions are included with many tasks, so they can be used for other assessments.

A similar chart precedes each of the other two sections of this chapter, Biology Investigation Tasks and Biology Extended Investigation Tasks. The four skills categories—planning performing, analyzing, and applying—are illustrated in Figures 4.5 and 4.6 (pages 62 and 63). Note that the "applying" category here means more than numerically solving an equation with collected data. It includes skills such as relating or integrating results to underlying themes or models, proposing additional investigations/hypotheses, and suggesting applications beyond the context of the specific investigation.

Biology Skills Tasks

Skills Categories	Chromatography (page 85)	Cell Size (page 87)	Sugar or Starch? (page 92)	Pulse (page 95)	Natural Selection (page 99)	Using a Dichotomous Key (page 102)	Kernels of Corn (page 105)
Planning			✔				
Performing	✔	✔	✔	✔	✔	✔	✔
Analyzing	✔	✔	✔	✔	✔	✔	✔
Applying							

Chromatography

This task was used in the Second International Science Study (Kanis, et al. 1990) as part of the skills testing of students in grade 9. The task is a very simple one using commonly available materials. You can easily vary the colors and solubilities of the dots to enhance the "problem" nature of the task. A scenario could be developed around a series of black marker pens, such as the GEMS activity in crime lab chemistry (Lawrence Hall of Science 1985).

The scoring rubric is clear and can be changed easily if one changed the composition of the dots. It is a good activity for students and teachers just beginning alternative assessment.

Chromatography
Task Information

Time: 10–15 minutes

Materials:

- 1 small (plastic) cup 10 ml with water less than 1 cm deep
- 1 circular filter paper at least 9 cm in diameter

Preparation:

Cut filter paper with four tabs (1 cm × 3 cm) as shown in the illustration on the student task sheet (below). Place a different colored dot 1 cm from the end of each of the four tabs (using three water soluble marker pens—black, yellow, and green—and one non-water soluble marker pen—red). The outline of each dot should be highlighted in indelible ink (blue or black). This outline is the beginning position of each dot.

Chromatography
Student Task Sheet

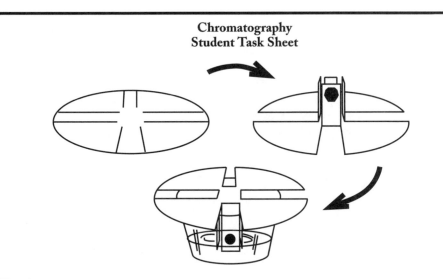

Directions:

Before you are a small cup of water and a piece of cut filter paper. Bend the tabs with colored dots upward as shown in the diagram. Next, turn the paper upside-down and place the four tabs into the small cup. (Be sure the colored dots are <u>above</u> the water surface.)

DO NOT LIFT THE CUP!

1. By carefully turning the cup around on the table, determine if the coloring from each of the dots moves at the same rate. According to what you observe, circle the correct response below:

SAME RATE OF MOVEMENT   DIFFERENT RATE OF MOVEMENT

When the first color reaches the top of the tab, remove the filter paper and flatten it out on a paper towel.

2. Describe what happened to the color of each dot. (Did it move? Did it change?)

   A. Black dot

   B. Red dot

   C. Yellow dot

   D. Green dot

3. Write an explanation for what happened to the black dot.

Chromatography
Scoring Rubric

Item Number	Answer	Scoring
1	Different Rate should be circled	1 pt. for correct answer
2	A. Black dot separated (changed/turned) into several colors *or* it moved up the paper B. Red dot did not move *or* did not change colors C. Yellow dot did not separate *or* yellow dot moved up the paper D. Green dot separated (changed/turned) into several colors *or* moved up the paper Acceptable: black, yellow, and green dots turned light or faded away	1 pt. for each correct answer Total possible points - 4 pts.
3	The black ink is composed of (is a mixture of) two colors (pigments/dyes/chemicals).	1 pt. for correct answer

Total possible points – 6 points

Cell Size

This task is part of a "test sampler" prepared by the New York State Education Department (NYSED 1999) that illustrates the kinds of tasks to be used beginning in May–June 2001 as part of statewide testing at the intermediate level. The official statewide test, *Grade 8 Intermediate Level Science Test*, is made up of a written test (with multiple-choice and constructed-response items) and a performance test (three tasks, with students given 15 minutes to complete each one).

The sampler tasks can be used by grades 5–8 science teachers as part of a unit or as final exams. The tasks illustrate the kinds of skills that should be part of standards-based instruction, the kinds of scientific equipment to be used, and the direction of future statewide exams. (The other two tasks from the test sampler are "Soaps and Water," page 223, and "Experimenting with a Ball and Ramp," page 211). Although these tasks are located in specific content chapters in this book, the skills they require have relevance and applications across all areas of science teaching and are aligned with the *National Science Education Standards* (NRC 1996).

The cell-size task requires that a student have some knowledge of and skill using a compound light microscope. Students are expected to find and focus on cellular features and to determine the average length of some cells, after they determine the diameter of the microscope's field of view. This task promotes the use of microscopes as a quantitative tool, extending the use of hand lenses (at the elementary grades) to observe and describe organisms and objects. All student and teacher print-materials presented here (including the station diagram) can be found on the NYSED website (*www.emsc.nysed.gov/ciai/mst/sci.html*). Feel free to use the electronic version instead of the hard copy version here.

The task information is generally used only by teachers and administrators, as they are the ones who select tasks, obtain equipment and material, and set up and administer the tasks to students. Note that most microscopes used in middle/intermediate-level schools have two or three objective lenses in addition to the eyepiece lens. The eyepiece lens is usually 10x, so the total magnification using the various objective lenses is 10 times the magnification for each objective lens. One very common model has these three objective lenses: 4x (also called the scanning lens), 10x, and 40x (or 43x), resulting in a total magnification of 40x, 100x, and 400x (or 430x). As there is some variation of these values, the science educators who designed this task used the descriptors "lowest power" and "highest power" of the two lenses available for student use. The teacher can certainly stress the use of each lens separately, but it was assumed that students had had that experience and could select among the two and use them easily. Similarly, students may have already prepared "wet mount" slides in class, so prepared slides are used here (prepared by the teacher or a science supplier). The skills involved in making wet mount slides can be assessed by a teacher using a checklist; we chose to focus on the skills of measuring and estimating length of cells. The frog skin or frog blood slides were chosen because they contain very similar cells throughout the sample. This is important as students are asked to sketch (accurately) one cell under high magnification.

This test sampler uses a station diagram so that students and teacher can make sure that the necessary materials are always present and in the appropriate place. Naturally, the equity of the assessment is documented by having a testing situation that is the same for each student.

Similarly, the test sampler provides detailed directions for teachers to read when administering the tasks and suggestions on how to set up the materials around a room (e.g., classroom or library). With the microscopes, either a window (for light) or an electrical outlet (for microscope bulb) is needed. If a set of three tasks is set up, three tables or desks need to be arranged for easy and unhindered student movement. These matters should be taken care of at least one day prior to the testing day. (Detailed directions can be found on the NYSED website, given on page 87.)

Cell Size
Task Information

Description:

Students will measure the size of a microscope's field of view and estimate the size of a cell in a prepared slide. Students will then draw accurate sketches of different cells that they observe under the lowest power (about 100x) and the highest power (about 400x).

Time: 15 minutes

Materials for one station:

- 1 mm graph paper
- transparent tape
- compound microscope with a low-power lens (about 100x total magnification) and a high-power lens (about 400x total magnification)
- prepared stained slide of onion skin tissue (allium leaf epidermis) (at least 3 mm x 3 mm)

- prepared stained slide of animal tissue (such as frog skin or frog blood) (at least 3 mm x 3 mm)
- blank slide
- 3" x 5" index cards

Preparation (to be done prior to the test date):

1. Prepare a permanent slide of a section of graph paper ruled every 1 mm. Cut out a 2 cm x 2 cm section of the graph paper. Use the transparent tape to mount the graph paper section in the center of the blank slide. Label this Slide A.

2. Prepare a wet mount slide of stained onion skin, or purchase a prepared slide of allium leaf epidermis. Be sure the sample is much larger than the field of view under low power (at least 3 mm x 3 mm). Label this Slide B.

3. Prepare or purchase a slide of stained animal tissue such as frog skin or frog blood cells. Label this Slide C.

4. The compound microscope should have only two objectives, about 10x and about 40x. Combined with the 10x eyepiece, these will provide total magnification of about 100x and about 400x. If the microscope has additional objectives, cover them securely with lens paper so the objective cannot be used.

5. When setting up the room, locate this station first for each group. This is important because the microscopes may need an electrical outlet for the light source or good natural lighting if mirrors are used. Do not place the microscopes where direct sunlight could hit the mirror and reflect into students' eyes.

6. Use masking tape to secure the Station Diagram in the lower left corner of the desk/table.

7. Place the equipment at the station so its location agrees with the Station Diagram.

Safety:

1. Position microscopes carefully. Do not place them where direct sunlight could hit the mirror at any time during the testing period.

2. Alert students to sharp edges of microscope slides.

3. Monitor the students for safe use of the microscopes.

Station Diagram: Cell Size

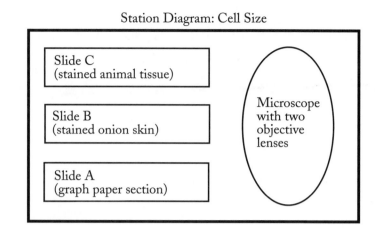

Make a photocopy of the Student Task Sheet for each student. This sheet includes directions, questions, and spaces for students to write their answers. (The directions are highly detailed because the task was being used for the first time as part of a statewide assessment. These directions could be simplified *if* your students are used to performing investigations independently.) Space is provided to re-write measurements from previous steps, if that data is to be used again later (e.g., step 9).

Cell Size
Student Task Sheet

Task: At this station you will measure the size of a microscope's field of view, estimate the size of a cell, and draw pictures of cells that you observe under the lowest and highest powers.

Directions:

1. Pick up Slide A, hold it up to the light, and look at the squares.
2. Slide A is a prepared slide of a tiny piece of graph paper. The lines of the graph paper are all spaced 1.0 mm apart.
3. Place slide A on the microscope stage and bring the graph paper into focus, using the lowest power.
4. When you look into the microscope, the whole area you see is the "field of view." Knowing that the lines of the graph paper are 1.0 mm apart, estimate the diameter of the lowest power's field of view to the nearest 0.25 mm. _____ mm
5. Return Slide A.
6. Place Slide B on the microscope and bring it into focus under the lowest power. Slide B is a piece of onion skin tissue that has been stained and mounted for viewing.
7. Look closely at Slide B under the lowest power. Find one row of cells that goes across the middle of the field of view from one edge of the field of view to the other edge. These cells may go from side to side, from top to bottom, or diagonally across the diameter. In the circle below, carefully sketch only *one row* of cells whose lengths go across the field of view.

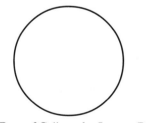

One Row of Cells under Lowest Power

8. How many cells did you see under lowest power in the row that you drew above?

9. In step 4, you estimated the diameter of the lowest power's field of view. Record that value again here: _____ mm.

10. Based on the values you recorded in steps 8 and 9, use the space below to calculate the average length of <u>one</u> onion cell in your diagram to the nearest 0.1 mm. _____ mm/cell

11. Return Slide B.

12. Place Slide C on the microscope stage. Bring Slide C into focus under the lowest power. Now bring the slide into focus under the highest power. In the box below, draw an enlarged view of one typical cell on this slide under the highest power. Your drawing should accurately show the shape and structures of the cell.

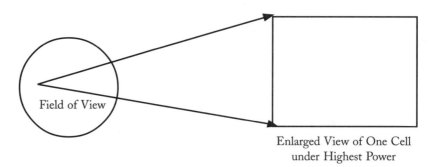

Field of View

Enlarged View of One Cell
under Highest Power

13. When you are finished, put the microscope back to the lowest power. Return all materials to their positions as shown on the Station Diagram.

Cell Size
Scoring Information and Rubric

This task appears to be "just another lab activity," which is exactly how students perceive it. What makes it an assessment task is a set of scoring guidelines (sometimes called "rubrics") for use in evaluating students' written responses. Although there are many ways to focus and organize rubrics, **the rubric below is for items 4, 8, 9, and 10 only** (the items related to diameter of field of view and length of single cell calculation). Rubrics for the other questions are on the NYSED website: *www.emsc.nysed.gov/ciai/mst/sci.html*

4. Estimate the diameter of the field of view. Maximum points: 2

Criteria: The student estimates the diameter of the field of view with precision. (*Note:* The teacher must check the fields on the microscopes in the testing room to be sure that they are all about 1.5 mm (about 1.5 squares) for a 100x magnification.)

- student estimates the diameter of the field of view in the range 1.25–1.75 mm: 2 points
- student estimates the diameter of the field of view either in the range 1.00–.24 mm or in the range 1.76–2.00 mm: 1 point
- student estimates the diameter of the field of view either as less than 1.00 mm or as more than 2.00 mm: 0 points

8. How many cells are in a row?   1 point

Criteria: The student's response matches the number of cells in the student's diagram (± 1 cell). (*Note:* Evaluate the student's response based on the student's diagram in #7.)

9. Record the field of view value determined in #4.   0 points

10. Calculate the length of one onion skin cell.   3 points

Criteria: The student shows work that indicates a correct approach to the problem and obtains a solution by dividing the value in #9 by the value in #8. (*Note:* Evaluate the student's response based on the student's data in #8 and #9).
- Allow 2 points if the student shows a correct approach and arrives at a correct answer.
- Allow 1 point if the student shows a correct approach and arrives at an incorrect answer.

OR
- Allow 1 point if the student arrives at a correct answer but does not show work.
- Allow 0 points if the student shows an incorrect approach regardless of the answer provided.
- Allow 1 point if the student expresses the answer to the nearest 0.1 mm.

Sample correct approaches:

mm/cells = 1.5 mm/5 cells = 0.3 mm/cell

5 cells/1.5 mm = 1 cell/X mm
5X = 1.5
X = 0.3 mm

Sugar or Starch?

This task was included in *Assessing Science Process Laboratory Skills at the Elementary and Middle/Junior High Levels* (Kanis, et al. 1990). It is one in a family of tasks that uses indicators to identify unknowns. The indicators are iodine solution (for starch) and test strips/sticks (for glucose). (This task is also appropriate as a chemistry assessment task. The chemical aspects of the starch and glucose are important biochemical pathways that impact on nutrition and health.)

While the solutions can be purchased commercially, they can also be made with cornstarch (from a grocery store) and glucose (from a drug store). Purchasing the solutions saves preparation time and guarantees similar samples in the various kits and classrooms. The glucose strips are relatively expensive, but could lead to discussions of diabetes, as the major users of the strips are diabetics.

A more structured task could be developed for middle level students who are relatively unfamiliar with planning investigations.

Sugar or Starch?
Task Information

Materials:

- dropper bottles labeled A, B, and C
- dropper bottle with iodine–labeled "<u>Iodine</u> POISON"
- glucose test strip
- transparency test card (see preparation, below)
- Solution A—distilled water
- Solution B—glucose
- Solution C—starch
- paper towels
- safety goggles
- waste container (cup or small pail)

Preparation:

- Label waste container: "Used test strips."
- Glucose and starch solutions can be obtained from a science supply company. Glucose solution can also be made by adding glucose powder to distilled water (about 1 tsp. per liter). Test with glucose strips and dilute just until you get a positive reaction. Starch solution can be made by adding cornstarch to distilled water. Stir and filter. Test with iodine and dilute (use 1 tbsp. to 1 liter of water).
- Fill bottles with solutions (bottle A–water; bottle B–glucose; bottle C–starch.
- Glucose test strips can be obtained from a science supply company or your local drugstore. Glucose test strips are <u>not</u> sensitive to table sugar, which is mainly sucrose.
- Keep the glucose strips away from the iodine, which will turn the strips black or green.
- Be sure to test glucose and starch solutions before using them with the students.
- Diluted solutions are more effective than full strength.

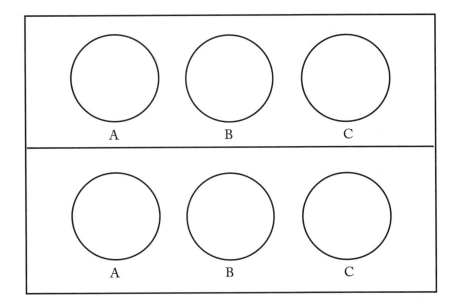

- The transparency test card can be made by drawing small circles the size of nickels on a piece of paper (see above). Place three circles in a row. You will need two rows of circles. Label the circles A, B, C, and copy onto a transparency. Six or eight sets of circles will fit in one overhead transparency. Cut the sets apart and place one at each station. Discard after one use.

Safety:
- Students must wear safety goggles when working with iodine.

Modifications and Extensions:
- Glucose test strips are very expensive so a teacher demonstration may be more appropriate.
- To do a teacher demonstration, you might use an overhead projector with a transparency sheet with three circles marked "A", "B", and "C". Use only two drops of each solution. The students could then check the color on the strips as well as see the iodine change color when the materials were added. Use the glucose strips first, then add the iodine. You could divide the task into two components: finding sugar and finding starch.

Sugar or Starch?
Student Task Sheet

Iodine solution is used as an indicator to test for starch. It will turn a starch solution blue-black in color. The test strips turn from yellow to green in the presence of a certain type of sugar. Before you are three bottles labeled A, B, and C. The bottles may contain a sugar solution, a starch solution, neither starch nor sugar, or starch and sugar. You are to determine the contents of each bottle.

1. Using the information above, what will you do to determine which bottle contains starch and which contains sugar? Write down your plan.

2. Carry out the experiment. Record your observations in a table.

3. On the basis of the information in your table, answer the following questions.
   A. Which sample(s) contain sugar?
      What are your reasons for this conclusion?
   B. Which sample(s) contain starch?
      What are your reasons for this conclusion?

Sugar or Starch?
Scoring Guide

Item No.	Answer	Scoring
1.	Place a test strip in each circle of the top row. Place a drop of iodine in each circle of the bottom row.	1 pt. for adequate plan using iodine. 1 pt. for plan using test strip. Total possible points – 2 pts.
2.	Circle Test strip Iodine solution A no change no change/brown, red, orange B turns green or brown/black no change/brown, red, orange C no change brown solution turns blue-black, purple/gray	1 pt. for no change in circle A (either column). 1 pt. for correct observation with test strip, circle B. 1 pt. for correct observation with iodine solution, circle C. Total possible points – 3 pts.
3A.	Bottle B contains sugar. Reason: The solution caused the strip to turn green or brown/black.	2 pts. if correct sample is identified and correct reason cited. 1 pt. for correct identification with incorrect explanation. 0 pts. for incorrect identification. Total possible points – 2 pts.
3B.	Bottle C contains starch. Reason: Because the solution turned blue-black when iodine was added.	2 pts. if correct sample is identified and correct reason cited. 1 pt. for correct identification with incorrect explanation. 0 pts. for incorrect identification. Total possible points – 2 pts.
		Total possible points – 9 points

Pulse

This task is from the collection used in the Third International Mathematics and Science Study (TIMSS) (Harmon, et al. 1997). TIMSS was one of the largest international education studies ever conducted, with over 40 countries conducting the testing at three levels of schooling: grade 4, grade 8, and the last year of secondary school (usually grade 12). In addition to using objective tests with multiple-choice and constructed-response items, TIMSS included a set of performance assessment tasks. These tasks were an optional component. Twenty countries participated in this component at the fourth and eighth grade levels; most of the tasks were used at both grade levels, with slight modifications for the different grades. (The TIMSS performance tasks can be found in *Performance Assessment in IEA's Third International Mathematics and Science Study* [Harmon, et al. 1997]. A review of the TIMSS eighth-grade performance testing is also available [Chan, et al. 1999]).

Performance assessment in the life science area is complicated by the need to include live organisms (in at least some of the tasks). Growing and monitoring plants and animals for specific tasks is difficult, especially for state, national, or international assessments. In this task, the organism is the students completing the task. (Note the need to screen for physical conditions that may preclude some students from doing this task). The materials for the task are very simple: a stopwatch and a step or bench (about 20–25 cm high). The task is designed to measure a student's ability to

- collect and record data at appropriate intervals;
- summarize and describe the trends or patterns in the data; and
- interpret the data, using knowledge about the human body (heart, circulatory system, respiratory system, or muscle system) to explain the results.

Students have 20 minutes to complete the task. Students are also expected to develop an appropriate table to present the data collected.

This task was relatively difficult for most students in the United States. Their performance was strong for the questions that required collecting and recording data and less strong for questions that required interpreting data and explaining results. These findings were similar to ones from other TIMSS performance tasks.

Below is the information provided for the teacher regarding necessary equipment and prior preparation. In this task, the only preparation is that the teacher review with students the procedure for taking one's own pulse, ensuring that students will be able to complete the task meaningfully.

Pulse
Task Information

Materials:
- A watch that measures time in seconds, or a stopwatch.
- A stable step or bench, about 20–25 cm (8–10 in) high. Students will be stepping up onto it, so it should be able to take the weight and it should not easily slide on the floor.

Before Testing:
1. Before administering the test, tell the students that some of them will be doing a task requiring that they count their pulse. Demonstrate *for all students* how to find their pulse and give them one

or two minutes to locate it and practice counting it. Tell the students who will be participating to ask for help during the test if they are unable to find their pulse.

2. Determine if any students have physical conditions that would make it inadvisable for them to participate in this exercise.

During Testing:

3. Even with advance instruction, students may have difficulty in finding their pulse. They may need to ask for help. Show them how to find it on their neck. However, do not assist them in completing the task—that is, do not show them how to find and record changes in their pulse.

Pulse
Student Task Sheet

Your task: Find out how your pulse changes when you climb up and down a step for five minutes.

Procedure:

1. Find your pulse and be sure you know how to count it. *If you cannot find your pulse ask a teacher for help.*

2. Count your pulse for 10 seconds. Write down the number of counts.

3. Climb up and down on the step for about five minutes. Stop after each minute and write down your pulse.

4. Make a table and write down the times at which you measured your pulse and the measurements you made.

5. Write down your answer to this question: How did your pulse change during this exercise?

6. Write down your answer to this question: Why do you think your pulse changed in this way?

7. *Put everything back the way you found it so that someone else can use the station.*

Pulse
Scoring Rubric

Step 2: Count your pulse for 10 seconds. Write down the number of counts.

Complete response (1 point):
- Any response that indicates that the pulse beats within the range of 2 and 25 counts per 10 seconds.

Incorrect response (0 points):
- Pulse not within range (or other incorrect response).

Step 3: Climb up and down on the step for about five minutes. Stop after each minute and write down your pulse.

(Note to the teacher: If the rates recorded are erratic [the number of pulse beats goes up and down with increasing exercise time and there is no consistent pattern], assume that the student does not know how to measure pulse, and score as an incorrect response. Evidence in a later step may show another reason, such as "resting between every measurement," but this is still an error in procedure and is incorrect for this question.)

Complete response (3 points):
- Pulse counts within range of 7 and 25 counts per seconds.
- Pulse range is recorded at least four different times during the exercises—that is, the table contains five entries, including an "at rest" entry.

- Pulse rate increases with exercise (it may level off or slow down near the end).

Partially correct response (2 points):
- Fewer than five measurements are recorded. Other responses are given.

Minimally correct response (1 point):
- Entries are complete but there are slight errors (e.g., one or two of the pulse beats recorded may be inconsistent with the rest, but there are enough measurements recorded to show the general trend).
- Records only the beginning and the final sets of measurements.
- Describes rate qualitatively rather than quantitatively, but indicates general trend (e.g., *slow, medium, fast,* or *up/down.*)

Incorrect response (0 points):
- Pulse rates not reasonable because number of beats is erratic (e.g., student reported pulse as whole numbers per second).
- Merely repeats responses given earlier.

Step 5: Answer the question How did your pulse change during this exercise?

Complete response (2 points):
- Number of pulse beats increases with exercise.
- Number of pulse beats increases at first, then stabilizes or slows.

Partially correct response (1 point):
- Stabilizing in pulse rate shown in data but not mentioned in Step 5 or inconsistencies in data are not addressed.
- Describes pulse at specific time intervals instead of summarizing trend (e.g., *At 2 minutes slow; at 4 minutes faster. At 2 minutes 60/minute; at 4 minutes 70/minute.*)

Incorrect responses (0 points):
- Not consistent with data.
- Merely repeats information from a previous step.

Step 6: Answer the question Why do you think your pulse changed in this way?

Complete response (3 points):
A complete response includes the following three elements that relate to the change in pulse rate because of the physiological needs of the body during exercise: (1) role of muscle action—that is, exercise results in the need for more energy in the muscles (and therefore more oxygen or food); (2) role of blood—that is, more oxygen or food (or removal of waste products) is provided by an increase in blood flow; (3) connection with heart action or pulse rate—that is, increased pulse means that the heart is pumping faster to supply more blood.
- Makes a scientific connection between heart rate, blood supply, and muscle action or exercise. Example: *For exercise, the body needs more oxygen and the heart must pump blood faster to get it there.*

Partially correct response (2 points):
- Mentions need for oxygen or energy but does not relate it to heart action. Example: *The heart got faster because I needed more energy.*
- Change in pulse is related to the fact that the heart works harder/faster to pump more blood, but the connection to the need for more energy is not made. Example: *The heart works faster to pump more blood.* OR *More blood must be pumped, so the heart works harder.*

Minimally correct response (1 point):

- Mentions that the pulse increases because the heart works faster, without mentioning blood or energy or oxygen needs. Example: *The pulse increases because the heart is working harder/faster.*

- A correct interpretation of student's own data without explicit reference to circulatory system, heart, etc.

Incorrect responses (0 points):

- Reports on change in pulse related to something in the body, but not explicitly to the heart. Example: *The body speeds up.* OR *Everything inside the body works harder.*

- Gives descriptive response or repeats procedure or data rather than explaining cause of the results. Example: *Because I walked.* OR *Because you get tired.*

Natural Selection

This task was developed in a doctoral dissertation (Saha 2001) in response to an initiative by the New York State Education Department to include performance assessments in the final exams for each high school science course. The station format of this task was easy to fit within preexisting school schedules. This task is a simulation or model of the effect of environmental factors on evolution of organisms by natural selection.

The materials used within this task are readily available.

Natural Selection
Task Information

Materials:

- seeds: 10 each of 7 types (variety of color and sizes—e.g., kidney beans, lima beans, pinto beans, green beans)
- box tops (e.g., from copier paper boxes) or cafeteria trays
- shredded paper: green, yellow, or white work well, as does cellophane "Easter" grass.
- tweezers: (size compatible with seeds) metal or plastic
- timer
- 1 index card (5"x 8" or larger)
- Seed Type Card (one seed of each type—i.e., seven seeds in all—glued to card, with name or description of each)

Station Diagram:

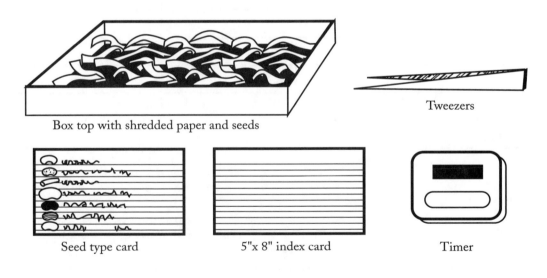

Box top with shredded paper and seeds

Tweezers

Seed type card

5"x 8" index card

Timer

The Students' Task Sheets include background information, a few procedural directions, and a set of questions to answer. The questions are organized so that they begin with very simple observations and descriptions, and culminate with questions that direct students to interpret data and make predictions. Students are provided with a labeled data table. Teachers may modify the task by asking students to develop their own data table.

Natural Selection
Student Task Sheet

Background:

The origin of species by means of natural selection is an element of the theory of evolution developed by Charles Darwin and Alfred Russel Wallace in the 19th century. That theory states that the existence of an innate tendency toward over-reproduction starts the "struggle for existence" among organisms. Small differences in structures and abilities result in greater fitness for a given environment. Evolutionary theories hypothesize that changes occur over millions of years and ultimately culminate in the formation of a new species. Multiple environmental factors—including predators, food supply, diseases, and weather—influence this evolutionary process.

Procedure:

1. Put shredded paper and 70 seeds (10 each of 7 types) in the box top. Shake up so that all seeds are not on top.

2. Using tweezers, pick up as many seeds as possible from the box top within two minutes, trying to move the shredded paper as little as possible. Place the seeds on the index card provided.

3. Using your data, complete the following table (seed description will include shape, size, and color):

No. of Each Seed Type	Seed Description	Number Collected	Number Remaining in the Environment
10			
10			
10			
10			
10			
10			
10			

Questions:

1. Which description(s) helped you pick out more of certain seeds than of others? In this activity, what represents the predator and what represents the prey?

2. What interpretations can you make about how natural selection might work on these seeds in the simulated environment? Refer to column 3 of the above data table in answering this question.

3. If predators continue to prey on the seed ecosystem, would some of the seed species be in danger of extinction? What may happen over time? Is this is a positive or a negative result for this ecosystem?

Natural Selection
Scoring Rubric

Filling out the data table:
Possible number of points: 3

1. (Column 2 of the table) Descriptions represent shape, size, and/or color—1 point
2. (Column 3 of the table) Data reported for at least three kinds of seed—1 point
3. (Column 4 of the table) Number of seeds remaining was determined accurately—1 point

Question #1 Listing the descriptions of the seeds that were collected in the greatest quantities:
Possible number of points: 2

1. Descriptions given of the seeds that were collected in the greatest quantities (e.g., "large and brown color beans")—1 point
2. If the descriptions correspond to the student's data (most collected seeds)—1 point

Question #2 Naming the predator and the prey:
Possible number of points: 2

1. Tweezers/student is the predator—1 point
2. Seeds are the prey—1 point

Question #3 Interpretation of possible effect of natural selection process in the box top environment:
Possible number of points: 3
1. *Elements of natural selection* (e.g., masking/hidden/stuck out/camouflaged/fittest/unfit/more visible/ less visible/visible/ blended/adapted/not adapted)—1 point
2. *Link to descriptions* (e.g., size, color, and/or shape)—1 point
3. *Possible effect of #1 and #2 on natural selection process in the environment* (e.g., could not find/difficult or hard to find or catch or get or pick/easy to find/help prey/can or can't be attacked or seen/ easily collected/not collected, etc.)—1 point

Question #4 Effect of predators on the prey in the environment:
Possible number of points: 3

1. Predictions (what will happen over time): Possible answers—"Eventually there will be no large seeds left" or "Seeds will be extinct" or "There would be eventually no seeds left" or "Some species, those that are preyed upon more, may become endangered ultimately." – 1 point
2. Indication of the type of effect (either directly or indirectly): Possible answers—"Some of the seeds would be extinct. This would 'disrupt the ecosystem'— a negative effect" or "In this ecosystem diversity of the population will be reduced" or "Less array of food choices for predator"— 1 point

Using a Dichotomous Key

Classification is an important tool in all science fields. Geologists classify rocks as igneous, sedimentary, or metamorphic. Chemists classify elements based on observable and measurable characteristics; the periodic table presents the elements in their respective groups and families, based on atomic properties. Physicists classify the several interactions among matter in terms of the forces involved: gravitational, electrostatic, or nuclear. Biologists, however, use different criteria for classifying living organisms. In this task, students classify very simple organisms.

Beginning in elementary school, students learn to sort or group objects based on simple characteristics such as size, shape, and color. Students then may sort and group animals based on whether they fly, swim, or walk. This skill is built upon, with increasingly sophisticated observations, through middle school and into high school. In the example below, students use a microscope to examine very small organisms. They are given a dichotomous key—a very helpful tool for scientists in many disciplines of study (as well as for "weekend biologists," who use the dichotomous keys in field guides to identify birds, flowers, and trees).

In this task (designed for middle-level and high school students), the teacher provides three unknown/unlabelled slides, a brief introduction, and the classification key. The language in the key is representative of the conceptual knowledge derived from an introductory study of microbiology at the middle or high school level. The task assesses students' manipulative skills (students use a microscope) and their conceptual understanding (students identify the organisms on three slides). The organisms on the three unlabeled slides are sampled from the four organisms described in the key. This task was developed in a doctoral dissertation (Wright 2002).

Dichotomous Key
Task Information

Background: Biologists estimate that there are as many as 40 million different species of organisms on Earth. Even though there is variation among species, there also are many similarities. These similar characteristics make it possible to place organisms into categories.

Materials (for teachers only):
- microscope
- three slides (euglena, bacteria, paramecium) labeled A, B, and C.

Dichotomous Key
Student Task Sheet

Task: Your task is to use a dichotomous key to identify some single-celled or unicellular organisms.

Directions: Using the microscope, observe and identify each organism. The dichotomous key below provides characteristics common to each organism.

Dichotomous Key
Unicellular Organisms

1 Prokaryotic: lack cellular organelles such as a nucleus	*Bacteria*
Eukaryotic: contain cellular organelles such as a nucleus	**Go to 2**
2. Autotrophs: photosynthetic (contain chlorophyll)	*Euglena*
Heterotrophs: absorptive or ingestive	**Go to 3**
3. Locomotion: ciliated movement	*Paramecium*
Locomotion: extended pseudopodia	**Go to 4**
4. *Amoeba*	

Questions:

1. What is the organism on Slide A? Explain the reasons for your answer.
2. What is the organism on Slide B? Explain the reasons for your answer.
3. What is the organism on Slide C? Explain the reasons for your answer.
4. List two characteristics you observed that are similar in these three organisms.
5. Can more than one organism occupy the final place in this dichotomous key? Why or why not?

Dichotomous Key
Scoring Rubric

Question 1: What is the organism in Slide A?   **2 points total**
- Allow 1 point for the correct answer (depends on preparation of slide)
- Allow 1 point for a plausible reason

Question 2: What is the organism in Slide B?   **2 points total**
- Allow 1 point for the correct answer
- Allow 1 point for a plausible reason

Question 3: What is the organism in Slide C?   **2 points total**
- Allow 1 point for the correct answer
- Allow 1 point for a plausible reason

Question 4: List two cellular characteristics that are similar in the three organisms.   **2 points total**
- Allow 1 point for each characteristic.
    - Acceptable characteristics include: having a nucleus, having a cell membrane, having vacuoles
    - Unacceptable characteristics include: very small, microscopic, causing diseases

Question 5: Can more than one organism occupy the final place on the key? Why or why not?

     2 points total

- Allow 1 point for "no"
- Allow 1 point for the statement that there will always be a single characteristic that categorizes the organism from all other organisms.

To discourage the "borrowing" of answers, provide a table with slides labeled with letter and number, so all A slides were <u>not</u> the same organism. The following table illustrates this approach:

	LETTER		
	A	B	C
Slide 1	E	P	B
Slide 2	P	E	B
Slide 3	B	P	E
Slide 4	P	B	E
Slide 5	E	B	P
Slide 6	B	E	P

E = Euglena
P = Paramecium
B = Bacteria

Kernels of Corn

Genetics is an important topic in biology. Many student activities focus on calculations based on data from a Punnett square. This task is designed to assess students' ability to apply or transfer genetic concepts to a common object—an ear of corn. The ears described and used in this example have yellow and purple kernels. Teachers can also use "bread and butter" corn (with white and yellow kernels), a variety of corn found in many parts of the United States. Students are expected to determine dominant color, phenotype ratios, and possible genotype. They are also called on to use scientific inquiry skills in questions about likely errors and the effect of using a larger sample. This task was developed in a doctoral dissertation (Wright 2002). The materials used are very simple and commonly available.

Kernels of Corn
Task Information

Materials:

- 1 ear of corn with purple and yellow kernels in a 3:1 ratio
- 1 ear of corn with purple and yellow kernels in a 1:1 ratio

Note: The ears of corn can be purchased from many science suppliers. Leaving the ears wrapped in plastic sheeting will prolong the life of the ears.

Kernels of Corn
Student Task Sheet

Task: You are going to use corn kernels to examine principles of Mendelian genetics. Kernel color is just one characteristic determined by the combination of alleles inherited from each parent. You need to determine whether yellow or purple is the dominant color.

Directions:

1. Fill in the data table with an <u>estimate</u> of kernels. (Do not attempt to count all the kernels). Use a rubber band to identify the fraction of the ear you will count.

	# of purple kernels	# of yellow kernels
Ear 1		
Ear 2		

2. Which is the dominant kernel color? Explain your decision.
3. What is the phenotypic ratio for Ear 1 and the phenotypic ratio for Ear 2?
4. What are the most likely parental genotypes for Ear 1 and Ear 2?
5. Suppose you repeated the activity using a bushel of corn ears (many more corn ears) of the same genotype. How would your results be affected?
6. What are some sources of error that may have affected your conclusions?

Kernels of Corn
Scoring Rubric

Question 1: Fill in the data table with an estimate of kernels.   **4 points total**
Correct range plus or minus 5%.
Allow 1 point for the correct estimate in each cell.

	# of purple kernels	# of yellow kernels
Ear 1		
Ear 2		

Question 2: Which is the dominant kernel color?   **1 point total**
Purple kernels are dominant.

Question 3: What is the phenotypic ratio for Ear 1 and the phenotypic ratio   **2 points total**
for Ear 2? (The phenotypic ratio is the ratio of the number of
purple kernels to the number of yellow kernels.)
Allow 1 point for the correct ratio of Ear 1 and for the correct ratio of Ear 2
(one will be 1:1, the other 3:1).

Question 4: What are the most likely parental genotypes for Ear 1 and Ear 2?   **2 points total**
Allow 1 point for ear of corn with purple and yellow kernels in a 3:1 ratio
purple/yellow, Pp for both parents.
Allow 1 point for ear of corn with purple and yellow kernels in a 1:1 ratio
purple/yellow and yellow/yellow, Pp and pp for parents.

Question 5: Suppose you repeated the activity using a bushel of corn ears   **1 point total**
(many more corn ears) of the same genotype. How would your
results be affected?
Allow 1 point for explaining that a bushel count would give a more accurate
count of kernels.

Question 6: What are some sources of error that may have affected   **1 point total**
your conclusions?
Allow 1 point for explanation of a miscount or an inaccurate estimation.

Biology Investigation Tasks

These tasks require students to complete an entire inquiry or solve a problem, and are authentic in that they involve students in all phases of research as scientists. Most of the tasks take one or two class periods and are designed to fit within school schedules.

Students should already be familiar with laboratory and measuring equipment used in a task, as well as the science concepts and principles. This form of assessment task determines if students understand the relevant content and are proficient with investigative skills by their level of success in extending or applying these ideas to new situations. These assessment tasks can range from those that are quite similar to the instructional task to those that are very different from instruction in class. (See the Novelty portion of Chapter 2, page 26.)

These tasks can be modified using varying amounts of information and directions (called degrees of structure; Chapter 2, page 24). The level of structure in assessment tasks should be similar to that of the laboratory and fieldwork done in class. Students can learn to work with less-structured instruction and assessment, but they need to be instructed and encouraged to handle this "challenging" approach. Most students prefer a teacher-structured approach as there is less work required on their part.

Most of the tasks included here are for use at the high school level, but can be adapted for use with middle school students by adjusting the directions, labels, and the number of unknowns. While most tasks begin with the planning stage, you can make minor changes so they can begin with students collecting their own data, using a set of experimental procedures, or analyzing previously collected data.

For most of these tasks, students will need to record their answers in either their laboratory logbook or on two blank sheets of paper. Specific instructions for what students should record, and the labels they should use, are given in each task. Generally, students will be asked to record their hypothesis, their procedure (including any diagrams), and their data table (including their observations) on one sheet in a reasonably finished form. The other sheet is to be used as scratch paper. If the task has a Part B, students will usually need a piece of graph paper and a third sheet for recording their conclusions. You may wish to hand out prepared answer sheets with the headings already in place.

The chart below identifies the skills assessed by the five biology Investigation Tasks that follow.

Biology Investigation Tasks

Skills Categories	Sowbug Habitats (page 108)	Perspiration and Cooling (page 114)	Respiration (page 116)	Using Indicators (page 120)	Diffusion/Osmosis (page 125)
Planning	✔		✔		✔
Performing	✔	✔	✔	✔	✔
Analyzing	✔	✔	✔	✔	✔
Applying	✔	✔			✔

Sowbug Habitats

This task can be used with middle-level or high school students depending upon their instructional experiences. Sowbugs, also called pillbugs, are crustaceans, like lobsters, crabs, and crayfish. As a subject for student investigation, they have the advantage of not biting, not slithering, and being kind of cute. Invertebrates such as sowbugs are all around us, and perform many functions crucial to maintaining the balance of nature. The success of particular invertebrates in particular habitats is an important indicator of environmental health.

In this task, students focus on designing and conducting an experiment about the preferential environment inhabited by some organisms. The organism used here should be quite familiar to the students from class and from outdoors. The only materials needed, beyond sowbugs, are materials you find in almost every science room. The scoring guide is in a detailed format and specific to this task. While the criteria in the scoring guide seem long and involved, teachers find it very helpful for scoring the first few tasks. By then, most teachers have "internalized" most of the scoring criteria and can score student responses quickly, accurately, and reliably.

Sowbug Habitats
Task Information

Content: Organisms exist in certain environments with certain characteristics.

Purpose: Conducting an experiment to determine what type of environment sowbugs prefer.

Skills: **Primary:** Predicting, interpreting data
    Secondary: Collecting data, recording data, inferring

Time: 30–40 minutes

Materials:

- beaker of water
- eyedropper
- 1 extra petri dish lid
- masking tape
- a petri dish with 10 sowbugs

- scissors
- clock/timer
- stack of paper towels
- 1 sheet black construction paper

Preparation:

Sowbugs/pillbugs are scavengers and are easy to culture. You can order a kit from various science supply houses. Another option is to establish your own culture. These animals can be easily found under rocks and rotting logs. A plastic shoe box with holes melted in the lid with a hot dissecting needle will serve as a container. Place several centimeters of soil in the bottom of the box. The soil should be from a wooded area with much organic matter. There should be wood chips, leaves, and stones. Be certain to keep the soil moist since sowbugs are crustaceans and use gills to breathe. Sprinkle a little oatmeal on the surface of the soil and add some potato slices and a few lettuce leaves or carrot peels. Place your culture where it won't be disturbed, being certain to keep it moist and to periodically add vegetable scraps.

Sowbugs can be placed into the petri dish a day or two ahead of time <u>only</u> if the sowbugs are provided with a source of moisture. A wet piece of paper towel can be used. The teacher should remove the towel prior to the start of the experiment. To remove sowbugs from the paper towel, gently move them with forceps or small paint brush. At the end of the experiment, return wet paper towel to the petri dishes. Approximate time to set up 10 petri dishes with 10 sowbugs in each: 20–30 minutes.

Sowbug Habitats
Student Task Sheet

Task: At this station, you will be conducting an experiment to determine what type of environment sowbugs prefer. Sowbugs are crustaceans and close relatives of crabs and lobsters. Like their relatives, sowbugs use gills for respiration. But, unlike most crustaceans, they live on land and <u>not</u> in the water.

Materials:

- beaker of water
- scissors
- stack of paper towels
- 1 sheet black construction paper
- 1 extra petri dish lid

- eyedropper
- clock/timer
- masking tape
- 1 petri dish with 10 sowbugs

Directions:
Part A

1. Answer questions 1–2 on the answer sheet on page 110.

Part B

1. Using the extra petri dish lid as a pattern, trace two circles on a piece of paper towel.
2. Cut out the two circles. Fold each circle in half. Saturate one folded circle with water. It should be moist, but not soaking wet. The second folded circle should remain dry.
3. Arrange the folded circles in the extra petri dish lid to create a habitat which is half moist and half dry.
4. Remove the lid from the petri dish lid containing the sowbugs and replace it with the wet/dry habitat lid you prepared.
5. Invert the petri dish so the wet/dry lid becomes the <u>bottom</u> and the petri dish bottom becomes the <u>top</u>.

Before   Invert   After

6. Using black construction paper, cover the <u>moist side</u> of the petri dish to make it dark.
7. Note the time on your clock, or start your timer now. Record your start time in the data table on your answer sheet.
8. The sowbugs should remain undisturbed for five (5) minutes. While you are waiting, check your answers to questions 1–2.
9. At the conclusion of the five (5) minute time period, record the time and the location of the sowbugs in the data table on your answer sheet.
10. Complete the remaining questions in Part B of the lab.

Sowbug Habitats
Answer Sheet

Part A

1. Using complete sentences, predict what you think the sowbugs will do if they are released into a habitat with different areas of moisture and light.

2. Using complete sentences, explain why you think the sowbugs will be arranged in the way you predicted.

Part B
Data Table

	Environment	Number of Sowbugs
Start time _____	Moist/Dark	
Stop time _____	Dry/Light	

3. Did the animals prefer one environment to another? State evidence for your answer in complete sentences.

4. For this question, answer <u>either</u> (a) or (b).
   a) If most of the animals were found on the dark, moist side of the container, is this proof that sowbugs prefer a moist environment to a dry one? Explain your answer in complete sentences.
   b) If most of the animals were found on the illuminated, dry side of the container, is this proof that sowbugs prefer light to darkness? Explain your answer in complete sentences.

5. Based on the way this experiment was run, can you say the sowbugs' behavior was due to differences in light conditions alone? Answer Yes or No.

6. Using complete sentences, explain your answer to question 5.

7. How can the variables in this experimental setup be changed to allow for better conclusions to be drawn? Answer in complete sentences.

8. For this question, answer <u>either</u> (a) or (b) depending on your results.
   a) If there is a preference, how does it relate to the sowbugs' survival? In other words, how do the environmental factors of light/dry or dark/moist make it possible for sowbugs to be better able to survive?

   b) If there is no preference, explain why this is the case in terms of sowbug survival and life processes.

Sowbug Habitats
Scoring Rubric

Maximum score – 29 points

Student Setup.   **3 points total**

Scoring should be done by teacher observation during the exercise.

3 points – Successfully (1) sets up the petri dish with the arrangement of (2) wet/dry paper towels and (3) construction paper screen

2 points – Has two factors correct

1 point – Has one factor correct

0 points – Incorrect setup; no factors correct

Answer Sheet Part A

Question 1.   **3 points total**

3 points – Predictions relate to both variables.

A prediction might be: (a) "The sowbugs seek the moist/dark side of the petri dish," (b) "The sowbugs will be all over the setup," (c) "The sowbugs will move toward the dry/light side of the petri dish," etc. Answers should be written in complete sentences; deduct 1 point if complete sentences are not used.

2 points – Has a prediction for only <u>one</u> factor. A prediction might be: "The sowbugs seek the dark side of the petri dish." Answers should be written in complete sentences; deduct 1 point if complete sentences are not used.

0 points – Incorrect response, even if in complete sentences, or no response provided.

Question 2.   **3 points total**

3 points – Provides a sound rationale for both factors based on biological principles. Possible answers include (a) "They prefer the dark because it is cooler or because they can hide from predators or they normally feed at night." (b) "They scatter all over because they are disoriented due to being handled or they are attempting to find their home area." (c) "They seek moisture because they require the dampness for respiration or to keep from drying out." Predictions should be written using complete sentences.

2 points – Identifies only one factor in explanation. Answers should be written in complete sentences; deduct 1 point if complete sentences are not used.

0 points – Incorrect response, even if in complete sentences, or no response provided.

Answer Sheet Part B

Data Table   **2 points total**

2 points – For completing table with both sets of times and numbers.

1 point – One part of the data is missing.

0 points – More than one part missing.

Question 3.   **3 points total**

3 points – "Yes, most or all of the sowbugs are on the moist/dark side or dry/light side." Students may say "Yes, 7 of the 10 sowbugs are on the moist/dark side." or "No, 6 bugs are on the moist/dark side and 4 were on the illuminated/dry side." The students should use the numbers of sowbugs located in the various parts of the setup, as long as they have an appropriate response based on what they observed and recorded on their chart, and answers are written in complete sentences.

2 points – In the case of partial answers, for correctly deciding "yes or no" based on their numbers for preference.

    or

For properly using the numbers of bugs in various locations as evidence but with a weak explanation. Answers should be written in complete sentences; deduct 1 point if complete sentences are not used.

0 points – Incorrect response even if in complete sentence, or no response provided.

Question 4a. 3 points total

3 points – "No. Movement to the moist/dark side is evidence that the sowbugs prefer darkness and have nothing to do with the moisture." Students indicate that there are two variables involved, not just one. Answers should be written in complete sentences.

2 points – Identifies only one of the above variables. Answers should be written in complete sentences; deduct 1 point if complete sentences are not used.

0 points – Incorrect response, even if in complete sentences, or no response provided.

Question 4b. 3 points total

3 points – "No. Movement to the dry/light side indicates preference for a dry environment. It may not be related to the amount of light available." Again, students should indicate that there are two variables involved, not just one. Answers should be written in complete sentences.

2 points – Identifies only one of the above variables. Answers should be written in complete sentences; deduct 1 point if complete sentences are not used.

0 points – Incorrect response, even if in complete sentences, or no response provided.

Question 5. 1 point total

1 point – Student responds "No"

Question 6. 2 points total

2 points – Student explains that two (2) variables are used at the same time. Answers should be written in complete sentences.

1 point – Student gives a correct explanation for answer, but not in complete sentences.

0 points – Incorrect answer, even if written in complete sentences.

Question 7. 2 points total

2 points – Student suggests a procedure to eliminate the problem of two (2) variables, such as, "The construction paper screen could be left off the petri dish. That way the sowbugs would be selecting between a moist and a dry environment."

> or

"The towels on the bottom of the petri dish could all be dry or all moist, with the construction paper shading on one side and the other side illuminated." Answers should be written in complete sentences; deduct 1 point if complete sentences are not used.

0 points – If student responds that the design is fine as it is, even if it is written in complete sentences.

Question 8a. 2 points total

2 points – "The sowbugs prefer a moist environment because they respire with gills. They require moisture to keep their gills moist so the diffusion of gases can occur."

> or

"The sowbugs prefer a dark environment because it keeps them from being easily spotted by predators. It also keeps them cooler and prevents them from drying out."

or

"The sowbugs prefer dry environments so that they do not drown. They must have the proper moisture level." Answers should be written in complete sentences; deduct 1 point if complete sentences are not used.

NOTE: There are other possible correct answers. Use your discretion in deciding if the answer is reasonable based on experimental findings and whether the survival factors are based on sound biological concepts.

Question 8b.   2 points total

2 points – "There is no preference since neither the moist and dark conditions nor the dry and light conditions are detriments to the sowbugs' survival, and neither condition is needed for their survival."

      or

"In order to maintain homeostasis, the sowbugs must move back and forth between the two environments." Answers should be written in complete sentences; deduct 1 point if complete sentences are not used.

0 points – Choice (a) or (b) is selected on the Answer Sheet but the answer is not based on a reasonable interpretation of the lab observations, even if it is written in complete sentences.

0 points – Incorrect response, even if written in complete sentences, or no response provided.

Perspiration and Cooling

This task can be used with middle-level or high school students. The equipment used is simple, and available in almost any science classroom. Perspiration, or sweating, is the loss of fluid through normal skin in humans. Fluid loss occurs from sweat glands secreting, or by diffusion through other skin structures. However, we seldom think of this process in terms of its implications for the temperature equilibrium of our bodies. Since science is perceived to be useful and relevant when we use its concepts and principles to explain phenomena and observations that personally affect us, this task challenges students to use science concepts to explain a phenomena they experience daily—making the task authentic and relevant.

This task requires students to demonstrate competence with several skills: collecting data, graphing data, and formulating conclusions. The scoring guide is based on these skills with specific criteria that relate to this activity.

Perspiration and Cooling
Student Task Sheet

Task: Collect and analyze data on perspiration.

Materials per student:

- 2 test tubes
- eye dropper
- newspaper strips, width the length of the test tubes
- hot water in Styrofoam cups
- paper towels
- room temperature water
- 4 rubber bands
- timer or clock
- test tube rack
- thermometer
- funnel

Background:

When you get hot you perspire, and this is your body's way of maintaining normal temperature. But how effective is perspiration in maintaining your body temperature?

Directions:

1. Examine the apparatus at this station.
2. Place the test tube rack on a paper towel. Prepare your test tubes by wrapping each one with a strip of newspaper. Use two rubber bands to hold the paper on the test tubes.
3. Quickly fill both test tubes with hot water. Take care not to spill any water on the newspaper.
4. Place one thermometer in each test tube. Record the starting temperature for each test tube on a data table. In the next step, one (1) test tube becomes the "wet" test tube and one (1) remains dry.
5. Use the eye dropper to quickly wet the newspaper of one (1) of the test tubes with room-temperature water. The newspaper on the test tube should be completely saturated with water.
6. Measure the water temperature in each test tube at intervals of one minute for the next 12 minutes, and record your measurements in a data table you construct.
7. Construct a line graph of your data, and answer questions 8–13.
8. From your data table, what is the temperature of the water in both the wet and dry tubes at 6 minutes?
9. From your graph, what is the temperature of the water in both tubes at 9.5 minutes?
10. Use your graph to predict what the temperature would be in the dry tube after 15 minutes. Using complete sentences, suggest an explanation for your prediction.
11. Using complete sentences, describe and compare the cooling patterns of the two test tubes.
12. Using complete sentences, explain what causes the differences in water temperature between the water in the two tubes.
13. Using complete sentences, describe what comparison you can make between the effect of perspiration on the skin of the human body, and the newspaper on the wet test tube. Relate your answer to body temperature control.

Perspiration and Cooling
Scoring Rubric

Maximum score – 23 points

1: Data Table .... 2 points total

Allow 1 point for each of the following:
*   table completed
*   data consistent with expectation of results

2: Graph .... 5 points total

Allow 1 point for each of the following:
*   appropriate title
*   axes labeled with correct variables (units included)
*   appropriate scale
*   points plotted accurately
*   curves are appropriate to data trend

3: Data transfer from table .... 2 points total

Allow 1 point for each of the following:
*   correct 6-minute dry tube reading based on data collected
*   correct 6-minute wet tube reading based on data collected

4: Graph Interpretation/Prediction .... 2 points total

Allow 1 point for each of the following:
*   corresponds to student's dry tube graph at 9.5 minutes
*   corresponds to student's wet tube graph at 9.5 minutes

5: Extrapolation Prediction .... 3 points total

Allow 1 point for correct temperature prediction based on student's graph/data.
Allow 2 points if explanation refers to extrapolation from graph/data and is in complete sentences.
Allow 1 point if explanation refers to extrapolation from graph/data and is not in complete sentences.
Allow 0 points if explanation is not correct even if it is in complete sentences.

6: Data Interpretation/Comparison .... 4 points total

Allow 1 point for each of the following:
*   states pattern for dry tube readings
*   states pattern for wet tube readings
*   states relationship/comparison
*   correct statement or statements and all in complete sentences

7: Data Explanation .... 2 points total

Allow 2 points if the explanation is correct and in complete sentences.
Allow 1 point if the explanation is correct, but not in complete sentences.
Allow 0 points if the explanation is incorrect even if it is in complete sentences.
Correct statements may include:
*   the wet tube is cooled by evaporation, or
*   heat energy is removed more quickly from water in wet tube, or
*   the dry tube temperature is maintained by better insulation

8: Comparison .... 3 points total

Allow 1 point for each of the following:
*   States correct comparison between wet paper towel and perspiration on human skin
*   Relates to process/role of evaporation to cooling/heat loss
*   Correct statement or statements in complete sentences
Allow 0 points if the explanation is incorrect even if it is in complete sentences.

Respiration

This task is from the set developed as part of the University at Buffalo/National Opinion Research Center joint project (UB/NORC; see *High School Science Laboratory Performance Tasks*, Doran, et al. 1993). Respiration is a key metabolic characteristic of both plants and animals, and is a source of energy, carbon dioxide, and water. This task uses a microorganism—yeast—as it is easy to use safely and humanely. Methylene blue is a standard indicator used to confirm the presence of oxygen in solutions.

The task is organized into two parts: the first is planning and designing the investigation and the second is collecting data using a safe, workable set of procedures, and reporting the experimental findings. The time for the entire task is 80 minutes (30 minutes–A, 50 minute–B), which fits nicely into a double lab period. A modified format where students use their own plans can be developed easily by eliminating steps from the detailed procedures in this version. Be sure your students have had some prior experience with planning investigations before trying this modification. This can be an excellent task to use with pairs of students.

There is quite a bit of equipment involved with this task. The yeast (microorganism) culture should be prepared about an hour ahead of time. If you do this with several classes, you may need to start several cultures so they can be viable and growing. Hot plates are sometimes difficult to maintain at relatively constant temperatures. You may need to test this out ahead of time, perhaps changing the volume of water in the bath. Try out the entire investigation yourself to troubleshoot experimental "glitches," and to know what each tube looks like at different stages of the reaction. Commercially prepared buffer solutions are excellent but not critical for the success of this investigation.

Respiration
Task Information

Prepare the following: 0.5% solution (aqueous) of methylene blue.

General Materials:

- 1 beaker, 800 ml
- 8 test tubes – 16 mm by 150 mm
- test tube holders
- adjustable hot plate, solid surface
- thermometer (°C)
- stopwatch/clock
- pencil
- graduated cylinder, 10 ml
- 8 rubber stoppers (solid), to fit test tubes (size 6)
- test tube rack
- paper towels
- wax marking pencil
- graph paper

Special Materials:

- 1 package dry yeast, mixed with 100 ml distilled water (approx. 30°C)
- 100 ml distilled water
- 0.5% methylene blue (aqueous) solution, 40 ml in dropper bottle
- pH solutions of 2, 4, 6, 8, 10 in plastic dropper bottles (60 ml)

1. Plastic dropper bottles are 60 ml size. Label and place at the student station with the caps removed.

2. Prepare the yeast suspension approximately one hour before testing. Stir the package of dry yeast into 100 ml of distilled water at about 30° C. **NOTE:** Use a fresh package of dry yeast.

3. Prepare the 37° C water bath by filling the 800 ml beaker with approximately 200 ml of tap water.

4. Locate work station near water source and sink.

Respiration
Student Task Sheet

Part A

Time: 30 Minutes

Materials:

General Materials:

- 1 beaker
- 8 test tubes
- test tube rack
- adjustable hot plate
- graph paper
- wax marking pencil

- graduated cylinder
- 8 clean stoppers for the test tubes
- test tube holders
- paper towels
- thermometer

Special Materials:

- microorganisms in suspension
- methylene blue solution, 40 ml in plastic dropper bottles
- pH solutions of 4, 6, 8, and 10 in dropper bottles

Introduction:

This laboratory test presents a problem. Your task in Part A is to plan and design an experiment to solve the problem. You have 30 minutes to complete Part A. At the end of the 30 minutes, your answer sheet will be collected. You will then receive separate directions for Part B. In Part B you use materials and equipment provided in the laboratory kit to collect experimental data for this problem. Write your plan on your answer sheet.

Problem:

Sometimes biologists use indicators to test the effect of various factors on chemical reactions. Your problem is to design an experiment to test the effect of various pH levels on the rate of respiration in microorganisms, using methylene blue as an indicator. During respiration oxygen combines chemically with some compounds. Methylene blue is an oxygen indicator. When oxygen is present, it remains blue. When oxygen is absent, it loses its blue color. There may remain a blue ring at the upper edge of the test tube. Design an experiment to test the effect of various pH levels on the rate of respiration in the organisms.

a) State a HYPOTHESIS for this investigation as to the effect that various pH levels may have on the rate of respiration in organisms.

b) Under the heading PROCEDURE list in order the steps you will use to solve the problem. You may include a diagram to help illustrate your plans for the experiment. Include any safety procedures you would follow.

c) Construct a DATA TABLE or indicate any other method that you can use to record the observations and results that will be obtained.

NOTE: In Part A you are <u>NOT</u> to proceed with any part of the actual experiment. You are just to plan and organize a way to investigate the problem.

Part B

Time: 50 Minutes

You have 50 minutes to complete this part. Record your work for Part B on your answer sheet under the appropriate headings. Perform the experiment by following the steps outlined in the procedure (listed below). Under the heading RESULTS record your observations and measurements for the experiment. Use written statements, descriptive paragraphs, tables of data, and/or graphs where appropriate. Construct a GRAPH that presents the relationship between the data you have collected. Under the heading CONCLUSIONS write an interpretation of your results. State the effect that pH level has on respiration of microorganisms. At the end of 50 minutes, your answer sheet for Part B will be collected.

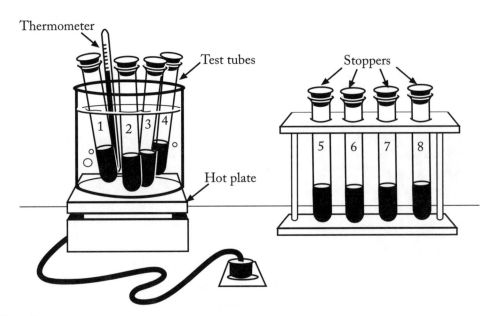

Procedure:

1. Check the temperature of the water bath in the 800 ml beaker (on the hot plate). The temperature <u>must</u> be between 35°C and 39°C. Record the temperature on the answer sheet.

2. Prepare 4 test tubes each with 5 ml of the microorganism in suspension, and 4 test tubes each with 5 ml of distilled water (for the control). Use the wax pencil to label each test tube with a number from 1 to 8.

3. Place 5 ml of prepared pH solutions in each test tube according to the chart below. The pH in each test tube should be as follows:

Microorganism Suspension		Control: Distilled Water	
Test Tube #	pH	Test Tube #	pH
1	4	5	4
2	6	6	6
3	8	7	8
4	10	8	10

NOTE: Thoroughly RINSE the graduated cylinder after filling EACH test tube.

4. Now add two drops of methylene blue to each test tube (1 through 8). Place stoppers on each test tube. Mix by carefully inverting each test tube several times.

5. Place test tubes 1 through 4 in the water bath. Record the time at which you placed the test tubes in the water bath on the answer sheet. Observe how long it takes for the blue color to disappear in each test tube. Record the times in a data table. Continue timing for 10 minutes.

6. Take test tubes 1 through 4 out of the water bath and place in the test tube rack. Invert each tube several times. What do you observe? Record your observations in your data table.

7. Repeat steps 5 and 6 for test tubes 5 through 8.

8. Enter the RESULTS (your times and observations) in your data tables.

9. Construct a GRAPH of your results.

10. Based on your data and your graphing of the results, write your CONCLUSION about how pH affects the time for the indicator to change.

Respiration
Task Specific Scoring Rubric

Part A: Experiment Design

1: Statement of Hypothesis

- Effect linked to variable
- Directionality of effect
- Expected effect/change
- Independent variable
- Dependent variable

The relationship between the variables and the expected effect is clearly and correctly expressed (i.e., rate of respiration increases as pH increase).
Rate increases or decreases.
Rate of respiration changes with changes in pH.
pH is the <u>independent</u> variable. Constant temperature is needed.
Rate of respiration as measured by the time it takes to change the color of the indicator methylene blue.

2: Procedures for investigation

- Detailed procedure/experimentally feasible
- Sequence to plan

- General strategy
- Safety procedures
- Use of equipment/diagram

Treatment and controls are specified. A suggested time frame and optimal temperature are given.
Steps are presented sequentially with adequate detail (i.e., includes temperature, concentrations, volumes, replications).
Treatments (at least 2 pHs) and controls are suggested. Observe color change.
Care and use of hot plate might be mentioned.
Procedure suggests appropriate use of materials such as yeast, methylene blue, test tubes, pH solutions.

3: Plan for recording and organizing observations/data

- Space for manipulation of data or qualitative description
- Matched to plan
- Organized sequentially
- Labeled fully (units included)
- Variables identified

Space available for observations and notations of time.
Plan fits procedure outlined in step 2 above.
Sequence allows student to record data as it is generated.
All data recorded, including time and observations for each test tube.
pH, temperature, time and/or rate reaction all indicated.

4: Quality of observations/data

- Consistent data

- Accurate measurements/observations
- Completed data table

- Correct units
- Qualitative description

Microorganism suspension: Time disappearance of color decreases with increasing pH. Control: Color remains blue in each tube.
Observations of color change are noted in detail.
All data should be included; time and observations for each test tube should be recorded.
Time labeled as minutes or seconds.
Not scored.

5: Graph

- Curve is appropriate to data trends
- Points plotted accurately
- Appropriate scale
- Axes labeled with variables
- Variables placed on correct axes

Curve drawn through data points with best-fit line.
Plotted points are equal to data values found in student's table.
Value of scales fit to range of data, suitable intervals.
pH in scale units, time in minutes or seconds.
pH, the independent variable on x-axis, time on the y-axis.

6: Calculations

Not required for this task.

7: Conclusion

- Consistent with scientific principle
- Sources of error
- Consistent with data
- Relationship among variables stated
- Variables stated in conclusion

Rate of respiration (O_2 consumption) increases with increased pH.
Not scored.
Conclusion reflects student's experimental results.[1]
The higher/lower the pH, the faster/slower the rate of respiration.[1]
Mentions pH and rate of respiration or time to color change of methylene blue.

[1] A point can be earned for each of these elements if the conclusion reflects results of student's experiment.

Using Indicators

This task was developed as part of a National Science Foundation project dedicated to preparing prototype examinations for high school science. The project was jointly conducted by educators at the University of Buffalo and the National Opinion Research Center (NORC), with the laboratory assessment components centered at the University of Buffalo (Doran, et al. 1993). Most of the tasks are of the Part A–Part B format, whereby students plan and then conduct and report on an investigation. In Part A, the student plans an investigation to solve a problem using existing materials and equipment. Teachers then review the student's plan to ascertain whether it is viable and includes appropriate safety cautions. In Part B, the student conducts the investigation by using his or her experimental plan.

A variation of this approach is to have workable plans prepared and available for students, but to have them formulated in such a way that they need to be improved upon if they are to be implemented successfully. With this variation, all students have an opportunity to demonstrate their achievement and skills, thereby experiencing some measure of success.

Once these basic skills are mastered, students can be assessed on their ability to use them in inquiry or problem-solving situations (with real or unknown foods) and/or investigate using these indicators for quantitative results.

This task begins with a review of the three indicators with "standard" solutions of starch, sugar, and protein. This procedure eliminates the need to memorize the results of these indicators. It also reviews the lab skills needed for safer and more reliable testing in the second stage. The indicators used here are the most widely used ones for these substances.

Using Indicators
Task Information

Teacher Materials:

- 60 ml plastic dropper bottles each containing 50 ml of the following:

    1% - 5% Glucose solution, labeled SUGAR

    1% - 5% Starch suspension, labeled STARCH

    1% - 5% Albumen solution, labeled PROTEIN

    1% - 5% Starch suspension, labeled UNKNOWN

- Red food coloring
- 60 ml plastic dropper bottles each containing 50 ml of the following:

    Iodine solution, labeled Iodine (POISON)

    Biuret reagent, labeled Biuret Reagent

    Benedict's reagent, labeled Benedict's Reagent

- hot plate (solid/ceramic surface type)
- 250 ml beaker – 1/4 filled with water
- 6 clean test tubes – size: 24 ml (16 mm × 150 mm); test tubes must be labeled with permanent ink as indicated under PREPARATION below.

- permanent ink marking pen – black or blue
- test tube rack and holder
- safety goggles
- paper towels

Preparation:

Prepare sufficient quantities as indicated:

1. Prepare 100 ml solutions of sugar, starch, and albumen. For the albumen solution, stir 5 grams of albumen powder into 100 ml of warm water.

2. Place 50 ml of the glucose solution in a plastic dropper bottle. Label the bottle with permanent ink SUGAR, using capital letters.

3. Place 50 ml of the albumen solution in a plastic dropper bottle. Label this bottle PROTEIN.

4. Place 50 ml of the starch solution in a plastic dropper bottle. Label the bottle STARCH.

5. Place the remaining 50 ml of the starch solution in a plastic dropper bottle. Label this bottle UNKNOWN. Color the UNKNOWN with red food coloring to produce a pink/light-red color.

6. Remove the caps on the bottles at the student station.

7. Fill the 250 ml beaker 1/4 full with hot tap water for the hot water bath. Adjust the hot plate to provide a hot water bath that is near boiling (80° C). Caution: Be certain the water level in the bath is maintained. Allow sufficient time for the water to be brought up to temperature prior to the start of testing.

8. Label the test tubes, using permanent ink and in capital letters, as follows:
   Label: A, B, C — for testing the standard solutions
   Label: 1, 2, 3 — for testing the unknown
   NOTE: Clean test tubes must be provided for each student to be tested.

9. Set up the station using the following layout. An area should be selected that has convenient access to an electrical outlet. Prior to each session, be certain materials and equipment are returned to the layout below.

Student Materials:

- plastic dropper bottles labeled:
  SUGAR solution
  STARCH solution
  PROTEIN solution
  UNKNOWN solution
- plastic dropper bottles labeled:
  Iodine solution
  Biuret reagent
  Benedict's reagent
- hot plate and hot water bath
- test tube rack with 6 clean test tubes labeled:
  A, B, C; 1, 2, 3
- test tube holder
- paper towels
- safety goggles

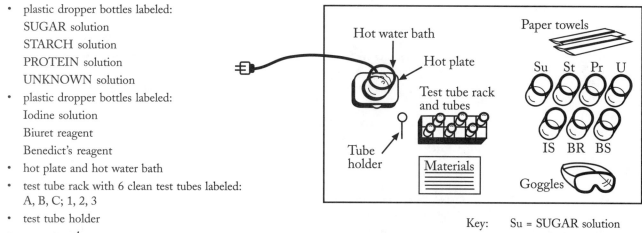

Key: Su = SUGAR solution
St = STARCH solution
PR = PROTEIN solution
U = UNKNOWN solution
IS = Iodine solution
BR = Biuret reagent
BS = Benedict's reagent

General Information:

1. Have extra supplies available in case they are needed (i.e., labeled dropper bottles and solutions, labeled test tubes, materials lists, pencils and/or pens, paper towels, water to refill hot water baths).

2. Test each solution and reagent to determine that a positive result will occur.

CAUTION: SAFETY GOGGLES MUST BE WORN AT ALL TIMES AT THIS STATION. BIURET REAGENT MAY CAUSE SKIN BURNS. FLUSH WITH WATER IF CONTACT IS MADE WITH THE SKIN.

Using Indicators
Student Task Sheet

Introduction:

This laboratory test presents a problem, lists materials, and outlines the sequence to be followed in solving the problem and writing your observations and conclusions. You will have a total of 40 minutes to complete this test. Record your answers on a separate sheet of paper.

Problem:

Biologists often use indicators to identify the properties of an unknown substance. Your problem is to conduct an experiment to determine which organic compound is present in the dropper bottle marked UNKNOWN.

Materials:

- 4 dropper bottles, each with 50 ml of solution and labeled
    - SUGAR
    - STARCH
    - PROTEIN
    - UNKNOWN
- dropper bottles of:
    - Iodine solution
    - Biuret reagent
    - Benedict's reagent

- 250 ml beaker—water bath
- hot plate
- 6 clean, labeled test tubes
- test tube holder
- test tube rack
- goggles
- paper towels

CAUTION: SAFETY GOGGLES MUST BE WORN AT ALL TIMES AT THIS STATION. BIURET REAGENT CAN CAUSE SKIN BURNS. FLUSH WITH WATER IF CONTACT IS MADE WITH SKIN.

Record your work on the answer sheets under the appropriate headings.

a) Perform the experiment by following the steps outlined in the procedure below.

b) Under the heading RESULTS record the findings of the experiment. Use statements, descriptive paragraphs, and measurements where appropriate.

c) Under the heading CONCLUSION give an interpretation of your results. What was the unknown? What was your evidence for this identification?

d) At the end of 40 minutes, your papers will be collected.

Procedure:

1. Start your water bath. It needs to be boiling for the test procedure.

2. Transfer 2 ml (50 drops) of the sugar solution to a clean test tube (labeled A) and add 2 ml (50 drops) of Benedict's reagent. Heat for 2 minutes in the water bath (water should be boiling). Record your observations in Table A.

3. Transfer 2 ml (50 drops) of the protein solution to a clean test tube (labeled B) and add Biuret reagent one drop at a time until a change is noted. Record your observations in Table A.

4. Transfer 2 ml (50 drops) of the starch solution to a clean test tube (labeled C). Add iodine solution one drop at a time until a change is noted. Record your observations in Table A.

5. Take the unknown solution and transfer 2 ml (50 drops) to each of three test tubes numbered 1, 2, and 3.

   (a) Add 2 ml (50 drops) of Benedict's reagent to test tube #1 and heat for 2 minutes. Record your observations in Table B.

   (b) Add Biuret reagent, one drop at a time, to test tube #2 (up to 20 drops). Record your observations in Table B.

   (c) Add iodine solution, one drop at a time, to test tube #3 (up to 10 drops). Record your observations in Table B.

Table A: Standard Solutions		
Test Tube	Solution	Observations
A	SUGAR (+ Benedict's reagent and heat)	
B	PROTEIN (+ Biuret reagent)	
C	STARCH (+iodine solution)	

Table B: Unknown Solution		
Test Tube	Indicator Used	Observations
1	Benedict's reagent	
2	Biuret reagent	
3	Iodine solution	

Results:

Conclusion:
Identify the unknown. Give reasons for your answer.

Using Indicators
Scoring Rubric

Solution Testing Guidelines:

Unknown Test Tube 1 (Sugar test)   _____

Based upon the information below, award 0 to 3 points if the student has:

- no change; unknown solution stayed the same color − 1 point
- expected change for sugar was not observed − 1 point
- unknown is not sugar − 1 point
- award zero (0) points if none of the above is met

Unknown Test Tube 2 (Protein test)   _____

Based upon the information below, award 0 to 3 points if the student has:

- no change; unknown solution stayed the same color − 1 point
- expected change for protein was not observed − 1 point
- unknown is not protein − 1 point
- award zero (0) points if none of the above is met

Unknown Test Tube 3 (Starch test)   _____

Based upon the information below, award 0 to 3 points if the student has:

- solution turned blue-black after adding the indicator − 1 point
- color change in solution − 1 point
- unknown solution changed color consistent with it containing starch − 1 point
- award zero (0) points if none of the above is met

Conclusion: _____

Award 0 to 3 points for the conclusion based upon the following:

- unknown solution is starch (contains starch) − 1 point
- unknown solution turned blue-black after iodine was added − 1 point
- blue-black solution is an indicator of the presence of starch − 1 point
- award zero points if none of the above is met

Total Points: _____

Diffusion/Osmosis

This task was developed as part of the UB/NORC project (Doran, et al. 1993), and revised for use here. Diffusion is one of the key processes for allowing material to move from one system to another toward a uniform distribution throughout the available volume. Diffusion happens relatively quickly among liquids and gases, and more slowly among solids. On the other hand, osmosis is a physiological process through which substances enter and leave cells across a semipermeable membrane. In this task, potassium permanganate ($KMnO_4$) moves from a solution into cubes of raw potato. There are many other combinations of solutions and vegetables that will work well. This combination produces a drastic, visible "diffusion" effect. The $KMnO_4$ solution can be kept and used for several classes. The effect of time and concentration of the solution on the diffusion distance is dramatic when viewed qualitatively. As the diffusion "line" is not smooth due to variations in the potato, precise measurements are difficult. Students can examine the effect of time with lower concentrations on different vegetables, woods, and other materials.

This investigation begins with one cycle of data collecting so students can use the procedure as a foundation for this experimental work. The teacher should supply some other indicators, such as cabbage juice and strong coffee, and some other materials, such as zucchini and radishes. It is hoped that student can prepare many other materials for investigation. The teacher should encourage groups of students to use different materials so the sharing of group results is more interesting and comprehensive.

The scoring of the task is based on a report that includes the hypotheses, procedure, data, and conclusions. If an oral presentation is part of the project, it can be added to the scoring procedure.

For this Investigation Task, students will need to record their answers either in their laboratory logbooks or on two blank sheets of paper. Specific instructions for what students record, and the labels they use, are given in the task. Generally, students are asked to record their hypothesis, their procedure (including any diagrams), and their data table (including their observations) on one sheet in a reasonably finished form. The other sheet is to be used as scratch paper. If the task has a Part B, students usually need a piece of graph paper and a third sheet for recording their conclusions. You may wish to hand out prepared display sheets with the headings already in place, such as the one below.

Diffusion
Display Sheet

	1% solution	5% solution	10% solution
5 Minutes			
10 Minutes			
15 Minutes			
20 Minutes			

Diffusion/Osmosis
Student Task Sheet

Introduction:

This laboratory test presents a problem. Your task is to plan and conduct an experiment to solve the problem.

Problem:

Osmosis is a process (a kind of diffusion) by which substances enter and leave cells across a semi-permeable membrane. Your problem is to design an experiment to test the effects of two variables (time and concentration) on diffusion of potassium permanganate into potato cubes.

Materials:

- 2 firm potatoes
- metric ruler (30 cm)
- 1%, 5%, and 10% solutions of potassium permanganate (in beakers)
- paper towels
- waste container

- stopwatch/clock
- 3 small beakers (approx. 150 ml)
- forceps
- scalpel
- graph paper
- prepared display sheet (optional; see page 125)

a) State a HYPOTHESIS for this investigation that can be used to test the effects of time and concentration on osmosis.

b) Under the heading PROCEDURE list in order the steps you will use to solve the problem. You may include a diagram to help illustrate your plans for the experiment. Include safety procedures you would follow.

c) Construct a DATA TABLE or indicate any other method that you can use to record the observations and results that will be obtained.

d) Perform the experiment by following the steps outlined in your procedure.

e) Under the heading RESULTS record your observations and measurements for the experiment. Use written statements, descriptive paragraphs, tables of data, and/or graphs where appropriate.

f) Construct a GRAPH which presents the relationship between the distance $KMnO_4$ moved into the potatoes and time and concentration.

g) Under the heading CONCLUSIONS write an interpretation of your results. State the effects of time and concentration on osmosis.

Additional Investigations:

You have learned a set of experimental procedures from investigating diffusion of $KMnO_4$ into potato cubes. Now prepare some additional investigations. Consider the possibility of other variables in addition to time and concentration. Have your procedure and materials checked by your teacher. When completed, write a lab report of your investigations to share with your teacher and classmates.

Diffusion/Osmosis
Task Specific Scoring Rubric

1: Statement of Hypothesis

- Effect linked to variable — As concentration of $KMnO_4$ and time increases, distance of movement of $KMnO_4$ inside the cubes increases

- Directionality of effect — $KMnO_4$ distance increases
- Expected effect/change — Distance of $KMnO_4$ varies with concentration and/or time
- Independent variable — Time, concentration
- Dependent variable — Distance of $KMnO_4$ that travels into the cubes

2: Procedures for investigation

- Detailed procedure/ experimentally feasible — Plan includes measurement of diffusion distances from a combination of concentrations (1%, 5%, 10%) and time (i.e., 5m, 10m, 15m, 20m) that the cubes stay in the solution. Potato cubes should be at least 5 mm in size

- Sequence to plan — Plan includes at least two times and two concentrations
- General strategy — Plan includes varying times and concentrations
- Safety procedures — Care not to spill $KMnO_4$, wearing an apron and goggles, care in using scalpel
- Use of equipment/diagram — Appropriate use of equipment and materials

3: Plan for recording and organizing observations/data

- Space for manipulation of data — Qualitative description may be included
- Matched to plan — Observations and data are consistent with the plan
- Organized sequentially — Organized so that recording follows data generated
- Labeled fully (units included) — All columns and rows are identified, correct units of measurement are used
- Variables identified — Time, concentration, and $KMnO_4$ distance are clearly indicated

4: Quality of observations/data

- Consistent data — Distance increases with increasing concentration and time
- Accurate measurements/observations — Accurate measurement of the distance reached by the $KMnO_4$ every five minutes
- Completed data table — All data entered in the tables
- Correct units — Distances labeled in mm
- Qualitative description — Variability of distance $KMnO_4$ travelled within a single cube may be mentioned

5: Graph

- Curve is appropriate to data trends — Curve drawn best fits data points
- Points plotted accurately — Plotted points are accurate
- Appropriate scale — Value of scales are appropriate to ranges of data, suitable intervals
- Axes labeled with variables — Time in minutes; concentration in percentages; distance in mm
- Variables placed on correct axes — Dependent variable, distance $KMnO_4$ travelled, is the y-axis; Independent variables, time and concentration (on the x-axis), can be placed on separate graphs or combined as three separate plots of concentration within one graph with time as the x-axis

6: Calculations

Not required for this task

- Calculated accurately
- Substituted correctly into relationship
- Relationship stated or implied

- Units used correctly
- Use all data available

7: Conclusion

• Consistent with scientific principle	As concentration and time increases, distances $KMnO_4$ travelled also increases
• Sources of error	Measurement of distance may be hard to measure accurately
• Consistent with data	Consistent with student's experimental results
• Relationship among variables stated	Distances $KMnO_4$ travelled are related to concentration of $KMnO_4$ and/or time
• Variables stated in conclusion	Distance and concentration of $KMnO_4$ solution and time

Biology Extended Investigation Tasks

Most extended investigation assessments are outgrowths of successful instructional activities. You can supplement or adapt some "chunk" of instruction with scoring rubrics—so student performance can be reviewed from a slightly different perspective. At least three ways of scoring are possible, each requiring a separate rubric. The first method is to use rubrics on student work at particular points or lessons (i.e., planning an experiment or graphing results). This has been called "snapshot assessments," as it is composed of separate probes of student skills. Another way is to rate the product of student work ranging from written reports, an object or model, or an oral presentation of their work. Each mode needs a separate rubric. A third way is with a follow-up test assessing the student's ability to apply or transfer concepts and skills learned to a new situation or context. This technique has been used with much success (Baron 1991). When writing your own tasks attempting to assess transfer, refer to the Novelty section in Chapter 2, page 26. For a discussion of the use of extended investigations, see Chapter 3, page 32.

Biology Extended Investigation Tasks		
Skills Categories	Vitamin C Testing (page 130)	DNA Extraction (page 137)
Planning	✔	✔
Performing	✔	✔
Analyzing	✔	✔
Applying	✔	✔

Vitamin C Testing

This assessment task was modified from a collection of laboratory investigations developed by teachers during a summer institute at Cornell University. The task is included here because vitamin C is of high interest regarding its role in human health. Recent research, for example, suggests that vitamin C acts as a "free radical" scavenger, a property that suggests a role in cancer prevention and treatment. From a teacher's point of view, vitamin C also serves as a model for discussing both water soluble and fat soluble vitamins.

The Vitamin C task consists of two parts. In the first part, students become familiar with relevant experimental procedures by measuring the vitamin C content of orange juice. Students then plan and design their own experiments to determine the effects of various environmental factors on the vitamin C content of different juices. (Vitamin C testing also appears in the Golden State Examination [GSE] of the California Department of Education. That examination asks students to analyze the amount of vitamin C in juice through titration and to make recommendations about the packaging and storage of a new breakfast drink. See the website for the department's Standards, Curriculum, and Assessment Division at *www.cde.ca.gov/cilbranch/sca*.)

Vitamin C Testing
Task Information

Background:

This task involves vitamin C. Vitamins, and in particular vitamin C, have generated a great deal of controversy in our health care. There have been numerous claims for the role of vitamin C in our health, from the prevention of the common cold to a possible "cure" for certain forms of cancer (vitamin C is a water soluble antioxidant on account of its high reducing power). Many of these claims appear in "mass-market" publications and are often based on anecdotal evidence.

Most vertebrates synthesize vitamin C from their diet. Humans and monkeys are the exception; they do not have the capability to synthesize vitamin C from glucose as they lack the enzyme gulono lactone oxidase. Vitamin C participates in a number of oxidation reactions, including the hydroxylation of proline to hydroxyproline and of lysine to hydroxylysine. As such, synthesis of collagen is compromised in vitamin C deficiency. Collagen is a protein necessary for the formation of connective tissue in the skin, ligaments, and bones. Vitamin C also helps connective tissue form during the healing of wounds and in the growth and repair of tissues. Other functions of vitamin C include aiding in red blood cell formation, preventing hemorrhaging, and fighting bacterial infections. Vitamin C also participates in the synthesis of carnitine, tyrosine, adrenal hormones, leukocyte functions, and folate metabolism.

The Recommended Daily Allowance (RDA) of vitamin C is 75 mg/day for females and 90 mg/day for males. Smokers suffer increased oxidative stress and metabolic turnover of vitamin C, and the recommended intake is increased by 35 mg/day in both male and female smokers to decrease the effect of reactive oxygen.

In this task on vitamin C, you have an opportunity to use your science knowledge, apply your inquiry skills, and gain more insight into a popular vitamin.

Part A

In this part of the investigation, you will analyze the vitamin C content of orange juice. This task can be completed in one class period of 45 minutes. It gives you an opportunity to manipulate materials and equipment, and learn science concepts necessary for you to design your own experiment in the second part of the investigation.

Task:

You are provided with appropriate materials and equipment to:

- Measure and compare the vitamin C content in some juice samples.
- Determine the effect of various factors that influence the vitamin C content in food samples.

Please work in your assigned pairs and follow the suggested procedures to complete your task.

Materials:

- vitamin C indicator solution
- 4, 50 mL beakers
- 1, 10 mL graduated cylinder
- 4 medicine droppers
- 1 stirring rod
- calculator
- 4 sources of vitamin C: orange juice (freshly squeezed, bottled, frozen, and canned)
- *Optional:* container for waste solutions and source of clean water for rinsing medicine droppers.

Procedure:

1. Pour 15 mL of the vitamin C indicator into a 50 mL beaker.
2. Using a clean medicine dropper, add a drop of one of the orange juice samples to the indicator in the 50 mL beaker. Gently swirl the liquids to mix.
3. Continue to add orange juice, drop by drop, until the indicator changes from blue to colorless. *Note: Be sure to swirl after each drop is added.*
4. Observe and count the number of drops of orange juice you needed to add to the indicator to cause it to lose all of its color. Juices low in vitamin C will begin to dilute the indicator. The indicator will start to take on the color of the juice. If this occurs, indicate that no satisfactory end point was reached. Record the number of drops added in the chart on your data table.
5. Repeat step 4 two more times and calculate the average number of drops (to the nearest tenth) required to change the indicator.
6. Repeat the above steps for each orange juice sample being tested. *Note: Be sure to rinse your medicine droppers between tests and to use clean beakers for each trial!*
7. Record the following information on a separate sheet of paper for each type of orange juice.

Brand Name _____ Type: _____ (canned, etc.)

Serving Size _____ ounces = _____mL

Milligrams per serving size _____

Data Table/Graph:

Relative Vitamin C Content of Foods
Number of Drops Needed to Change the Indicator

Type of Juice	Trial 1	Trial 2	Trial 3	Average

Convert the data table into a *bar graph* below to compare the relative amounts of vitamin C in each sample tested.

Relative Vitamin C Content of Foods

Analysis of Data:

On your own paper, answer the following questions using complete sentences:

1. Which type of orange juice was the best source of vitamin C? The worst source?

2. Before this activity, which type of orange juice did you think would be the best source of vitamin C? Why?

3. Briefly explain how you know that the different orange juices did not contain the same amount of vitamin C.

4. What are some factors that may have converted a good source of vitamin C into a poor one?

5. If you had to develop a label that told consumers how much vitamin C is present in the fresh orange juice you tested, how would you determine the actual vitamin C content?

6. As a result of doing this activity, suggest two questions someone might ask about vitamin C concentrations in food?

Part B

Problem:

1. Working in pairs, your task is to determine which juice (X or Y) contains more vitamin C. Each person in the pair submits an individual report.

   • Decide on a procedure using the materials provided (see next page).

   • List the steps in sequence that you will use in your procedure.

   • Set up a table in which to record your results.

   • Write one or more sentences comparing the amounts of vitamin C in the two juices. Use information from your data table to support your answer.

2. Discuss with your partner what variables you might like to test and what your experiment should include. You may use juices and chemicals available in the classroom or bring in your own.

Materials:

Check your lab station to be certain you have the following materials:

- 4, 50 mL beakers
- unknown juice X
- unknown juice Y
- 10 mL graduated cylinder
- 1 stirring rod

- pH paper
- container of hydrogen peroxide
- 1 container of vitamin C indicator
- iodine (Lugol's) solution
- 3 clean medicine droppers

(Note: You may not need to use all of the materials available at your station.)

Before doing the lab, please submit the following information to your teacher:

- The question your experiment will try to answer and your hypothesis.
- A list of the materials you will need.
- A description of your experimental procedure.

Use the Scoring Guide for Laboratory Report (page 135) to assist you in the planning and writing process. After conducting the experiment, submit a final report that includes the following:

- title
- initial question
- hypothesis
- methods and materials
- results including a data table and graph
- a discussion and conclusion that answers the following questions:

a. Does your data support your hypothesis? Use data from your experiment to support your response to this question.

b. What conclusions can be made based on the results of your experiment?

c. What especially surprising information did you discover as a result of your investigation?

d. What could be done to make your procedure and/or findings more reliable?

e. As a result of your investigation, what questions do you have that need to be answered through further experimentation?

Question:

Assume that everyone in the class tests the same two juices. Describe three specific things that could result in your data being very different from those of other students.

Please note: Each person submits his or her own individual report.

**Vitamin C Testing
Scoring Guide**

Part A

1. *Which type of orange juice was the best source of vitamin C? the worst source?*

   Answers will vary. The juice with the smallest number of drops is the best source while the juice requiring the most drops to decolorize the indicator is the worst source of vitamin C.

2. *Before this activity, which type of orange juice did you think would be the best source of vitamin C? Why?*

   Answers will vary. Allow any reasonable response.

3. *Briefly explain how you know that the different orange juices did not contain the same amount of vitamin C.*

   Different juices required different numbers of drops to make the indicator turn clear. If they all had the same amount of vitamin C, they would have taken the same number of drops to turn the indicator clear.

4. *What are some of the factors that may have converted a good source of vitamin C into a poor one?*

   Processing, sitting around, temperature, decomposition (bacteria spoiling it), sunlight, and so forth are all reasonable responses. Students should provide two or more factors.

5. *If you had to develop a label that told consumers how much vitamin C is present in the orange you tested the fresh juice from, how would you determine the actual vitamin C content?*

Students should mention that they would use the average number of drops they obtained for the fresh orange juice and the information about vitamin C content on the label of the juice they referenced on the student part of the lab. They should then use the commercial juice drop/ concentration along with the fresh juice vitamin C concentration. They would also need to know the volume of juice they could get out of an average fresh orange.

6. *As a result of doing this activity, what are some questions you have about vitamin C concentrations in food?*

Answers will vary.

Graph Scoring Guide

_____ Independent variable is on the horizontal axis.

_____ Horizontal axis is labeled.

_____ Horizontal axis label includes units of measure.

_____ Appropriate scale appears on the horizontal axis (even intervals).

_____ Vertical axis is labeled.

_____ Vertical axis label includes units of measure.

_____ Appropriate scale appears on the vertical axis (even intervals).

_____ Points are plotted accurately.

_____ Graph connects data points and does not go beyond.

_____ Legend indicates meaning of each line if there is more than one.

Part B

Use the Scoring Guide for Laboratory Report on the next page to evaluate student lab reports. Student responses to questions (a) through (e) will depend on the results of their experiment. In terms of making the experiment more reliable, students might suggest more replicates of the same foods, more foods, better control over the variables, better calculations, and so forth. The total value of these questions is up to the teacher.

In Part B of this laboratory investigation, students design an experiment to demonstrate the effect of various factors on the vitamin C levels. Some things students might investigate include the following:

1. *Determine the effect of pH on the vitamin C content of juice.*

   Things to consider if you choose this experiment:

   a. How are you going to have a control in this experiment?

   b. What type of acid/base will you use?

   c. How much acid/base will you add to how much juice? Does it matter?

   d. What information needs to be recorded?

   e. Are there other factors you need to consider?

2. *Determine the effect of light on the vitamin C content of juice.*

   Things to consider if you choose this experiment:

   a. How you are going to vary the amount of light to which the juice is exposed?

   b. What will you use for your light source?

   c. For how long will you expose the juice?

   d. What information needs to be recorded?

   e. Are there other factors you need to consider?

3. *Determine the vitamin C content of assorted vegetables and fruits.*

   Things to consider if you choose this experiment:

   a. How are you going to convert solid fruits and vegetables into liquids?

   b. How can you standardize these preparations?

   c. What information needs to be recorded?

4. *Determine the effect of heat processing on the vitamin C content of foods.*

   Things to consider if you choose this experiment:
   a. Are you going to use processed foods or process your own?
   b. If you process your own, how are you going to prepare and treat the samples?
   c. What safety measures need to be considered?
   d. What information needs to be recorded?

5. *Perform a cost analysis to find out which orange juice is most economical, based on its vitamin C content.*

Scoring Guide for Laboratory Report

Rating Scale: 4 = Excellent   3 = Very Good   2 = Acceptable   1 = Unacceptable   0 = Missing

Note that not all items are worth the same number of points.

Section of Report	Score	Comments
Initial Question: Clearly states the question being addressed.	3 2 1 0	
Hypothesis: Clearly stated in appropriate "if/then" or "cause/effect" format.	3 2 1 0	
Methods and Materials: Statements provide a concise series of procedural steps that others could repeat.	4 3 2 1 0	
The control(s) and variables are clearly indicated.	2 1 0	
Repeat this 2 or 3 times for unknown X.	2 1 0	
Repeat this 2 or 3 times for unknown Y.	2 1 0	
Student uses chemicals appropriately.	2 1 0	
Results: Clearly understood and concisely stated.	4 3 2 1 0	
Data tables and graphs are utilized.	4 3 2 1 0	
Data Table Scoring Guide Title; column headings indicate what is being measured; column headings indicate units of measurement; independent variable in increasing order; data correctly and completely entered.	4 3 2 1 0	
Graph Scoring Guide Title; independent variable is on the horizontal axis; horizontal axis is labeled; horizontal axis label includes units of measure; appropriate scale on the horizontal axis (even intervals); vertical axis is labeled; vertical axis label includes units of measure; appropriate scale on the vertical axis (even intervals); points plotted accurately; connects data points and does not go beyond; legend indicates which data is indicated by each line if there is more than one.	4 3 2 1 0	
Discussion/Conclusion: There are details about what happened and why it happened.	4 3 2 1 0	
There is a clear statement of whether or not the hypothesis was supported.	3 2 1 0	
There is a summarization of trends or patterns in the data. There is an explanation of how the trends or patterns support or refute the hypothesis.	4 3 2 1 0	

(continued on next page.)

Possible sources of error are mentioned.	4 3 2 1 0	
What could be done to further clarify and support the results?	4 3 2 1 0	
Presentation:	4 3 2 1 0	
The lab report is well organized, clearly written, and easy to follow. Appropriate vocabulary is used.	4 3 2 1 0	
Total Points		

Preparation of Starch-Iodine Solution

There are two different preparations (starch-iodine or indophenol) that may be used for the vitamin C indicator solution. Neither solution is more accurate than the other. The starch-iodine mixture is much cheaper. It can be made ahead and stored in a dark, cool place in 2-liter soda bottles and dispensed in liter containers at the lab stations. Both indicators vary from one preparation to the next, so an accurate measure of vitamin C is not possible using this protocol. Students can only compare relative amounts of vitamin C in different food sources.

- Add 2 g of cornstarch or potato starch in 200 mL of cold, distilled water. Bring the mixture to a full boil in a glass beaker.
- To 1 liter of water, add 8 mL of the starch solution and 1 mL of tincture of iodine.

Note: Specific amounts are given here but variations that produce a royal blue color of the starch-iodine indicator may also be used. The color of the starch indicator should be a royal blue. Just before doing the lab, check the indicator and dilute the concentration so that a workable number of drops of fresh orange juice (5 to 25) turn the indicator colorless.

Preparation of Tincture of Iodine

- Add 2 g of iodine crystals to 45 mL of ethanol and dissolve.
- Dissolve this mixture in 55 mL of distilled water.
- Add 2.4 grams of KI to this mixture and dissolve.

Preparation of Indophenol

- Stock solution : Dissolve 100 mg of 2,6 dichloro-indophenol salt in 100 mL of distilled water.
- Prepare a working solution by diluting the stock solution at a 1:10 ratio with distilled water.

Hints

- When testing the juices of citrus fruits for vitamin C content, the blue indophenol may turn pink before turning colorless because of the presence of substances other than vitamin C.
- Plastic medicine cups and coffee stirrers work well as substitutes for beakers and stirring rods. Medicine cups have volume levels indicated and make the task easier for students.
- Demonstrate for students how to do the titration. Show them what an appropriate end point would look like. You may want to establish at how many drops they can stop adding juice and just indicate that the food contains an insignificant level of vitamin C (perhaps 50 drops).
- Depending on your lab situation, you may want to provide students with a container in which to dump waste solutions and clean water in which to rinse materials between trials.
- Caution students to use clean containers, medicine droppers, and stirring rods for each trial. Discuss with them why this is important.
- Indicate to students whether they are to pour waste chemicals directly down the drain or dump them into a temporary waste container.
- Other materials and equipment will be necessary for the student-generated investigations. For example, if students decide to test foods such as strawberries or peppers, they will need a blender and cheesecloth. If the impact of temperature is to be investigated, they will need a hot plate, larger beakers, and a thermometer.
- A vitamin C tablet dissolved in water and the same solution diluted multiple times works well for the unknowns. That way you can vary the concentration of the solutions from station to station and there will be no external cues, such as color or aroma.

DNA Extraction

This task is adapted from a collection of laboratory investigations developed by biology teachers during a summer institute at Cornell University. The task is based on an instructional model of the 5 Es of problem solving:

- *Engage*: Initiate the learning task and engage the learner.

- *Explore*: Identify and explore concepts, and manipulate materials.

- *Explain*: Develop explanations and test hypotheses.

- *Elaborate*: Broaden understanding and conduct experiments.

- *Evaluate*: Assess understanding and review.

We have modified this inquiry-based task so that it is appropriate for an advanced-level high school biology course as an example of an extended investigation using a two-part model.

In part A of the extended investigation, students explore concepts and experimental techniques involved in DNA extraction. This part of the extended investigation engages students in a learning task and gives them the opportunity to explore new concepts and skills in detail. Part A is the "recipe" component of the investigation, and students can complete it in one class period of about 45 minutes.

Part B is the planning and performing component of the investigation, in which students use the concepts and skills from Part A to come up with possible solutions to a problem. In Part B, students have the opportunity to engage in a task that allows them to transfer their inquiry skills to a problem. Students need about two to three class periods of 45 minutes to complete Part B.

DNA Extraction
Task Information

Part A

Preparation of Materials and Solutions:

- Set up materials and glassware to accommodate student pairs.

- **Baking soda solution** preparation—Dissolve small amounts of baking soda in 500 mL water and check the pH. A pH of approximately 8 is desired. Continue to add baking soda until a pH of 8 is reached.

- **DNA standard solution**—We recommend a DNA standard (e.g., Sigma D-3159 or Carolina Biological). Add 0.02 g DNA standard to 200 mL distilled water. Add one drop of glacial acetic acid. If required, heat gently to dissolve the DNA.

- **Diphenylamine** can be purchased (e.g., Fisher 0-2611)—Dissolve 3.2 g diphenylamine in 200 mL of glacial acetic acid. Add 3 mL of concentrated sulfuric acid. Store in a dark bottle. On the day of use, prepare a solution of fresh acetic acid (add 1 mL of acetic acid to 500 mL distilled water), and add 1 mL of fresh acetic acid to 100 mL of the already prepared phenylalanine solution.

- **Sodium chloride**—Add 2 g of NaCl to 50 mL distilled water to make a 4% salt solution.

- **Raw wheat germ**—Purchase from a grocery story or health food store.

- Make hot plates available to students. Point out appropriate safety precautions when using hot plates (e.g., do not touch the surface of hot plates).

- Additional steps in the experimental procedure can be (1) the addition of controls, such as a test tube lacking wheat germ; (2) another test tube lacking detergent; or (3) a third test tube without meat tenderizer. No DNA can be extracted in the control test tubes. Students can even set up controls with wheat germ and meat tenderizer but no detergent.

Part B
Experimental Tips:
When DNA isolations are attempted, one of the following three outcomes can result:
- There is no DNA yield.
- DNA collected is "fluffy" or sheared.
- DNA collected is in the shape of long, continuous threads.

DNA in the form of long, continuous threads is the desired experimental result.

There are three basic steps in DNA extraction and isolation:

1. The cell must be broken or lysed to release the DNA. Detergents and salt solutions lyse the lipid cell membrane.

2. The nuclear membrane, if present, must be ruptured. Stirring breaks down cell walls, cell membranes, and nuclear membranes.

3. The extracted DNA must be protected from enzymes that can shear the DNA strands. The enzyme DNAase denatures at 60°C. It is therefore important to pay attention to this lower temperature so that the DNAase is not inactivated.

Safety:
- Work areas should be clean, with a clear area to conduct the investigation.
- Students must wear safety goggles.
- Students are required to clean up materials after completing the investigation, and return all materials and equipment to the appropriate location in the science laboratory.

DNA Extraction
Student Task Sheet

Background Information: DNA stores genetic information, which controls cellular growth and reproduction in all living cells and organisms. DNA is found in the nucleus of plant and animal cells. DNA can be extracted from plant and animal cells by breaking apart the nuclear membrane. Detergents are used to break apart the nuclear membrane, allowing the DNA of a cell to be collected for analysis. During collection of DNA, enzyme activity must be inactivated so the DNA strands are kept intact as long, thin fibers. The collected DNA in the shape of long, thin fibers allows for ease of observation and analysis.

Part A

Your Task: In Part A of this investigation, you extract deoxyribonucleic acid (DNA) from raw wheat germ. You manipulate materials and equipment, record observations and data, and evaluate your data. You are asked to work in pairs using the materials in the Materials section below.

Safety Precautions: You are required to wear safety goggles. Be sure to handle materials and glassware carefully to avoid spillage of any materials. Do not touch the surface of the hot plate or the beaker containing hot water with your bare hands.

Materials per Pair

- 2, 250 mL beakers (or similar container, such as a plastic cup)
- hot plate
- 1.5 g non-roasted (raw) wheat germ
- thermometer
- pH meter or pH paper (pH range 5–9)
- 5 mL clear, colorless detergent
- test tube rack (or something to hold test tube at a 45° angle—e.g., beaker)

- 6 mL ice-cold 95% ethanol (denatured ethyl alcohol)
- 3 g natural meat tenderizer
- 2, 15 mL (small) test tubes
- baking soda
- glass stirring rod or eyedropper or pipette
- 9 mL 4% sodium chloride solution
- 100 mL distilled water (preferable) or tap water

- graduated measuring cylinders—
  10 mL and 100 mL
- boiling hot water bath

- 9 mL diphenylamine solution
- 3 mL standard DNA solution

Procedure (Extraction of DNA):

1. Add 100 mL of water to the 250 mL beaker and heat to 50–60°C on the hot plate.

2. Add 1.5 g raw wheat germ to the warm 100 mL water in beaker and mix until dissolved.

3. Add 5 mL detergent to the wheat germ solution, maintaining a temperature of 50–60°C, and continue stirring for 5 minutes.

4. Add 3 g of meat tenderizer to the wheat germ/detergent solution.

5. Add 1 tsp. baking soda to 50 mL water in the second 250 mL beaker to make a baking soda solution. Add a few drops of the baking soda solution to the wheat germ solution to bring the pH of the wheat germ to approximately 8. Check pH of the solution with pH paper or pH meter.

6. Maintain the temperature of the wheat germ suspension from step 5 between 50° and 60°C and stir for 10 minutes.

7. Remove the wheat germ from the water bath, and place the wheat germ suspension in a clean test tube.

8. Pour 6 mL of ice-cold ethanol carefully down the inside edge of the test tube so that the ethanol layers on top of the wheat germ suspension.

9. Let the mixture stand *undisturbed* for 5 minutes. Observe. DNA strands appear at the interface between the ethanol-wheat germ suspension. Record your observations as directed below in the section entitled "Observations and Data Analysis."

10. Weigh a small piece of filter paper (approximately 3 x 3 cm) and label in pencil with your names. Record the weight of the filter paper as directed in "Observations and Data Analysis."

11. Use a pipette or eyedropper to draw up the DNA from the alcohol layer, and place the DNA on the filter paper. Set the filter paper aside and let it dry overnight. Reweigh the filter paper containing DNA the following day. Record your results as directed in "Observations and Data Analysis (3b)." Calculate the yield of DNA from the wheat germ.

12. Remove some of the DNA sample from the filter paper and place the DNA in a labeled test tube containing 3 mL of 4% salt solution, and add 3 mL diphenylamine solution. You may call this test tube X.

13. Into a second labeled test tube, place 3 mL of the standard DNA solution, and add 3 mL phenylamine. You may call this test tube Y.

14. To a third labeled test tube, add 3 mL 4% salt solution and 3 mL diphenylamine. You may call this test tube Z.

15. Place all the labeled test tubes—X, Y and Z— in a beaker with water at 50–60° C, and record any color changes.

16. Diphenylamine reacts with the deoxyribose of the DNA to produce a blue color, which indicates the presence of DNA.

Observations and Data Analysis

Use a separate piece of paper to write your answers.

1. Describe the appearance of the DNA strands (from step 9).

2. What can you infer about the solubility of DNA in ethanol from your observations?

3. Calculate the yield of DNA from the wheat germ.

    a. mass of filter paper   _____g

       mass of filter paper + DNA   _____g

       mass of DNA   _____g

    b. DNA yield (mass of DNA extracted/mass of wheat germ)   _____g

4. What is the purpose of heating the wheat germ solution?

5. Why is it important to stir the wheat germ solution for 5 minutes (step 3)?

6. Why is ice-cold alcohol used instead of room-temperature alcohol?

7. State whether DNA was present/absent in test tubes X, Y, and Z (refer to step 15 in the procedure section).

Part B

Your Task: In Part B, you apply the skills and concepts from Part A to a problem. Each group *chooses one* of the following tasks for completion in two to three class periods of 45 minutes.

1. Plan and design an experiment to improve the extraction procedure of DNA from wheat germ without reducing the DNA yield.

OR

2. Use different sources of DNA and apply the original procedure to determine if another source of DNA produces a higher yield of DNA/gram of material compared to wheat germ.

Hypothesis or Prediction

Use a separate piece of paper to write your answers.

A. From the information you now have regarding DNA extraction, develop a hypothesis you can test in a controlled experiment that will allow you to gather quantitative data.

B. Explain the reasoning behind your hypothesis.

Plan of Investigation

In planning your investigation, remember that you will need to (1) design a controlled experiment based on your hypothesis, (2) list detailed steps so that someone else can follow your procedures, and (3) consider the design for the table(s) or graph(s) that is appropriate for recording your data. Consider the following questions in drawing up your plan:

- What will you measure?
- What materials will you need?
- How will you proceed with the investigation?
- How will you show your results in data tables and graphs?

Submit your experimental plan to your teacher before starting your investigation. Your evaluation will be based on the quality of your experimental plan, results, analysis of results, and conclusions.

When you have completed your investigation, prepare a report based on the scoring rubric obtained from your teacher.

DNA Extraction
Scoring Rubric

Part A (see questions 1-7 under "Observations and Data Analysis"):

1. Description of appearance of DNA isolated	0-2 points
2. Inferences about the solubility of DNA in ethanol	0-2 points
3a. Calculation of the dry weight of DNA	0-3 points
3b. Calculation of yield of DNA	0-2 points
4. Statement of the purpose of heating DNA solution	0-2 points
5. Statement of the purpose of stirring wheat germ solution	0-2 points
6. Statement of the purpose for using room-temperature alcohol	0-2 points
7. Statement regarding presence/absence of DNA in test tubes X,Y, and Z	0-3 points
Total	0-18 points

Part B: Experimental Plan

1. Appropriate hypothesis (e.g., *DNA yield might be increased depending on DNA source compared to wheat germ yield.*)	0-2 points
2. Explanation behind hypothesis	0-2 points
3. Variables identified	0-2 points
4. Appropriate DNA source	0-2 points
5. Safety precautions	0-1 point
6. Feasible experimental plan	0-4 points
7. Appropriate data collected	0-2 points
8. Data organized appropriately for analysis	0-2 points
9. Conclusions aligned with data collected	0-2 points
Total	0-19 points

Notes for Using Scoring Rubric:

Options for the student experimental plan in Part B of the investigation:

- Use alternative materials as a source of DNA (e.g., aqueous solution of lima beans [for bacteria cultured within the aqueous solution], beef liver, onion, beef thymus)
- Use a buffer (e.g., Bufferin) to alter pH during extraction
- Use a different liquid detergent to improve yield
- Substitute fresh papaya juice for meat tenderizer
- Vary the temperature
- Use 1.5 mL Eppendorf centrifuge tubes to collect centrifugate, then dry and weigh it
- Use mini centrifuge
- Replace detergent with SDS (sodium dodecyl sulfate) 10%
- Use reusable coffee filter as a strainer

Potential hypotheses:

- *The yield of DNA per gram of original material might be increased by a change (improvement) in the procedure.*
- *The yield of DNA per gram of DNA source might be improved if a different DNA source were used.*

Potential alternative procedures:

- Eliminate or alter the heating step. How does this affect DNA yield?
- Choose a different DNA source. How does another DNA source produce a greater amount of DNA per gram of material used?

Potential data analysis and interpretation:

The raw wheat germ appears to be the best source of DNA for use in this extraction procedure. Of the various sources of DNA, raw wheat germ is the least expensive, easiest to use, and seems to provide the greatest yield per gram. Although results may vary, all the suggested sources should provide excellent yield of DNA.

The teacher should also note the following:
- DNA strands appear as long threads if unsheared or as fluffy pieces when cut.
- DNA appears to be relatively insoluble in alcohol.
- The value of DNA extracted should be approximately 0.2–0.3 g per 1 g of wheat germ used.
- Heat helps accelerate the destruction of the cell wall, cell membrane, and nuclear membrane when present.
- Stirring helps to break up the cell parts containing the DNA.
- Iced alcohol helps to rapidly decrease the temperature and provide an interface across which the DNA will move.

Works Cited

Baron, J. 1991. Performance Assessment—Blurring the Edge of Assessment, Curriculum, and Instruction. In *Science Assessment in the Service of Reform*, Kulm, G., and Malcolm, S., eds. Washington, DC: American Association for the Advancement of Science.

Chan, A., Doran, R., and Lenhardt, C. 1999. Learning from the TIMSS. *Science Teacher* 66 (1).

Doran, R., Boorman, J., Chan, A., and Hejaily, N. 1993. *High School Science Laboratory Performance Tasks*. Buffalo: University at Buffalo.

Harmon, M., Smith, T., Martin, M., Kelly, D., Beaton, A., Mullis, I., Gonzalez, E., and Orpwood, G. 1997. *Performance Assessment in IEA's Third International Mathematics and Science Study (TIMSS)*. Chestnut Hill, MA: TIMSS International Study Center.

Kanis, I., Doran, R., and Jacobson, W. 1990. *Assessing Science Process Laboratory Skills at the Elementary and Middle/Junior High Levels*. Washington, DC: National Science Teachers Association.

Lawrence Hall of Science. 1985. *GEMS Crime Lab Chemistry*. Berkeley, CA: Lawrence Hall of Science.

National Research Council (NRC). 1996. *National Science Education Standards*. Washington, DC: National Academy Press.

New York State Education Department (NYSED). 1999. *Intermediate Level Test Sampler*. Albany: NYSED.

Saha, G. 2001. *Implementing the Science Assessment Standards: Developing and Validating a Set of Laboratory Assessment Tasks in High School Biology*. Doctoral diss., University at Buffalo.

Wright, A. 2002. *Development of Performance Tasks—An Alternative Assessment for the New York State Regents Biology Course*. Doctoral diss., University at Buffalo.

Suggested Readings

Jacob, R. A. 1994. Vitamin C. In *Modern Nutrition in Health and Disease*, 8th ed., edited by Shils, M.E., Olson, J. A., and Shike, M., 432–48. Philadelphia: Lea and Febiger.

Food and Nutrition Board. 2000. *Dietary Reference Intakes for Vitamin C, Vitamin E, Selenium, and Carotenoids*. Washington, DC: National Academy Press.

CHAPTER 6

Illustrative Assessment Tasks for Chemistry

This chapter is organized in three parts: skills tasks, investigation tasks, and extended investigation tasks. All three parts contain models or templates of chemistry assessment tasks, many of which are "complete." These models may be used as is, incorporated into existing assessment programs, adapted and modified to address additional educational objectives, or completely redesigned to form entirely new and innovative assessments.

We include three small-scale assessment tasks from the American Chemical Society's Division of Chemical Education, Examination Institute (Silberman 1996): "Drop Size" (page 160), "Unknown Powders" (page 162), and "Antacids" (page 173). These laboratory tasks challenge students to plan, design, and perform experiments using small-scale laboratory techniques. The use of small-scale laboratory techniques makes it possible for students to practice their inquiry skills in solving authentic assessment tasks. Small-scale techniques also are environmentally friendly, especially when students use common household materials. We suggest that students carry out the tasks in pairs.

In all our chemistry tasks, safety concerns are minimized but not completely eliminated. Students must be required to follow appropriate safety precautions such as wearing safety glasses (goggles) and aprons. Chemistry teachers should ensure that laboratories contain eyewash stations as well as appropriate means for disposal of chemicals.

Chemistry Skills Tasks

The chart below shows the skills tasks in this chapter and the skills they assess. The skills tasks usually focus on one skill, or on a small set of skills assessing a single event or experience. Most skills tasks assessments include student directions, answer sheets, material preparation guidelines, and scoring rubrics. Possible revisions are included with many tasks, so they can be used for other assessments.

A similar chart precedes each of the other two sections of this chapter, Chemistry Investigation Tasks and Chemistry Extended Investigation Tasks. The four skills categories—planning performing, analyzing, and applying—are illustrated in Figures 4.5 and 4.6 (pages 62 and 63). Note that the "applying" category here means more than numerically solving an equation with collected data. It includes skills such as relating or integrating results to underlying themes or models, proposing additional investigations/hypotheses, and suggesting applications beyond the context of the specific investigation.

Chemistry Skills Tasks							
Skills Categories	Acid-Base Testing (page 146)	Missing Labels (page 149)	Measuring (page 151)	Observing Reactions (page 154)	Rate of Solution (page 158)	Drop Size (page 160)	Unknown Powders (page 162)
Planning		✔		✔		✔	✔
Performing	✔	✔	✔	✔	✔	✔	✔
Analyzing	✔	✔	✔	✔	✔	✔	✔
Applying						✔	

Acid-Base Testing

This task has been used with many students, with slight variations in amount of directions (structure). This version was used with the Second International Science Study (SISS) (Kanis, et al. 1990). Using common indicators (i.e., litmus paper and phenolphthalein) is a common activity in chemistry classes. This version is only slightly structured; more or less structure can be used depending on normal class activities.

You can also vary the structure by not giving the information about the behavior of the several indicators in acid, base, or neutral solutions. As students gain more experience with using indicators, they will know this information. With younger students, it is recommended that the teacher provide the information for a clearer focus on student proficiency with skills, the main purpose of the assessment task.

Another variation is to not tell students there is one solution that is acid, one that is base, and one that is neutral and vary from station to station the number of each. You can also have just two unknown solutions, or you can use more (four or five). Having just three, and specifying that there is one of each, does allow students to solve the problem without testing all the unknowns.

The rubric for this task has a total of ten points. The other task used in the SISS Project also had a maximum of ten possible points. This allowed for comparison of performance of different tasks on the same basis (10 point maximum).

The equipment used should match that used in the students' labs. The solution can be tested in test tubes or vials of the kind used frequently in chemistry classes. However, many classes use reaction wells, which use less solution and are easier to clean. Another variation is to use laminated index cards with circles marked for the solutions. As many laminating plastics are porous, a piece of wax paper can be laid over the card and disposed of after each student.

Acid-Base Testing
Task Information

Time: 15 minutes

Materials:

- solution A – base
- solution B – water
- solution C – acid
- plastic strip with three circles
- small plastic cup
- paper towels
- waste container

- red and blue litmus paper
- phenolphthalein
- dropper bottles
- water for cleaning
- goggles

Teacher Preparation:

1. Stock Solution Preparation: for thirty (30) students (60 ml) dropper bottles which can be used for 5 classes.
   a. Solution A – base solution – dilute limewater ($Ca(OH)_2$).
      For best results purchase just prior to the activity as limewater has a short shelf life; place in dropper bottles labeled "A."
   b. Solution B – water in dropper bottles labeled "B."

c. Solution C – acid solution - dilute citric or ascorbic acid

If using purchased citric acid, follow manufacturer's directions for making a dilute solution; if using "Fruit Fresh," dissolve 3 teaspoons in 1500 ml of water; test with litmus paper; place in dropper bottles labeled "C."

2. Materials Preparation:

a. Label dropper bottles "A," "B," "C," and "Phenolphthalein."

b. For best results, fill phenolphthalein bottles just prior to the activity.

c. Keep litmus paper in closed containers.

d. Cut litmus paper into strips; discard strips after using.

Safety:

- Students should wear safety goggles; laboratory safety procedures required.
- Check MSDS (Materials Safety Data Sheets) for further laboratory precautions.

Extensions/Modifications:

- Variations of this task can involve different degrees of structure.

Acid-Base Testing
Student Task Sheet

Introduction:

Phenolphthalein is a colorless indicator. When a few drops are added to a basic solution, the solution will turn pink. Litmus paper, another indicator, is used in the identification of acids and bases. Blue litmus paper turns red (pink) when dipped in an acidic solution. Pink litmus paper turns blue when dipped in a basic solution. Before you are three solutions, labeled A, B, and C. One contains a basic solution, another an acidic solution, and a third, water. Use the colorless indicator and litmus paper to determine which solutions are acid, base, or water.

Procedure:

Begin by following the instructions below.

1. Add a few drops of the indicator, phenolphthalein, to each circle (on the plastic strip with three circles). What changes do you observe? Record them.

2. What conclusions can you draw from these changes?

3. What will you do next? Write down your plan and carry it out.

4. What did you observe this time? Record your observations.

5. What conclusions can you draw? State your reasons for each one.

Acid-Base Testing
Scoring Rubric

Item No.	Answer	Scoring

1) Test tube A – solution turned pink (purple pink).*
   Test tube B – no change**
   Test tube C – no change**

1 pt. if observed changes reported correctly.
* = required for point
** = optional for point

2) Test tube A contains a basic solution.

1 pt. for correct conclusion.

3) Dip a piece of blue and/or pink litmus paper (blue must be used, pink is optional) into test tube(s) B and/or C. Testing A is not required. Other procedures may be acceptable (i.e., combining equal amounts from vial B (or C) with vial A).

2 pts. for complete plan.
1 pt. for partial plan.

4) 1. Test tube A – pink litmus paper turns blue.
   2. Test tube B – no color change with either.
   3. Test tube C – blue litmus paper turns pink.

2 pts. for listing 2 and 3.
1 pt. for listing 2 or 3.
(1 is optional.)

5) 1. Test tube A – contains a base.
   Reason: pink litmus turned blue when dipped in it or phenolphthalein turned solution pink.

   2. Test tube B – contains water.
   Reason: no color change with either pink or blue litmus paper.
   3. Test tube C – contains an acid.
   Reason: blue litmus paper turned pink.

Identification:
2 pts. for correct identification of 2 and 3 (1 pt. each).
(1 is optional.)

Explanation:
2 pts. for correct explanation of 2 and 3 (1 pt. each).
(1 is optional.)

10 points total

Missing Labels

This task was developed by Peter Mirando (1993) as part of his doctoral research . It has three additional solutions and a reaction information matrix. The reaction information matrix shows the observations that are known to exist for a set of chemicals. The ones used in this task are among those used in this matrix. A table of solubilities (in water) for some common compounds is also presented in the matrix. Examples of such data in table form are presented in the data table. They are used widely by chemists and are available in handbooks.

In this task students must write the procedure they will use to identify the unknowns, collect and record their observations, and state their conclusions. This is the approach used by many scientists as they solve a problem. This task was chosen because it is an authentic chemistry activity for middle-level and high school students. It also illustrates a quite unstructured assessment task.

Missing Labels
Student Task Sheet

The labels have fallen off three bottles of solution in our chemistry lab and we need help in identifying which is which. The three solutions are:

- sodium carbonate
- ammonium hydroxide
- barium chloride

For now, we have labeled the bottles P, Q, & R.

Materials available to use in your investigation:

- dropper bottles of copper (II) sulfate, sodium sulfate, and hydrochloric acid
- Reaction Information Matrix and Table of Solubilities in Water
- three unknown solutions (labeled P, Q, R)

1. Write the procedure you will follow to solve the mystery.

2. Record your data and observations.

3. Write out your conclusions, identifying the solutions in each of the bottles.

Reaction Information Matrix

	1A BaCl2	2A H2SO4	3A Na2CO3	4A NaOH	5A Phenol-pthalein	6A Na2SO4	1B HCl	2B K2CO3	3B KOH	4B FeCl3	5B NH4OH	6B (NH4)2SO4	1C CuSO4	2C (NH4)2CO3
1A BaCl2	XXX	white Ppt.	white Ppt.		N.C.	white Ppt.	N.C.	white Ppt.		N.C.		white Ppt.	Blue Ppt.	white Ppt.
2A H2SO4		XXX	effervescence		N.C.	N.C.	N.C.	effervescence		N.C.		N.C.	N.C.	effervescence
3A Na2CO3			XXX	N.C.		N.C.	effervescence	N.C.	N.C.	rusty Ppt.	N.C.	N.C.	Blue Ppt.	N.C.
4A NaOH				XXX	turns pink	N.C.	N.C.	N.C.	N.C.	rusty Ppt.	N.C.	N.C.	Blue Ppt.	N.C.
5A Phenol-pthalein					XXX	N.C.	N.C.		turns pink	N.C.	turns pink	N.C.	N.C.	
6A Na2SO4						XXX	N.C.	N.C.	N.C.	N.C.	N.C.	N.C.	N.C.	N.C.
1B HCl							XXX	effervescence		N.C.	N.C.	N.C.	N.C.	effervescence
2B K2CO3								XXX	N.C.	N.C.	N.C.	N.C.	Blue Ppt.	N.C.
3B KOH									XXX	rusty Ppt.	N.C.	N.C.	Blue Ppt.	N.C.
4B FeCl3										XXX	rusty Ppt.	N.C.	N.C.	rusty Ppt.
5B NH4OH											XXX	N.C.	Dk blue color	N.C.
6B (NH4)2SO4												XXX	N.C.	N.C.
1C CuSO4													XXX	Blue Ppt.
2C (NH4)2CO3														

Table of Solubilities in Water

i - nearly insoluble
ss - slightly soluble
s - soluble
d - decomposes
n - not isolated

	acetate	bromide	carbonate	chloride	chromate	hydroxide	iodide	nitrate	phosphate	sulfate	sulfide
Aluminum	ss	s	n	s		i	s	s	i	s	d
Ammonium	s	s	s	s	s	s	s	s	s	s	s
Barium	s	s	i	s	i	s	s	s	i	i	d
Calcium	s	s	i	s	s	ss	s	s	i	ss	d
Copper II	s	s	i	s	i	i	n	s	i	s	i
Iron II	s	s	i	s		i	s	s	i	s	i
Iron III	s	s	n	s		i	n	s	i	ss	d
Lead	s	ss	i	ss	i	i	i	s	i	i	i
Magnesium	s	s	i	s	s	i	s	s	i	s	d
Mercury I	ss	i	i	i	i	n	i	s	i	ss	i
Mercury II	s	ss	i	s	i	i	i	s	i	d	i
Potassium	s	s	s	s	s	s	s	s	s	s	s
Silver	ss	i	i	i	i	n	i	s	i	ss	i
Sodium	s	s	s	s	s	s	s	s	s	s	s
Zinc	s	s	i	s	s	i	s	s	i	s	i

Measuring

This station requires student skill with some measuring equipment commonly used in chemistry and other sciences: graduated cylinder, balance, and a centimeter ruler. The task has three sections using different equipment. As this task is organized, students are provided with a box of equipment and materials, except for the balances. Students work at their station, except when using the balance.

This task may be useful in a diagnostic assessment for a chemistry class in which students come from several different middle schools. It may also be used as a summative assessment for a middle level program.

Measuring
Task Information

Part 1: Using a Balance

- use of a balance
- using a container or weighing paper to determine the mass of a substance
- recording data to the highest degree of accuracy of a measuring tool
- using appropriate accuracy and precision in measurement and use of numbers for data
- using unit labeled accurately in recording data

Part 2: Determining Density

- skills from Part 1
- use of a graduated cylinder to measure liquid volume
- determining the density of an irregularly shaped object
- applying formula for density

Part 3: Laboratory Equipment and Measurement

- identifying and properly using beakers, flasks, graduated cylinders
- using a metric ruler to measure and report measurements to the highest degree of accuracy
- understanding and recording the highest degree of accuracy of measuring devices

Materials:

Per student:

- 25 ml graduated cylinder
- 100 or 150 ml beaker
- 100 or 150 ml Erlenmeyer flask
- dropping pipette
- slug of zinc metal in a plastic container
- 15 cm plastic ruler
- wax marking pencil
- several pieces of weighing paper

Each student will take and keep this kit at his or her work station throughout the exam.

- 1 small test tube or other container with a recorded pre-weighed amount of sand

  The students will most likely empty the container, so be sure to have enough containers of sand for each team of students taking the test in all classes.

  Each container should be numbered and the mass of the sand in each container recorded along with the number of the container.

This information will be used to check for accuracy in Part 1

- 2 or more balances – triple beam or electronic

  These should be set out in a convenient location for use by students as needed.

- calculators, 4 function – 1 per student

Measuring
Student Task Sheet

This task consists of three parts. You are to complete each part. The parts do not have to be completed in order. If balances are being used, work on that part that does not require the use of the balance until one is free. Be sure to be careful with your measurements, and show all work and formulas used. You will be graded on accuracy, completeness, and neatness.

Obtain a numbered box containing laboratory equipment from your teacher. The box contains all of the necessary equipment for the completion of this task (with the exception of a balance). You may or may not require every piece of equipment in order to complete this task. Use only the equipment and materials in your box. If there appears to be a problem with the materials, call your teacher.

Your box should contain the following equipment and materials:
- 1 25 ml graduated cylinder
- 1 100 or 150 ml beaker
- 1 100 or 150 ml Erlenmeyer flask
- 1 dropping pipette
- 1 plastic box containing a piece of metal
- 1 15 cm plastic ruler
- 1 wax marking pencil

- vial of sand
- empty vial
- calculator
- several sheets of weighing paper

Record the number of the box that you are using.

Part 1: Using the Balance
A. Obtain a numbered sample of sand from the teacher and record the number of the sample.

B. Determine the mass of the sand in the container to the highest degree of accuracy possible with your balance. Describe the procedure you used and show any calculations used.

Part 2: Determining Density
In your materials box is a numbered plastic box which contains a piece of metal. The metal may be any one of the following:

Metal	Density
Bismuth	9.80 g/cm^3
Lead	11.35 g/cm^3
Magnesium	1.74 g/cm^3
Mercury	13.55 g/cm^3
Zinc	7.14 g/cm^3

A. Record the number of the box containing the metal you used.

B. Determine the identity of the metal in the container by determining its density. Record the procedure that you used and show all the formulas and calculations.

Part 3: Laboratory Equipment and Measurement
A. Measure the length of the line below to the highest degree of accuracy and record its length.

B. Record the greatest degree of accuracy that can be measured with: the 25 ml graduated cylinder; the 15 cm ruler; and the balance.

Measuring
Scoring Rubric

Part 1: Using the Balance

Weighing procedure   8 points
• give 2 points for each of the following indicated:
taring weighing paper or container
using tared paper or container to weigh sand
subtracting mass of tared container or paper from combined mass of container and sand
calculations shown

Accuracy of answer   3 points
if =/− 0.2 gram error or less   (3 points)
if +/− >0.2 gram to 0.5 gram error   (2 points)
if +/− >0.5 grams to 1.0 gram error   (1 point)
if >1.0 gram error   (0 points)

All numbers with appropriate unit labels   1 point

                                                       Total points Part 1   12 points

---

Part 2: Determining Density

Give credit for each of the following steps as indicated: 8 points
determining the mass of the metal   (2 points)
determining volume of metal by water displacement or   (2 points)
determining volume of metal by measuring with ruler   (1 point)
correct formula for density   (2 points)
appropriate units in the formula for density   (2 points)

Accuracy of answer   3 points
if < 10% error   (6.43 g/ml − 7.95 g/ml)   (3 points)
if >10% − <16% error   (6.08 g/ml − 7.96 g/ml   (2 points)
if > 16% − 20% error   (5.73 g/ml − 8.55 g/ml)   (1 point)
if >20% error   (0 points)

Correct name of metal (for above data—zinc)   2 points
All numbers with appropriate unit labels   1 point

                                                       Total points Part 2   14 points

---

Part 3: Laboratory Equipment and Measurement

Measurement   3 points
if answer is 4.00 cm   (3 points)
if answer is 4.0 cm   (2 points)
if answer is 4 cm   (1 point)
if answer is other than 4.0, but 3 significant figures   (2 points)

Unit label on answer   1 point

Degree of accuracy   6 points
• for each of the following, allow 1 point for each correct degree of accuracy
and 1 point for each correct unit label
    25 ml graduated cylinder: 0.1 ml   (2 points)
    15 cm ruler: 0.01 cm or 0.1 mm or 0.0001 M   (2 points)
    Balance: (variable with balance used)   (2 points)

                                                       Total points Part 3   10 points
                                                       Maximum score   36 points

Observing Reactions

Observing is one of the most basic and pervasive skills in science, and reactions are the phenomena most commonly viewed in chemistry. The following task could be used at the middle or high school levels, depending on prior experience with related (not the same) instructional activities.

The task begins (Part I) with a typical chemical activity in which common materials are mixed and changes occur: sometimes there are changes in color or temperature, sometimes solutions or precipitates are formed. The inquiry part of the task is found in Part II: students must determine which substances caused which changes. Students describe the steps in their planned experiment, develop a data table, and state their conclusions. We describe this as a "relatively unstructured" format, in contrast to the all-too-common structured (recipe-like) approach. (The researcher did develop a structured task parallel to the one given here [Zichitella 2002]).

The materials used are very common and present no safety issues when used with structured science lab procedures (goggles, washing hands, etc.).

Observing Reactions
Task Information

Materials:

- phenol red (an indicator)
- water
- 2 solids ($NaHCO_3$ and $CaCl_2$)
- graduated cylinder
- resealable plastic sandwich bag
- beaker
- pipettes
- scale

Note: It is not necessary to use all of the equipment, but the student may not use additional equipment.

The students first follow directions to observe the planned reactions. These recorded observations are an important basis for the inquiry that follows. If students haven't been prepared to determine and write their own procedures, construct data tables, and so forth, this form of the task may be inappropriate. Related instructions could be planned or the directions enhanced/structured to provide a successful inquiry. There are many stages between structured and unstructured activities both for instruction and assessment. Although students can be challenged (with a less-structured version in an assessment as compared with instruction), many students are not able to make such a shift. As teachers, we need to help students to become skilled with less and less structured tasks.

Observing Reactions
Student Task Sheet

Introduction: This laboratory exercise is designed to give you practice in making accurate and complete observations of physical and chemical processes. You will

- formulate a hypothesis that will account for these observations,
- develop a plan to be used to solve a problem, and
- construct a data table.

Part I: Observations

1. Observe the two solids ($NaHCO_3$ and $CaCl_2$) and the two liquids (water and phenol red); note all possible physical properties of these substances. Place your observations into Table 1 under "Step 1: Properties."
2. Mix the liquids together in a beaker in the following amounts: 2 drops of phenol red with 10 mL of water. Observe any changes that occur and record the physical properties of this mixture in Table 1 ("Step 2: Mixture" [top box]).
3. Mix the solids together in a resealable plastic sandwich bag in the following amounts: 2 g of $NaHCO_3$ and 2 g of $CaCl_2$
4. Observe any changes that occur and record the physical properties of this mixture in Table 1 ("Step 2: Mixture" [bottom box]).
5. Quickly pour the liquid mixture into the plastic bag with the solids, remove as much air as possible, and seal the bag. Record any changes that occur and list them in Table 1 ("Step 3: Mixture"). Observe carefully. (You should note a minimum of three changes.)

Table 1

Substance	Step 1 Properties	Step 2 Mixture	Step 3 Mixture
Water			
Phenol Red			
$NaHCO_3$			
$CaCl_3$			

Part II: Investigations

In this part of the investigation, you will determine what substance combinations resulted in the chemical changes in Part I.

1. Develop an experimental plan that you can use to determine which combinations of substances resulted in each of the changes that were noted when the four substances were added together in Part I. Indicate clearly your intended procedure. Another person should be able to follow your directions and obtain similar results. You will be provided with a small container of each of the substances. Use them and follow your plan to obtain and record data.

2. Construct a data table in which you will record the information that you obtained when following your experimental procedure.

3. State your conclusion clearly. (What combinations of substances do you believe resulted in each of the changes noted in Part I?)

Observing Reactions
Scoring Rubric

From the students' perspective, this activity is simply a nifty science lab (a part of instruction). When student responses are read carefully and scored with a rubric, however, this activity becomes an assessment task. The rubric developed by Zichitella (2002) is presented here. It has the format of a checklist, making it easy for a team of teachers to use simply and reliably.

Place a check mark next to each statement found on the student answer sheet and total the score for each section. Assign 1 point for each check mark.

Physical properties of substances

A) $NaHCO_3$
   White powder _____
   Solid _____

B) $CaCl_3$
   White powder _____
   Solid _____

C) Water
   Colorless _____
   Liquid _____
   Odorless _____

D) Indicator
   Transparent _____
   Color _____
   Liquid _____
   Odor _____

Observations of Change – Four Substances Mixed

Qualitative Description
   Notes color change _____
   Notes temperature change _____
   Notes gas generation _____

I. Planning and Design of Investigation:

1. Feasible plan for investigation
   Mixes water and indicator _____
   Mixes water and $NaHCO_3$ _____
   Mixes water and $CaCl_2$ _____
   Mixes $NaHCO_3$ and $CaCl_2$ (aq) _____
   Adds indicator to $NaHCO_3$ (aq) _____

Adds indicator to $CaCl_2$ (aq) _____

2. Demonstrates proper use of equipment and addresses safety issues
   Notes goggles must be worn _____
   Mixes substances in a beaker or well plate _____

II. Performance of Task

Records observations in a data table _____
Notes results of mixing water and indicator _____
Notes results of mixing water and $NaHCO_3$ _____
Notes results of mixing water and $CaCl_2$ _____
Notes results of mixing $NaHCO_3$ (aq) and $CaCl_2$ (aq) _____
Notes results of adding indicator to $NaHCO_3$ (aq) _____
Notes results of adding indicator to $CaCl_2$ (aq) _____

III. Analysis and Interpretation – Consistent with Observations

A. Gas Production $CaCl_2$ (aq) + $NaHCO_3$ (Aq) _____
B. Temperature Change $CaCl_2$ + water _____
                       or $NaHCO_3$ + water _____

C. Color Change $CaCl_2$ + indicator _____
                       or $NaHCO_3$ + indicator _____

Total Points _____

Rate of Solution

This task was included in the New York State Alternative Assessment in Science Project (Reynolds, et. al. 1996). Almost all chemical reactions occur when one or more of the substances are in a solution (usually an aqueous solution). This task explores the effect of two (of many) variables on the rate of solution (the size of the particle and agitation). Having students directly involved, by doing the shaking, is preferred to some black box or abstract application of the treatment.

In addition to the observation and counting, students are expected to enter the data into an appropriate graph and predict the rate of solution for a third sample. The students' predictions are based on their ability to understand the relationship between agitation and particle size.

This task could be modified to explore the effect of temperature, adding another variable to the task. Understanding that many variables are related to the complete understanding of most natural phenomena will help students identify, select, and control variables for other domains.

Sugar is another commonly available chemical, and one that is available commercially in several particle sizes. Salt, another common chemical, is also commercially available in several sizes (table salt, kosher salt, etc.). Students could grind table salt into a sample with even smaller particle sizes.

Rate of Solution
Task Information

Time: 15 minutes

Materials:

- 1 sugar cube
- waste container (cups or small buckets)
- graduated cylinder
- water (500 ml)
- 2 bottles with screw-on caps, labeled A and B (approximately 250 ml)
- granulated sugar in a sealed container
- teaspoon
- superfine sugar sample
- safety goggles
- hand lens

Preparation:

- Mark the sealed container of granulated sugar: "Sugar X–Do Not Open"
- Bottle size and water temperature <u>must</u> be consistent at every student station.

Safety:

- Safety goggles <u>must</u> be worn for this activity.
- Proper laboratory safety procedures are required.

Extensions/ Modifications:

- Different types of sugar may be substituted in the shaking process:
    - granulated and superfine – extrapolate to cube
    - granulated and cube – extrapolate to superfine
- Correlate particle size with surface area
- Use salt or other soluble material

Rate of Solution
Student Task Sheet

Task: At this station, you will determine the number of shakes necessary to dissolve various sized sugar particles.

Materials:

- 1 sugar cube
- sealed container labeled "Sugar X"
- waste cup
- teaspoon
- graduated cylinder

- water (500 ml)
- 2 bottles with caps, labeled A and B
- safety goggles
- superfine sugar sample

Procedure:

1. Put on safety goggles. Do not taste any substance in this activity. Clean up any spills immediately.
2. Use your hand lens to carefully observe the sugar cube and the superfine sugar. Which form of sugar has the smaller size particles?
3. Add 50 ml of water to the two (2) bottles.
4. Drop one sugar cube into bottle A and close the bottle tightly.
5. Count how many shakes it takes to totally dissolve the sugar cube.
6. Record your data in a table you construct.
7. Place one level teaspoon of superfine sugar into Bottle B and repeat steps 5 and 6.
8. Dump the contents of the two (2) bottles into the waste cup and rinse the bottles.
9. Draw a line graph showing the number of shakes needed to dissolve the two forms of sugar. Make sure you include the appropriate range and interval of numbers on the y axis.
10. Use your hand lens to carefully observe the particle size of Sugar X. Use the information from the line graph. Predict the number of shakes it would take to completely dissolve one level teaspoon of Sugar X in the same amount of water.
11. Write a generalized statement that explains the relationship between the particle size of the sugar and the number of shakes needed to dissolve the sugar.

Rate of Solution
Scoring Rubric

2: Identifying the smaller sized particle of sugar   1 point total
- Allow 1 point for identifying the superfine sugar as having the smallest particles.

6: Data Table   1 point total
- Allow 1 point for appropriate numbers showing a greater number of shakes for the sugar cube.

9: Graph   3 points total
- Allow 1 point for appropriate number range and interval on the y axis based on the student's data.
- Allow 1 point for correctly plotting <u>both</u> points
- Allow 1 point for correctly connecting <u>only</u> the two (2) plotted points.

10: Predicting   1 point total
- Allow 1 point for any number between the student-derived data for superfine and sugar cube shakes.

11: Relationship between particle size and number of shakes   2 points total
- Allow 2 points for the correct relation of both variables.
  Sample of acceptable answers:
  – as the particle size increases, shakes increase
  – as the sugar sizes get bigger, it takes longer to dissolve
- Allow 1 point for a restatement of data
  Sample of acceptable answers:
  – it took the cube longer to dissolve
  – it took less time to dissolve the superfine sugar

Maximum Score – 8 points

Drop Size

In the following task, students design and perform an experiment to investigate the relationship between surface tension and the number of drops from a micro-tip Beral-type pipette. They also describe the method they used to solve the problem. The task appears in *ACS Small-Scale Laboratory Assessment Activities* (1996), published by the American Chemical Society, Division of Chemical Education, Examination Institute. The publication was written by Robert G. Silberman and edited by Lucy Eubanks. The "Drop Size" task is reprinted with permission.

Drop Size

Problem Statement for Students:

Design and carry out an experiment to test the hypothesis that the surface tension of a liquid affects the drop size from a micro-tip Beral-type pipette. You have both water and a solution of detergent in water available to you. (Detergent is known to lower the surface tension of water.) Describe the method you developed to solve this problem.

Assessment Objectives:

This problem tests a student's ability to devise an experiment to test a specific hypothesis. Students will need to use a control and to vary the amount of detergent in solution. The student will also need to draw justifiable conclusions from the data and demonstrate understanding of the experimental relationship between surface tension and number of drops from a micro-tip Beral-type pipette.

Materials and Equipment:

Chemicals	Equipment	Possible Distracters
• water • clear liquid detergent such as Joy®, Dawn® or Ivory®	• calibrated Beral-type pipettes • 10 mL graduated cylinder • paper cups or other small containers to catch the drops and to make up the detergent solutions	• different sizes of Beral-type pipettes • 25 mL graduated cylinder • 10 mL measuring pipette • small screw cap vials • food coloring

One Likely Approach:

1. The student counts the number of drops of water that have a known volume of at least 1.0 mL.

2. The student prepares at least two other detergent solutions of known concentration in any convenient units such as percent by volume or parts per drop.

3. The student counts the number of drops of each concentration of detergent solution that will have a known volume of at least 1.0 mL.

4. The student repeats each procedure #1-3 as many times as is consistent with available time and materials, but at least once more for each procedure.

5. The student compares the number of drops of water with the number of drops for each of the different detergent solution.

6. The student draws a conclusion about the variation in the number of drops as the concentration of detergent varies. This, in turn, supports or refutes the hypothesis that the surface tension affects the drop size. NOTE: While not wrong, *calculation of drop size* is an unnecessary step. Since drop size is inversely proportional with the number of drops for a fixed volume, the same conclusion that surface tension of a liquid affects the drop size can still be reached.

Drop Size
Scoring Suggestions (Based on 5 Points)

1. Determination of number of drops of water that are needed for a known volume	1 point
2. Preparation of at least two detergent solutions of known concentration	1 point
(a) The student prepares two detergent solutions but no concentrations given.	0.5 points
(b) The student uses the *likely approach* procedure.	1.0 point
3. Determination of number of drops of detergent solution that are needed for a known volume	1 point
4. Conclusions about the relationship between surface tension and number of drops	2 points
(a) The student draws a conclusion about the correctness of the hypothesis, but does not support it with experimental data.	1.0 point
(b) The student completes the *likely approach* analysis.	2.0 points

Extra credit could be awarded if the student

(a) conserves variables by using the *same* Beral-type pipette (after rinsing with each liquid) for both water and increasingly concentrated detergent solutions.

(b) attempts to draw a graph to illustrate the experimental relationship.

(c) accurately explains at the molecular level how surface tension affects the drop size or number.

Notes:

1. If you elect to prepare and distribute the detergent solutions to the students, the problem becomes both somewhat easier and also shorter.

2. Use of the same pipette for all determinations will improve conservation of variables, but may not be practical for students.

3. It is *not* recommended that students have a balance available as a distracter. This has not been an effective distracter for this activity and for those students who did use it, simply weighing a fixed number of drops made the activity very simple.

Special Safety Considerations: None

Unknown Powders

In this investigation, students undertake a qualitative analysis of some common substances. The task appears in *ACS Small-Scale Laboratory Assessment Activities* (1996), published by the American Chemical Society, Division of Chemical Education, Examination Institute. The publications was written by Robert G. Silberman and edited by Lucy Eubanks. The "Unknown Powders" task is reprinted with permission.

Unknown Powders

Problem:

Identify five white powders, which may be ground-up chalk, Alka-Seltzer®, washing soda, baking soda, or vitamin C. The labeled pipettes contain water, vinegar, or phenolphthalein solution. Describe the method you developed to solve this problem.

Assessment Objectives:

This problem tests a student's understanding of qualitative analysis of some common substances. Students must demonstrate that their experimental plan takes advantage of simple reactions and that they can interpret their results to successfully identify the five white powders.

Materials and Equipment:

Chemicals	Equipment
• vinegar	• micro-tip Beral-type pipettes, 6 (one for each liquid reagent and 3 extras)
• water	
• phenolphthalein solution	• reaction plate, 24-well
• approximately 0.5 g of each powder:	• small vials (to hold solid samples)
pulverized chalk	
Alka-Seltzer®	
baking soda	
washing soda	
ascorbic acid	

One Likely Approach:

1. The student devises a general approach to see how the powders react (or fail to react) with water and with vinegar. Phenolphthalein is used to help identify the bases present.
2. The student notes that Alka-Seltzer® (sodium hydrogen carbonate and other ingredients) is the only white powder that reacts quickly with water.
3. The student notes that chalk (calcium sulfate) is the only white powder that is not soluble in water and does not react with water.
4. The student notes that washing soda (sodium carbonate) reacts with vinegar, and phenolphthalein solution turns pink.

5. The student notes that baking soda (sodium bicarbonate) reacts with vinegar, but phenolphthalein solution does not turn pink.
6. The student notes that vitamin C (ascorbic acid) does not react with either water or vinegar, but will react with the washing soda or baking soda if mixed with them and water.

Unknown Powders
Scoring Suggestions (Based on 5 Points)

1. Initial checking for reactions with water and vinegar   **2 points**
   (a) The student does not test the powders with either reagent   **0 points**
   (b) The student tests each powder with water or vinegar, but not both, or fails
   to use the phenolphthalein solution.   **1 point**
   (c) The student uses the *likely approach* procedure.   **2 points**
2. Presentation of evidence for identification of each white powder   **3 points**
   (a) The student does not present any reasonable evidence to support identification.   **0 points**
   (b) The student presents some reasonable evidence to support identification.   **1 point**
   (c) The student presents significant evidence to support identification.   **2 points**
   (d) The student presents reasonable evidence as in the *likely approach* analysis.   **3 points**

Extra credit could be awarded if the student

(a) writes chemical equations for each reaction, particularly net ionic equations.

(b) reasons that although the evidence supports the identification of each powder from the limited list of five possibilities, additional tests might be performed to double-check the identification.

Notes:
1. To keep this problem as simple as possible, just provide preweighed 0.5 g samples of each powder in small vials or possibly test tubes.
2. You may want to provide the chemical names, as well as the common names for the five white powders, depending on your assessment objectives.
3. Other soluble weak acids might be used, such as citric acid, rather than the ascorbic acid.
4. This problem becomes more difficult if students are limited to the minimum number of tests necessary to identify the white powders.

Special Safety Considerations: Be sure to follow usual safety rules for working with acids.

Chemistry Investigation Tasks

These tasks require students to complete an entire inquiry or solve a problem. These tasks are authentic, in that they involve students in all phases of research over one or two class periods. They are designed to fit within school schedules, many of which have at least one back-to-back double period per week.

Most of these tasks require students to demonstrate skills in each of the four categories: planning, performing, analyzing, and applying. While most begin with the planning stage, with minor changes, the tasks can begin with students collecting data (from a set of procedures provided) or with analyzing data (that is presented to the students).

For most of these Investigation Tasks, students need to record their answers in either their laboratory logbook or on two blank sheets of paper. Specific instructions for what students should record, and the labels they should use, are given in each task. Generally, students are asked to record their hypothesis, their procedure (including any diagrams), and their data table (including their observations) on one sheet in a reasonably finished form. The other sheet is to be used as scratch paper. If the task has a Part B, students will usually need a piece of graph paper and a third sheet for recording their conclusions. You may wish to hand out prepared answer sheets with the headings already in place. The chart below identifies the skills assessed by the three chemistry Investigation Tasks that follow.

Chemistry Investigation Tasks			
Skills Categories	Unknown Solutions (page 165)	Reaction Rates (page 167)	Solubility (page 169)
Planning	✔	✔	✔
Performing	✔	✔	✔
Analyzing	✔	✔	✔
Applying			✔

Unknown Solutions

This task was developed for use in a middle-level Science Olympiad in western New York State in 1996 (Doran and Anderson 1996), and was used in the experimental design category of the Olympiad. The scenario for the task was designed to be of interest to the students and consistent with a real lab problem.

Students are asked to design an appropriate experiment, conduct the experiment, and report the results. The purpose of this task is similar to that of acid-base testing, but here students must develop their own procedures for use. Students work on this task as a team of up to three students, and have 50 minutes to complete the entire experiment.

The scoring rubric included for this task is the rubric designed by the Science Olympiad Committee for the experimental design task. It is organized into ten skills that are part of designing and conducting experiments. Twelve of the total 27 points are for the design component, which is important to stress with middle level students.

Unknown Solutions
Student Task Sheet

Background:
A scientist found three unlabeled bottles in an area normally reserved for acids. We have labeled these bottles A, B, & C. In order to use or dispose of these solutions properly, your team is being asked to determine if these solutions are acidic, basic, or neutral.

Your task is to design an appropriate experiment to solve the above problem, conduct the experiment you have designed, and report your results. You may use any or all of the materials provided.

You will have 50 minutes for this task. Plan your time carefully.

Materials:
- three dropper bottles, labeled A, B, & C
- one dropper bottle with phenolphthalein
- vial with red litmus paper
- vial with blue litmus paper
- vial with pH paper
- acetate sheet with circles A, B, & C
- background sheet on indicators
- one dropper bottle with distilled water
- paper towel
- waste container

Unknown Solutions
Scoring Rubric

Portion Of Experiment	0	1	2	3
Problem	none stated	statement has many parts missing	statement has one part missing	stated correctly
Hypothesis	none	statement made, but can't be tested	good, but not complete	correct hypotheses for experiment
Independent Variable	incorrectly identified	correctly stated	NA	NA
Dependent Variable	incorrectly identified	correctly stated	NA	NA
Control	incorrectly identified	correctly stated	NA	NA
Procedure and Materials	none	3 or more steps missing	one or two steps missing	no parts missing
Qualitative Observations	none	given, but not relevant to data	given, but obvious ones left out	almost all included
Quantitative Observations	none	wrong calculations done or no calculations shown	correct calculations, but no work shown	correct calculations with work shown
Charts, Graphs, Diagrams	none	sketches with no labels at all	graphs OK, but not labeled	included with proper format and labels
Conclusion	none	incorrect conclusion from data	correct conclusion, but no supporting statements	correct conclusions and well supported
Recommendations	none	minor/trivial change from current experiment	logical, new plan for experiment	creative and feasible recommendation for further experimentation

1. Statement of problem	0 pts	1 pt	2 pts	3 pts
2. Hypothesis	0 pts	1 pt	2 pts	3 pts
3. Independent Variable(s)	0 pts	1 pt		
4. Dependent Variable(s)	0 pts	1 pt		
5. Control(s)	0 pts	1 pt		
6. Procedure and Materials	0 pts	1 pt	2 pts	3 pts
7. Results to included where appropriate:				
a) Qualitative observations	0 pts	1 pt	2 pts	3 pts
b) Quantitative observations	0 pts	1 pt	2 pts	3 pts
c) Use of diagrams, charts, & graphs	0 pts	1 pt	2 pts	3 pts
8. Analysis and Interpretation	0 pts	1 pt	2 pts	3 pts
9. Conclusion: to include why results did or did not support the hypothesis	0 pts	1 pt	2 pts	3 pts
10. Recommendations for further experimentation based on data	0 pts	1 pt	2 pts	3 pts

Total Points _____

Reaction Rates

This task is from the set of six chemistry tasks developed as part of the University at Buffalo/National Opinion Research Center (UB/NORC) joint project (Doran, et al. 1993). This project focused on prototype exams for high school science courses. These tasks assessing the laboratory skills outcomes are complemented by other tests with multiple-choice and free-response items developed as part of the project.

These lab assessments were organized into a Part A and Part B format with Part A requiring students to state hypotheses, plan procedures, and design appropriate data collecting charts for a specific problem. After Part A is complete, students do Part B. As students complete the experi-ment, they collect and record data, make calculations, construct graphs, and formu-late conclusions.

The concepts underlying chemical re-actions are important in chemistry. Factors that affect reaction rates—especially con-centration, temperature, time, and the na-ture of reactants—are important domains of study in chemistry. The application of these concepts in industry allows the effi-cient manufacture of chemicals, fertilizers, and pharmaceuticals. This serves as the context for the "Reaction Rates" task that follows. Students plan and conduct an ex-periment for investigating variables that affect reaction rates using magnesium rib-bon in an acid.

Reaction Rates
Student Task Sheet

Part A

Introduction:

This laboratory test presents a problem. Your task in Part A is to plan and design an experiment to solve the problem. You will have **30 minutes** to complete Part A. At the end of the 30 minutes, your answer sheet will be collected. You will then receive separate directions for Part B. In Part B you use materials and equipment provided in the laboratory kit to collect experimental data for this problem.

Problem:

In many industries, chemists are faced with the task of slowing down explosive reactions or speeding up slow reactions in order to synthesize a product. Your problem is to a) determine two factors that affect the speed of a chemical reaction and b) design an experiment, using the materials (and/or others) listed below, to determine quantitatively the effect of these two factors on the rate of a chemical reaction. Included relevant units appropriate to the data that will be collected.

a) State a HYPOTHESIS for this investigation that can be tested experimentally.

b) Under the heading PROCEDURE list in order the steps of the procedure you will use to solve the problem. You may include a diagram to help illustrate your plans for the experiment. Include any safety procedures you would follow.

c) Construct a DATA TABLE or indicate any other method that you can use to record your observations and results.

NOTE: In Part A you are <u>NOT</u> to proceed with any part of the actual experiment. You are just to plan and organize a way to investigate the problem.

Materials:

- 5 beakers, 100 ml
- graduated cylinder, 25 ml
- scissors
- safety goggles
- watch or stop clock with a second hand
- magnesium ribbon, 50 cm
- calculator

- 1 cm ruler
- hot plate
- graph paper
- thermometer
- balance accurate to 0.01 grams
- 1.0 M HCl, 250 ml

Reaction Rates
Student Task Sheet

Part B

You have 50 minutes to complete this part, in which you investigate the effect of temperature on reaction rates. You have been provided with a detailed Procedure, which you are to follow.

a) Perform the experiment by following the steps outlined in the procedure.

b) Under the heading RESULTS/OBSERVATIONS, record the results of the experiment. Use statements, descriptive paragraphs, and tables of data where appropriate.

c) Construct a GRAPH that demonstrates the relationship between reaction rate and temperature.

d) Under the heading CALCULATIONS, show all your equations and calculations.

e) Under the heading CONCLUSION, give an interpretation of your results. What did you learn from the experiment?

f) At the end of the 50 minutes, your answer sheets will be collected.

Materials:

- 5 beakers, 100 ml
- 1-cm ruler
- graduated cylinder, 25 ml
- hot plate
- scissors
- graph paper
- safety goggles
- thermometer
- watch or stop clock with a second hand
- balance accurate to 0.01 grams
- magnesium (Mg) ribbon, 50 cm
- 1.0 M HCl, 250 ml
- calculator

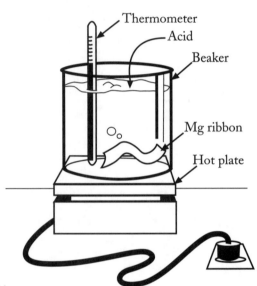

Procedure:

1. Determine the mass of 20 cm of magnesium ribbon.
2. Measure and cut four 5 cm lengths of Mg ribbon.
3. Heat 25 ml of 1.0 M HCl solution to about 20°C. Remove from the heat source. Immediately record the temperature and place one 5 cm length of Mg ribbon in the beaker. Measure the total time for all the Mg to react (disappear).
4. Record your data in table form. Pay attention to units.
5. Give acid to teacher after each stage of the experiment.
6. Repeat steps 3, 4, and 5 for temperatures of 25°C, 30°C, and 35°C.
7. Calculate the reaction rate for each temperature. Plot the collected data on graph paper.
8. Based on your data table and graph, formulate appropriate conclusions.

Safety: Acids and bases are highly corrosive! Students must wear safety goggles at all times. Avoid direct contact with reagents. If any acid touches skin, wash it off immediately with water. Always add acid to water, not water to acid. DO NOT HEAT ACIDS ABOVE 45°C.

Solubility

This task was developed as part of the UB/NORC Project (Doran, et al. 1993). Almost every chemistry activity and demonstration involves the use of one or more solutions. Most acids are used as solutions, as are most indicators. Chemists find it important to determine the solubility of solutes in solvent to make a solution. Water is often called the "universal" solvent, but many other liquids, including alcohol and acetone, also act as solvents. Factors such as temperature and stirring affect the rate at which a solute dissolves in a solvent, but there are limits to how much solute can be dissolved in given solvents at given temperatures. Sometimes when more solute is added to a solvent, a precipitate forms, as no further dissolving takes place. This is called a saturated solution. Graphs that describe these solubility limits are called solubility curves and are characteristic for particular compounds. Hence, they can be used as a method for identifying a compound. That is the purpose of this task.

When this task was designed as part of the UB/NORC project, it was composed of a Part A and a Part B. It could be revised into a "unified" format, in which students design a procedure, and then use it to collect data and identify an unknown salt. Despite the safety of the materials and equipment available, you need to monitor students as they conduct this task to ensure they take appropriate safety precautions. If students are not experienced with complete investigation formats, you can administer the task using the Part A–Part B format.

Solubility
Student Task Sheet

Part A

Introduction:

This laboratory test presents a problem. Your task in Part A is to plan and design an experiment to solve the problem. You have 30 minutes to complete Part A. At the end of the 30 minutes, your answers will be collected. You will then receive separate directions for Part B. In Part B, you use materials and equipment provided in the laboratory kit to collect experimental data for this problem. You may wish to do your preliminary planning on a scratch sheet.

Problem:

Chemists can identify substances by measuring a solubility of the substance in water. Solubility is usually measured in terms of the maximum amount of solute that can be dissolved in 100 grams of the solvent at a specified temperature. You are provided with an unknown substance X. Your problem is to plan and design an experiment using the materials (and/or others) listed below, and to construct the solubility curve for X. This information allows you to identify the unknown substance.

a) List in order the steps of the procedure you will use to solve the problem. You may include a diagram to help illustrate your plans for the experiment. Include any safety procedures you would follow.

b) Construct a data table or indicate any other method that you can use to record your observations and results that will be obtained.

NOTE: In Part A you are <u>NOT</u> to proceed with any part of the actual experiment. You are just to plan and organize a way to investigate the problem.

Materials:

- 4 boiling tubes (large test tubes)
- beaker, 400/500 ml
- stirring rod
- marking pencil
- thermometer
- balance accurate to 0.01 grams
- tongs
- distilled water

- Bunsen burner and mat
- graduated cylinder, 50 ml
- graph paper
- safety goggles
- spatula
- tripod
- beaker tongs or hot mitts
- unknown X

Part B

You have 50 minutes to complete this part. You are provided with a detailed Procedure (below) that you are to follow. Record your work for Part B on a sheet of paper.

a) Perform the experiment by following the steps outlined in the procedure.

b) Record the results of your experiment. Use statements, descriptive paragraphs, and tables of data where appropriate.

c) Construct a graph and plot the data on the graph.

d) Write out your conclusion, giving an interpretation of your results. What did you learn from the experiment?

e) At the end of the 50 minutes, your answers will be collected.

Materials:

- 4 boiling tubes (large test tubes)
- Bunsen burner and mat
- beaker, 400/500 ml
- graduated cylinder, 50 ml
- stirring rod
- graph paper
- marking pencil
- safety goggles
- thermometer
- spatula
- balance accurate to 0.01 grams
- tripod
- tongs
- beaker tongs or hot mitts
- distilled water
- unknown X

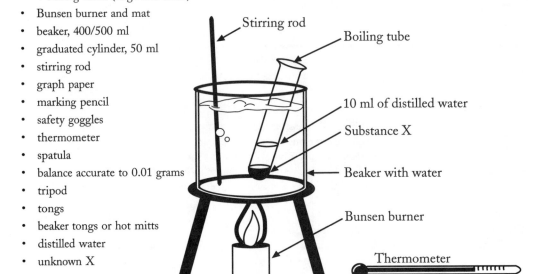

Procedure:

1. Half fill the 400/500 ml beaker with cold tap water.

2. Measure out the following approximate quantities of substance X: 4.0, 5.0, 6.0, and 7.0 grams.

3. Transfer each quantity of substance X into a labeled boiling tube.

4. Use a graduated cylinder to add 10 ml of distilled water to each boiling tube. Mix each tube with a stirring rod, then remove the rod.

5. Place the boiling tube containing the 4.0 gram sample of substance X in the beaker. Warm the water in the beaker gently using a medium flame. Stir the water in the beaker frequently with a stirring rod.

6. Place the thermometer into the boiling tube containing substance X. Use the thermometer to <u>GENTLY</u> stir substance X every 20 seconds.

7. Determine the temperature at which solid X disappears (one small crystal may still remain at the bottom of the test tube). Record this temperature. Remove the beaker from the heat source.

Leave water in the beaker for continuation of the experiment.

8. Repeat steps 5 through 7 for each successive mass of substance X. Begin with the water in the beaker at the temperature at the end of step 7.

9. Plot the collected data on the graph paper provided. Label the axes and solubility curve. Be sure to include this graph paper with your answers to Part B.

10. Raise your hand to contact your instructor. The instructor will check to see that your graph is completed, then give you a sheet labeled "Solubility Curves." Using your data and the information in the "Solubility Curves" figure, determine which substance was your unknown X.

11. State your conclusions.

Safety: Wear safety goggles at all times. Handle hot objects with tongs only. Don't place hot objects on the balance.

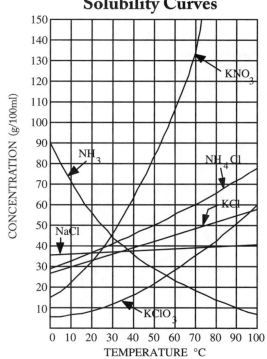

Chemistry Extended Investigation Task

Most extended investigation assessments are outgrowths of successful instructional activities. The teacher can supplement or adapt some "chunk" of instruction with scoring rubrics so that student performance can be reviewed from a slightly different perspective. At least three ways of scoring are possible, with each method requiring a separate rubric. The first method is to use rubrics on student work at particular points or lessons (i.e., planning an experiment or graphing results). This has been called "snapshot assessment," as it is composed of separate probes of student skills. A second way is to rate the product of student work (e.g., written reports, the design of an object or model, an oral presentation). Each of these assessment modes needs a separate rubric. A third way of assessing student work on an extended investigation is with a follow-up test that assesses the student's ability to apply or transfer the concepts and skills learned to a new situation or context. This technique has been used with much success (Baron 1991). When writing your own tasks to assess transfer of concepts, refer to the Novelty section in Chapter 2, page 26. For a discussion of the use of extended investigations, see Chapter 3, page 32.

Chemistry Extended Investigation Task	
Skills Categories	Antacids (page 173)
Planning	✔
Performing	✔
Analyzing	✔
Applying	✔

Antacids

This task appears in *ACS Small-Scale Laboratory Assessment Activities* (1996), published by the American Chemical Society, Division of Chemical Education, Examination Institute. The publication was written by Robert G. Silberman and edited by Lucy Eubanks. The "Antacids" task is reprinted with permission.

Antacids

The Problem:

Devise and carry out an experiment to determine how much magnesium hydroxide is in 1.0 mL of milk of magnesia. Describe the method you developed to solve this problem. [Students can then analyze the claims of various commercial antacids or design experiments to test those claims.]

Assessment Objectives:

The problem tests student understanding of titrations involving a dibasic material, simple experimental design, and the manipulation of titration data.

Materials and Equipment:

Chemicals	Equipment	Possible Distracters
• milk of magnesia • HCl solution (concentration should be between 0.1 M and 1.0 M, and indicated on the label) • phenolphthalein solution	• reaction place, 24-well • micro-tip Beral-type pipettes • graduated Beral-type pipettes	• standard base solution

One Likely Approach:

1. The student measures out a known volume of milk of magnesia, either by counting drops into a small graduated cylinder or by using a graduated Beral-type pipe.

2. The student adds a drop of indicator and titrates with the given acid solution, counting the drops from a micro-tip pipette or by using a graduated pipette, until a clear and colorless endpoint is reached.

3. The student determines the volume of acid used to neutralize the 1.0 mL of milk of magnesia by either counting the number of drops in 1.0 mL of acid or by determining the volume of a drop of acid.

4. The student repeats the titration and also repeats the volume determination.

5. The student calculates the number of moles in the average volume of acid used and uses proportions to determine how much $Mg(OH)_2$ is present in 1.0 mL of milk of magnesia.

Antacids
Scoring Suggestions
(based on 5 points)

1. Measurement of a known volume of milk of magnesia, either by using a graduated Beral-type pipette or by counting drops into a graduated cylinder — **1.0 point**

2. Titration to a phenolphthalein endpoint with acid of known concentration — **1.5 points**

   (a) The student reports only a single value for the number of drops used. — *1.0 point*

   (b) The student reports at least two determinations for the number of drops. — *1.5 points*

   NOTE: It is not strictly necessary to use any indicator, as the disappearance of the white precipitate is a reasonably accurate endpoint in itself.

3. Determination of the volume of acid used — **1.5 points**

   (a) The student reports only a single value for the number of drops in one mL or for the volume of a drop of acid. — *1.0 point*

   Rationale: Reproducibility of results is important in this determination.

   (b) The student reports at least two determinations for the number of drops in one mL or for the volume of a drop of acid. — *1.5 points*

4. Calculating the number of moles in the average volume of acid used and uses proportions to determine $Mg(OH)_2$ present in 1.0 mL — **1.0 point**

   (a) The student calculation neglects that $Mg(OH)_2$ is dibasic. — *0.5 point*

   (b) The student follows the *likely approach* calculation. — *1.0 point*

Extra credit could be awarded if the student

   (a) includes a net ionic equation for the reaction taking place.

   (b) discusses the possible sources of error in the determination.

Notes:

1. "Milk of magnesia" is not a true solution; it is mostly a suspension of the relatively insoluble magnesium hydroxide in water.

2. The problem can be made more challenging and also longer by supplying a standard base solution and an acid solution of unknown concentration. Then students will have to determine the acid's concentration before they proceed with the titration of the magnesium hydroxide.

Special Safety Considerations: Be sure to follow usual safety rules for working with acids and bases.

Works Cited

Baron, J. 1991. Performance Assessment—Blurring the Edge of Assessment, Curriculum, and Instruction. In *Science Assessment in the Service of Reform*, Kulm, G., and Malcolm, S., eds. Washington, DC: American Association for the Advancement of Science.

Doran, R. and Anderson, T. 1996. Design Task—Unknown Solutions. Unpublished document. Buffalo: University at Buffalo.

Doran , R., Boorman, J., Chan, A., and Hejaily, N. 1993. *High School Science Laboratory Performance Tasks.* Buffalo: University at Buffalo.

Kanis, I., Doran, R., and Jacobson, W. 1990. *Assessing Science Process Laboratory Skills at the Elementary and Middle/Junior High Levels.* Washington, DC: National Science Teachers Association.

Mirando, P. A. 1993. *Determination of Validity and Reliability of Four Performance Assessment Instruments Developed for General Chemistry.* Doctoral diss., University at Buffalo.

Reynolds, D., Doran, R., Allers, R., and Agruso, S. 1996. *Alternative Assessment in Science: A Teacher's Guide.* Buffalo: University at Buffalo.

Silberman, R. G. 1996. *American Chemical Society Small-Scale Laboratory Assessment Activities.* Edited by Lucy Eubanks. Clemson, SC: American Chemical Society, Division of Chemical Education, Examination Institute.

Zichitella, G. 2002. *Analysis of the Effect of Structure on Performance Assessment Tasks in High School Chemistry.* Doctoral diss., University at Buffalo.

CHAPTER 7

Illustrative Assessment Tasks for Earth Science

This chapter is organized in three parts: skills tasks, investigations, and extended investigations. All three parts contain models or templates of Earth science assessment tasks, many of which are "complete." These models may be used as is, incorporated into existing assessment programs, adapted and modified to address additional educational objectives, or completely redesigned to form entirely new and innovative assessments.

Earth Science Skills Tasks

The chart below shows the skills tasks in this chapter and the skills they assess. The skills tasks usually focus on one skill, or on a small set of skills assessing a single event or experience. Most skills tasks assess-

ments include student directions, answer sheets, material preparation guidelines, and scoring rubrics. Possible revisions are included with many tasks, so they can be used for other assessments.

A similar chart precedes each of the other two sections of this chapter, Earth Science Investigation Tasks and Earth Science Extended Investigation Tasks. The four skills categories—planning performing, analyzing, and applying—are illustrated in Figures 4.5 and 4.6 (pages 62 and 63). Note that the "applying" category here means more than numerically solving an equation with collected data. It includes skills such as relating or integrating results to underlying themes or models, proposing additional investigations/hypotheses, and suggesting applications beyond the context of the specific investigation.

Earth Science Skills Tasks						
Skills Categories	What's the Angle? (page 177)	How Much Time? (page 178)	Density of Minerals (page 179)	Crustal Sinking (page 182)	Probing under the Surface (page 185)	Earthquake Epicenter (page 189)
Planning						✔
Performing	✔	✔	✔	✔	✔	✔
Analyzing			✔	✔	✔	✔
Applying				✔		✔

What's the Angle?

This task was used in the performance section of New York State's *Earth Science Performance Exam* (NYSED 1991). This task counted for 10 percent of the final exam. It can be varied slightly depending on students' instructional experiences, adding an element of novelty to the task. (For a discussion of novelty, see page 26.)

In this task, students must find the angle between two points on a plastic hemisphere. For a class of 30 students, there would be six sets of five tasks among which students move at the end of five minutes. On each of the six "angle" tasks, a different angle is identified. Each hemisphere is coded for scoring purposes. This procedure eliminates any "leak over" or copying answers from neighbors. The student answer sheet is one piece of paper.

"What's the Angle?" is a straightforward approach to checking whether students are becoming proficient in the skill of measuring angles. The assessment has two strong attributes: it uses equipment that is common to many science laboratories, and it is different from that used during the normal course of instruction.

What's the Angle?
Student Task Sheet

Task: Determine, to the nearest whole degree, the angle between point "X" and point "Y" on the plastic hemisphere.

Materials:

- plastic hemisphere
- external or internal protractor
- marking pencil

Preparation:

To prevent erasure, mark and label point "X" and point 'Y" on the inside of the hemisphere.
The two points should <u>not</u> exceed 90°.
Code each hemisphere.

Scoring:

- A student response within plus or minus 2° of the teacher-determined angle will receive 2 points.
- A student response within plus or minus 4° will receive 1 point.
- A response range greater than plus or minus 4° will receive no credit.

How Much Time?

Time is used to determine reaction rates in chemistry, velocity and acceleration in physics, and rate of growth in biology. Measuring time is an essential skill in many scientific investigations. In this assessment, students are asked to determine how long it takes for a column of water to move through a tube between two points. Although measuring time as part of a student-planned project is more authentic, this task is a way to assess the skill in isolation. This task, like "What's the Angle?," was part of the *Earth Science Performance Exam* (NYSED 1991).

Teachers should be careful to monitor use of the apparatus to be sure it is ready for the next student to use. It is good to be familiar with equipment that might be used in a variety of contexts. However, teachers must be sure that students are skilled with equipment used in their school labs.

How Much Time?
Student Task Sheet

Task: Determine, to the nearest tenth of a second, the amount of time that it takes the column of water to flow through the tube from point A to point B.

Materials:

- stop watch (or wall clock with second hand)
- test tube clamps (2)
- beaker with water (250–500 ml)
- eye dropper tube or drawn glass tube (fire polished)
- plastic column (approximately 50–100 cm long × 4 cm in diameter)
- ring stand
- one hole stopper
- paper towels

Preparation:

1. Set up apparatus as in diagram at the left. Mark two permanent reference lines A and B on the plastic column.

2. Student should place a finger over the end of the narrow tube and add water to the plastic column well above reference line A.

3. Record the time, in seconds, it takes for the water to flow freely between lines A and B.

Cautions:

- Reference lines must be fine and horizontal. Amount of time should be in the range of thirty seconds.

Scoring:

- A student response within plus or minus 2 seconds of the teacher's determined duration will receive two points.
- A response within plus or minus 4 seconds will receive one point.
- A response range greater than plus or minus 4 seconds will receive no credit.

Density of Minerals

This is an excellent task for assessing student skills in measuring the mass, volume, and density of different mineral samples. Although this task is used in many forms, the format used here is from the "Earth Science Task Collection" (NYSED 1996) of the New York State Alternative Assessment in Science Project (Reynolds, et al. 1996).

In this assessment, the overflow cup is used to measure volume because many mineral specimens are too large for most graduated cylinders. (Using very large graduated cylinders can introduce a substantial margin of error.) While a variety of balances can be used, the triple beam balance used here is quite common in most high school lab facilities. Although quartzite and sandstone are used in the follow-up question, any number of sedimentary-metamorphic "pairs" can also be used.

Density of Minerals
Task Information

Preparation:

A. Selection of mineral samples

The samples must:

- fit the size of the overflow cups
- not be soluble
- be those that students are familiar with

B. Marking samples

- Use white paint and a fine tip permanent marker
- Mark the samples A1, B1; A2, B2; etc.

C. Measure mass and volume of samples and record data for use in scoring student work

Safety:

- If graduated cylinders are glass, place a small amount of modeling clay at the bottom of the cylinder to prevent breakage should a mineral sample be dropped.

Extensions/Modifications:

If small specimens of minerals are available and overflow cups are not, minerals may be lowered with a string into the graduated cylinders to get a volume reading.

Density of Minerals
Student Task Sheet

Task: You are to determine the mass, volume, and density of two (2) mineral samples. Record your data and calculations precisely and accurately within the limits of the measurement tools.

Materials:

- metric balance
- overflow cup
- mineral samples A and B
- graduated cylinder
- beaker with water
- calculator

Background:

Minerals are the different materials that make up the various rocks of the earth. Each mineral has its own set of identifying properties. Density is one of the properties often used to identify minerals. Rocks are composed of one or more minerals that have been formed in different ways. The properties of the rocks, made of the same minerals, may be different depending on how the rocks were made. Mineral densities are nearly always the same.

Directions:

1. Record the code number of each mineral sample and find the mass of each to the nearest tenth of a gram.

2. Record the code number and find the volume of each mineral sample to the nearest whole cm^3 (ml).

3. Write out a description of the procedure you used to find the volume of the minerals.

4. What is the <u>density</u> of the mineral samples? Record your answers to the nearest tenth place. Show all your work.

$$\text{density} = \frac{\text{mass}}{\text{volume}}$$

5. The metamorphic rock quartzite and a sedimentary rock sandstone are both made of the mineral quartz that has a density of 2.65 grams/cubic cm (g/cm^3). A geologist determined a sample of quartzite to have a density of 2.65 g/cm^3 and determined the sample of sandstone to have a density of 2.45 g/cm^3. In complete sentences, explain why the sample of quartzite has a different density from the sample of sandstone. In complete sentences, explain why densities of the quartz and the sample of quartzite are the same.

Density of Minerals
Scoring Rubric

Task 1: Mass   6 points total

Performance Standard: Students determine and record precise measurements of mass (to be compared with teacher-determined values).

Criteria:

A. Mass of mineral A

- allow 2 points if the mass is +/− 0.2 g
- allow 1 point if the mass is +/− 0.5 g
- no credit is given if the mass is +/− > 0.5 g

B. Mass of mineral B

- allow 2 points if the mass is +/− 0.2 g
- allow 1 point if the mass is +/− 0.5 g
- no credit is given if the mass is +/− > 0.5 g

C Labeling

- allow 1 point for labeling <u>both</u> measurements with units

D. Recording

- allow 1 point for all data accurately recorded to the nearest tenth of a gram

Task 2: Volume   6 points total

Performance Standard: Students determine and record precise measurements of volume using the displacement method (to be compared with teacher-determined values).

Criteria:

A. Volume of mineral sample A

- allow 2 points if the volume is +/− 1 cm^3
- allow 1 point if the volume is +/− 2 cm^3
- no credit is given if the volume is +/− > 2 cm^3

B. Volume of mineral B

- allow 2 points if the volume is +/− 1 cm^3
- allow 1 point if the volume is +/− 2 cm^3
- no credit is given if the volume is +/− > 2 cm^3

C. Labeling

- allow 1 point for labeling <u>both</u> measurements with units

D. Recording

- allow 1 point for all data accurately recorded to the nearest whole milliliter

Comment #1: The units cm^3 and ml are both acceptable based on the student's instruction.

Task 3: Volume Procedure   2 points total

Performance Standard: Students describe the displacement procedure for determining volume.

Criteria:

- allow 2 points for a clear, accurate description of the displacement method
- allow 1 point for a partially accurate or partially unclear description
- no credit is given if the answer is unclear, inaccurate, or not provided
- complete sentences are not required to receive credit

Task 4: Density Calculations   **8 points total**

Performance Standard: Students calculate the density of mineral samples and show work.

Criteria:

Mineral sample A:

A. Substitution

- allow 1 point for correct substitutions into the equation. (Units not required.)

B. Calculation (See comment #2 below.)

- allow 2 points if the density is +/− 0.2 g/cm^3 or g/ml
- allow 1 point if the density is +/− 0.5 g/cm^3 or g/ml
- no credit is given if the density is +/− > 0.5 g/cm^3 or g/ml

Mineral sample B:

A. Substitution

- allow 1 point for correct substitutions into the equation. (Units not required.)

B. Calculation (See comment #2 below.)

- allow 2 points if the density is +/− 0.2 g/cm^3 or g/ml
- allow 1 point if the density is +/− 0.5 g/cm^3 or g/ml
- no credit is given if the density is +/− > 0.5 g/cm^3 or g/ml

Labeling and Recording:

A. Labeling

- allow 1 point if both answers are labeled correctly

B. Recording

- allow 1 point if both answers are recorded to the nearest tenth of a g/cm^3 or g/ml

Comment #2: Double jeopardy: The student should not be penalized twice for the same error. Answers should be consistent with, and based on, data recorded in earlier parts of the question.

Task 5: Rock Differences   **3 points total**

Performance Standard: Students give a logical, scientifically accurate explanation for differences or similarities in rock densities.

Criteria:

A. Sedimentary rocks are composed of cemented grains and include pore space or other minerals between the grains. The density of the sandstone is likely to be lower than the quartzite bcause of the inclusion of pore space or less dense minerals in the sandstone. The metamorphic process which produces the quartzite causes a high amount of compaction.

- allow 2 points for a logical statement in complete sentences
- allow 1 point for a logical answer that is not given in complete sentences
- no credit for inaccurate answers

B. Both samples are made of the mineral quartz and the density of quartz is 2.65 g/cm^3. Quartzite contains very little or no pore space.

- allow 1 point for a correct response
- allow no point for an incorrect response

Maximum score – 25 points

Crustal Sinking

Models are an important intellectual idea in science. They allow scientists to examine characteristics of very large and very small natural objects using a more approachable size or time scale. In this task, a polymer—called glop, oobleck, or goop—is used to model crustal sinking. This allows students to view a phenomenon that takes much longer in nature.

Teachers should be very careful with this activity; the glop mixture is poisonous if ingested. If the material is accidentally consumed, call the local poison control center immediately. Borax is an eye irritant; any eyes that have been contaminated with glop should be flushed with water immediately. The students should thoroughly wash their hands after the task is completed. This task could be extended with different "recipes" of glop used by different students or two samples used for comparing results.

This task, from the "Earth Science Task Collection" (NYSED 1996) of the New York State Alternative Assessment in Science (Reynolds, et al. 1996), requires measurement and graphing skills, as well as skills at interpreting data and extending conclusions to new situations.

Crustal Sinking
Task Information

Materials:

Teacher:

- prepare "glop" (store in resealable plastic bags)
- prepare calibrated test tubes
- clear tape
- test tube with scale

Per Student:

- 1 250 ml beaker containing "glop"
- ring stand
- test tube clamp
- timer

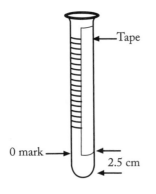

Preparation:

"Glop" recipe:

- dissolve 75 ml Borax in one liter of water and set aside
- mix equal parts of white glue and water; do not use fluorescent Elmer's glue
- add food coloring to the glue mixture
- combine the glue mixture and the Borax mixture in a 3:1 ratio

  – mix until the glop has the consistency of silly putty

  – a more concentrated solution of Borax will give you a "stiffer" mixture

  – try several recipes using modest volumes until you find one that works well

  – store the glop in an airtight container and refrigerate in sealed plastic bags for long-term storage

Calibrated test tube:

- make a transparency of the metric ruler from a reference table or textbook (cut to fit test tube used)
- insert the metric ruler inside test tube to have the zero mark about 2.5 cm above the bottom of the test tube (refer to diagram)
- tape transparency to inside of test tube. (the test tube is now ready for use and can be stored for future use)

Safety:

- the glop mixture contains Borax, which is poisonous if ingested. If this material is accidentally eaten, call the poison control center immediately
- Borax is also an eye irritant. Eyes that may have been contaminated with glop should be flushed with water immediately
- students should be cautioned and instructed to wash hands after the task

Extensions/Modifications:

You may change the consistency of the glop to produce different sets of data; keep detailed records of any changes you make. You may vary the rate of crustal sinking by putting weights or water inside the test tube.

Crustal Sinking
Student Task Sheet

Task: You will observe and analyze a model of the interaction between the Earth's crust and upper mantle.

Materials:

- 1, 250 ml beaker containing glop
- timer
- ring stand
- test tube clamp
- test tube with scale

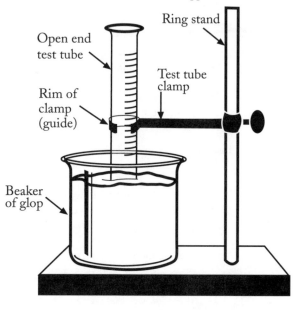

Background:

Some geologists believe the theory that there is a semi-fluid layer 100 to 300 kilometers below the Earth's surface. Due to high temperature and pressure, the rock in this region behaves both like a solid and a liquid. Slow movements in this region are thought to be related to changes in the upper crust and to fractures in the Earth's surface. The model in this activity may demonstrate how these changes can occur.

Directions:

1. Set up the equipment exactly as it appears in the diagram above.

2. Before placing the test tube clamp on the ring stand, adjust the opening of the clamp so that the test tube will slide easily through it; do <u>not</u> use the clamp to hold the test tube, but rather to guide its movement.

3. Place the test tube within the clamp and directly over the glop in the beaker. Hold the test tube above the glop, but do <u>not</u> allow it to rest on the glop yet.

4. Turn the test tube so that the lines and numbers can be read easily.

5. Carefully hold the test tube so that it just touches the surface of the glop. Using the bottom rim of the clamp as your guide, make sure that the scale on the test tube reads zero; move the clamp if necessary.

6. Release the test tube and start the timer.

7. Read the level of the test tube to the nearest tenth of a centimeter every 30 seconds. For each reading, record the level using the rim of the clamp as your guide (refer to above diagram). Take readings for a minimum of 5 minutes.

8. Construct a table, and record your observations regarding the level of the graduated test tube. Make a line graph of your data using time and change in level as your variables. Label both axes and include proper units.

9. Assume that your data is an accurate model for the behavior of a mountain range such as the Himalayas or the Adirondacks. How would the <u>rate</u> of sinking of the mountains early in their formation compare with the rate late in their development? Answer in complete sentences.

10. Based on your observations of this model, explain one possibility why the crust is usually pushed deeper into the earth below old mountains than under newly formed mountains. Answer in complete sentences.

11. List at least three factors in the natural world that have <u>not</u> been accounted for in this model.

Crustal Sinking
Scoring Rubric

Task 1–7: Directions   No credit

Task 8A: Data Table   3 points total

Standard: Students make precise measurements and record them accurately in a data table.

Criteria:

A. 2 points for a completed data table
- refers to five minutes of data recorded every half minute
- 1 point for recording data at all intervals
- 1 point for sequential and consistent data at all intervals

B. 1 point for accurately recorded data
- data must be recorded to the nearest tenth of a centimeter

Task 8B: Graph   6 points total

Standard: Students correctly set up graph axes, plot data points, and draw a line graph.

Criteria:

A. 1 point for correct labeling of both axes.

B. 1 point for correct units recorded on both axes

C. 1 point for appropriate scale on both axes

D. Data correctly plotted
- 2 points for 7–10 points accurately plotted
- 1 point for 3–6 points accurately plotted
- 0 points for 2 or fewer points accurately plotted

E. 1 point for accurately drawn line graph

Task 9: Relating Model   2 points total

Standard: Students relate the model to their knowledge of geologic processes.

Criteria:

- 2 points if the student indicates a change of the rate of sinking consistent with his or her graph in a complete sentence. Student should refer to the rate of sinking of mountains or land masses
- 1 point if answer is consistent with student's graph but not a complete sentence

Task 10: Crust Thickness   2 points total

Standard: Students explain how and why geologic processes occur based on their observations of the model.

Criteria:

- 2 points for a reasonable explanation that relates a knowledge of mountains to the model
- 1 point for a reasonable explanation that is not in a complete sentence

Samples:

– Crust is usually pushed deeper beneath old mountains because they have existed for a longer time. The test tube settles deeper over time

– Crust would be pushed deeper under older mountains but might be sinking at a slower rate. As time goes on this is similar to what is shown by the slope of the graph

Task 11: Other Factors   3 points total

Standard: Students identify two or more factors not addressed by the model.

Criteria:

- 3 points for three reasonable factors
- 2 point for two reasonable factors
- 1 point if only one factor is given

Samples:

– erosion	– weathering	– volcanism
– differing materials	– faults	

Maximum score – 16 points

Probing under the Surface

This task, from the "Earth Science Task Collection" (NYSED 1996) of the New York State Alternative Assessment in Science Project (Reynolds, et al. 1996), is an example of a "black box" in the Earth science area. It uses very common materials (shoe boxes, Styrofoam blocks, and straws) and can be prepared easily by teachers and students. A wide variety of box bottoms can be constructed for variety as well as security. While made of very common materials, it is a good model of the basic probing methodology.

Although this example contains just one series of holes for probing, several lines or entire fields could be developed with a larger box using a matrix of horizontal and vertical holes for probing.

Probing under the Surface
Task Information

Preparation:

Measuring Stick:

- use a small wooden dowel or skewer 0.3–0.6 cm in diameter and at least 5 cm longer than the box height.
- mark off the dowel in centimeters and label 0–15, using a fineline permanent marker.

Mystery Box:

- use regular size shoe boxes.
- cut and/or shape Styrofoam blocks to different levels; a handy knife or coarse file will do this (see diagrams, below)
- boxes must be all the same <u>or</u> coded to match student papers with an answer key
- glue Styrofoam blocks at 3 or 4 different levels inside the bottom of the box
- cover the tops of the styrofoam blocks with tag board, cardboard, or a manila folder; this keeps the measuring stick from poking into the Styrofoam
- the depth between hole three (3) and hole five (5) should show significant changes
- on the top of each box, place a row of 10 (ten) equally separated dots
- number the dots 1–10
- use a drill or sharp pair of scissors to poke holes through the top of the box on the <u>odd numbered dots</u>
- be sure that the holes are large enough for the measuring stick to fit through, but <u>not</u> so large that you can see into the box
- measure and record the actual depth reading of each box at each dot to serve as the answer key
- seal the edges of the box top on the box with clear packing tape
- students should not be able to see inside the box at all during the activity

Safety: Watch that the students don't push the probe down too hard, causing them to break the measuring sticks.

Extensions/Modifications: Students may wish to design their own hidden surfaces.

Materials:

Per Student:

- measuring stick
- mystery box

Sample Mystery Box Diagram:

(side view, inside of shoe box)

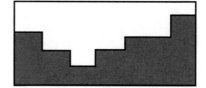

(top view)

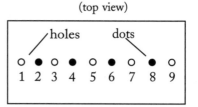

Probing under the Surface
Student Task Sheet

Task: You will use a measuring stick to determine the possible shape of the inside bottom of a box.

Materials:
- measuring stick
- mystery box

Background:

Scientists and engineers use remote sensing to create an image of objects that they cannot see. To observe the shape of the ocean bottom, oceanographers use the reflection of sound waves (sonar) or radio waves (radar) to "see" the ocean floor. In this activity you will use a stick as a remote sensor to indirectly observe the surface shape of the inside bottom of a mystery box that models a surface like the ocean bottom that we cannot directly observe.

Directions:

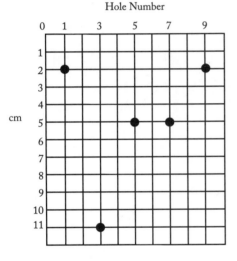

Hole Number

cm

1. Slide the measuring stick into each hole marked on the box lid.
2. Measure the distance to the nearest tenth of a cm to the bottom of the box for each hole.
3. Construct a data table, and record your measurements. Make a line graph of your data using hole number and distance to the bottom as your variables. Label both axes.
4. Use complete sentences to describe what your graph indicates about the shape of the bottom of the box.
5. Based on your graph, predict the depth of the inside bottom of the box at spot 4. In complete sentences, explain the reason for your prediction in the space below.
6. Make a drawing of what you think the inside bottom of the box looks like.
7. In complete sentences, explain how you determined the shape of the inside bottom of the box <u>between</u> the spots?
8. Below is a set of observations made on another box. Which of the drawings <u>could</u> represent the shape of the bottom of the box? (Circle the letters of as many choices that could be possible.)

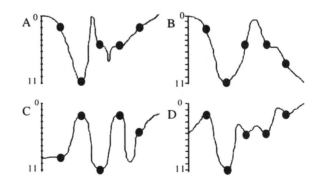

9. Suppose you were given a measuring tool that was only 6 cm long. In complete sentences, explain how this would change your drawing of the inside bottom of the box.

Probing under the Surface
Scoring Rubric

Tasks 1–2: Directions   No credit

Task 3a: Data Table   7 points total

Standard: Students measure the distance to the bottom of the box and record these data accurately and precisely in a data table.

Criteria:

A. 1 point for <u>each</u> accurate measurement +/− 1.0 cm (based on teacher's data)

B. 1 point if <u>all</u> measurements are rounded to the nearest tenth of a centimeter

C. 1 point if <u>all</u> measurements are labeled with the correct units

Task 3b: Graph   6 points total

Standard: Students use the data from their tables to draw a graph representing a profile of the surface of the bottom of the box.

Criteria:

A. 1 point if both axes are correctly labeled with variable

B. 1 point if both axes have appropriate scale

C. 1 point if both axes have correct units given

D. 2 points if 5 points are correctly plotted

    1 point if 4 points are correctly plotted

    0 points if fewer than 4 points are correctly plotted

E. 1 point if the line is correctly drawn; dot to dot or best fit curve may be acceptable

Task 4: Shape Description   2 points total

Standard: Students describe the shape of the bottom of the box using their data to draw inferences about the profile of an unobservable surface.

Criteria:

• 2 points if the statement is descriptive and is generally consistent with the table and graph using complete sentences

• 1 point if the statement is correct but is not complete sentences

• 0 points if statement is incorrect, even if it is in complete sentences

Task 5: Estimation   4 points total

Standard: Students predict the elevation of an unknown value between two known values, and justify that prediction. The prediction should be based on the student's graph.

Criteria:

A. 2 points for correctly estimating the value and unit at spot four (4), based on their line (+/− 0.1 cm) between holes 3 and 5

    1 point for correct value +/− 0.2 cm

B. 2 points for a reasonable explanation for their prediction in complete sentences

    1 point for a reasonable explanation that is not in complete sentences

    0 points for an unacceptable explanation

Continued on next page.

Task 6: Model Drawing   1 point total

Standard: Students draw a two-dimensional representation of a three-dimensional surface based on their graph data.

Criteria:

- 1 point for a drawing that matches the graph in #3

Task 7: Reason for Drawing   2 points total

Standard: Students explain inferences based on observations.

Criteria:

- 2 points for a reasonable explanation based on their data, using complete sentences
- 1 point for a reasonable explanation based on their data that is not in complete sentences
- 0 points for an unreasonable explanation

Task 8: Graph Representation   2 points total

Standard: Students interpret the data from the graph to make an inference.

Criteria:

- 2 points if both graphs A and D are selected with no other selections
- 1 point if only graph A or D is selected, with no incorrect selections
- 1 point if both graphs A and D are selected, and one incorrect selection is made
- 0 points if 2 incorrect graphs are selected

Task 9: Explanation of Limited Stick   2 points total

Standard: Students predict the results of the limits of measurement

Criteria:

- 2 points if a logical explanation is given that the graph would reflect the lack of data beyond the limits of the measuring stick using complete sentences
- 1 point if logical explanation is not in complete sentences
- 0 points if explanation is not logical

Maximum Score – 26 points

Earthquake Epicenter

This task, from the "Earth Science Task Collection" (NYSED 1996) of the New York State Alternative Assessment in Science Project (Reynolds, et al. 1996), is similar to related instructional activities, but with different locations of sites and different "lag times." This task does require use of some mathematical calculations and logic to locate an epicenter. It assumes students have studied earthquakes and have some understanding of epicenters. One can easily use maps of fictitious countries as well as supplemental maps with natural features, such as mountains and rivers, and manufactured features, such as cities and roads. This could allow a number of extensions beyond the basic task presented here.

Earthquake Epicenter
Student Task Sheet

Task: Using data in the chart below, the student will determine the location of the epicenter of an earthquake.

Background: When an earthquake occurs, scientists need to determine the location of its epicenter as soon as possible. The epicenter is the point on the surface of the Earth directly above the earthquake. Measurements from at least three seismographic stations allow scientists to locate the epicenter.

Materials:
- calculator
- compass
- map
- P–S wave graph

Safety: Use compasses appropriately.

Directions: The data in the table are the delay times between the P and S waves from an earthquake to three stations (A, B, and C).

Station	Delay Time Between P and S Wave Arrivals	Distance from Earthquake (km)	Distance on Map (cm)
A	5 minutes, 20 seconds		
B		1 minute, 40 seconds	
C	3 minutes, 20 seconds		

1. Find the distance of each station from the earthquake using the delay times between the P and S waves and the graph on the next page. Record these distances in the table. The delay time for a given distance is the time between graphs of that distance.
2. Locate the epicenter of the earthquake on the map on the next page. Calculate and record your map distances in the table. Indicate the epicenter location with the letter X. The scale of the map is 1 cm = 300 kilometers.
3. Write out a description of 3 procedures you used to locate the epicenter of the earthquake. Answer in complete sentences.

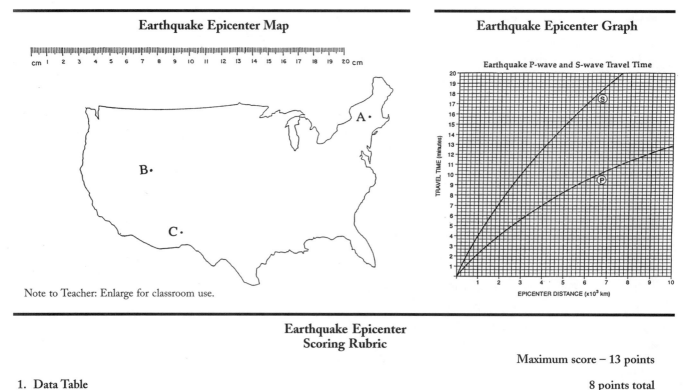

Earthquake Epicenter Map

cm 1 2 3 4 5 6 7 8 9 10 11 12 13 14 15 16 17 18 19 20 cm

A·

B·

C·

Note to Teacher: Enlarge for classroom use.

Earthquake Epicenter Graph

Earthquake P-wave and S-wave Travel Time

TRAVEL TIME (minutes)

EPICENTER DISTANCE (x10³ km)

Earthquake Epicenter
Scoring Rubric

Maximum score – 13 points

1. **Data Table**   8 points total

   Standard: The student will determine the distance from the earthquake epicenter.

   Criteria:

   Distance from earthquake

   Answers: A = 3700 km, B = 900 km, C = 2000 km

   • allow 2 points for each correct distance recorded within +\– 200 km
   • allow 1 point for each correct distance recorded within +\– 400 km
   • allow 0 points for distances recorded +\– > 400 km

   Distance on map

   Answers: A = 12.3 cm, B = 3.0 cm, C = 6.7 cm

   • allow 2 points if 3 of the distances recorded are within +\– 1.0 cm
   • allow 1 point if 2 distances are within +\– 1.0 cm
   • allow 0 points for 1 or less distances within range

2. **Location of epicenter**   2 points total

   Standard: By using the triangulation method, the student will identify the epicenter.

   Criteria:

   • allow 2 points for the correct placement of the letter "X" at the intersection of the 3 lines or a small triangle.
   • allow 1 point for the correct placement of the letter "X" where 2 lines intersect.
   • allow 0 points for the omission of the letter "X"

3. **Procedures**   3 points total

   Standard: Using complete sentences, the student will describe 3 procedures used to find the epicenter.
   (Three likely procedures are (1) used graph to find distances from stations; (2) converted distance from
   stations to distance for map, using map scale; (3) drew circles on maps with lines for each station.)

   Criteria:

   • allow 3 points if the student's response has three (3) logical and reasonable descriptions; the answers
     must be in complete sentences
   • allow 2 points if there are 2 logical and reasonable descriptions in complete sentences
   • allow 1 point for 1 logical and reasonable response in a complete sentence
   • allow 1 point for logical and reasonable answers <u>not</u> in complete sentences

Earth Science Investigation Tasks

The three Investigation Tasks presented here are designed for a double period (approximately 80 minutes). These tasks can be restructured, depending on the level of familiarity of students with planning and conducting investigations.

For most of these Investigation Tasks, students will need to record their answers in either their laboratory logbook or on two blank sheets of paper. Specific instructions for what students should record, and the labels they should use, are given in each task. Generally, students will be asked to record their hypothesis, their procedure (including any diagrams), and their data table (including their observations) on one sheet in a reasonably finished form. The other sheet is to be used as scratch paper. If the task has a Part B, students will usually need a piece of graph paper and a third sheet for recording their conclusions. You may wish to hand out prepared answer sheets with the headings already in place. The chart below identifies the skills assessed by the three Earth science Investigation Tasks that follow.

Earth Science Investigation Tasks

Skills Categories	Water Holding Capacity (page 192)	Angle of Insolation (page 194)	Weathering (page 196)
Planning	✔	✔	✔
Performing	✔	✔	✔
Analyzing	✔	✔	✔
Applying			✔

Water Holding Capacity

This task was developed and trial tested as part of a National Science Foundation–sponsored project—Prototype High School Science Assessment. The project was a joint venture of the University at Buffalo (UB) and the National Opinion Research Center (NORC). The task was initially organized into a two-part format as described by its developers (Doran, et al. 1993). It is presented here as a "unified" task with students proceeding on their own from beginning to end. This task is an example of many that relate several content areas—in this case, Earth science and biology. The materials are common to science labs and most homes. This task is quite unstructured, and can be modified or extended in many ways.

The scoring for this task is based on the analytical rubric developed by the UB/NORC project. The investigation model for all tasks in all science areas used the seven skills and the five elements of each skill that are seen in the scoring form on page 193.

Water Holding Capacity
Student Task Sheet

Introduction:

This laboratory test presents a problem. Your task is to plan, design, and conduct an experiment to solve the problem. You will have 80 minutes to complete the investigation. You may use any of the materials and equipment listed below to collect experimental data for this problem.

Problem:

The retention of water by different materials affects their use by plants and animals. Your problem is to determine the water holding capacity of sand, soil, and moss.

Materials:

- water, approximately 800 ml in a large beaker
- 100 ml graduated cylinder
- 3 funnels, 100 mm top diameter
- 3 funnel supports (ring stands or tripods)
- 3, 250 ml beakers
- 3 pieces of filter paper (18.5 cm in diameter)
- clock/timer
- balance (accurate to +/– 0.1 gram)

- dry potting soil, 100 g
- dry sand, 100 g
- dry sphagnum moss, 100 g
- wax marking pencil
- 1 spoon
- paper towels
- 3 paper cups

a) State a HYPOTHESIS for this investigation that relates to the water holding capacity of sand, soil, and moss.

b) List in order the steps you will use to solve the problem (PROCEDURE). You may include a diagram to help illustrate your plans for the experiment. Include any safety procedures you would follow. Make your procedure detailed enough so someone else could follow it easily.

c) Construct a DATA TABLE or indicate any other method that you could use to record the observations and results that will be obtained.

d) Perform the experiment by following the steps outlined in your procedure.

e) Under the heading RESULTS record your observations and measurements for the experiment. Use written statements, descriptive paragraphs, tables of data, and/or graphs where appropriate. Under the heading CONCLUSIONS write an interpretation of your results.

f) Note any limitations to your investigation.

g) Write a report of your experiment, including the sections mentioned above.

Water Holding Capacity
Scoring Form

1. Circle the NA code if a skill is _not assessed_ in a particular area.
2. The NR code is to be circled when _no attempt_ to respond to the question is apparent.
3. You may check each element present and sum up to determine a student's score for each skill.
4. There is _no_ need to determine a total score for a student.

1. Statement of hypothesis   NR   0   1   2   3   4   5 NA
   - Effect linked to variable   _____
   - Directionality of effect   _____
   - Expected effect/change   _____
   - Independent variable   _____
   - Dependent variable   _____

2. Procedure for investigation   NR   0   1   2   3   4   5 NA
   - Detailed procedure/experimentally feasible _____
   - Sequence to plan   _____
   - General strategy   _____
   - Safety procedures   _____
   - Use of equipment/diagram of set-up   _____

3. Plan for recording and   NR   0   1   2   3   4   5 NA
   organizing observations/data
   - Space for measured/calculated data   _____
   - Matched to plan   _____
   - Organized sequentially   _____
   - Labeled fully (units included)   _____
   - Variables identified   _____

4. Quality of the observations/data   NR   0   1   2   3   4   5 NA
   - Consistent data   _____
   - Accurate measurements/observations   _____
   - Completed data table   _____
   - Correct units   _____
   - Qualitative description   _____

5. Graph   NR   0   1   2   3   4   5 NA
   - Curve is appropriate to data trend   _____
   - Points plotted accurately   _____
   - Appropriate scale   _____
   - Axes labeled with variables and units   _____
   - Variables placed on correct axes   _____

6. Calculations   NR   0   1   2   3   4   5 NA
   - Calculated accurately   _____
   - Substituted correctly into relationship   _____
   - Relationship stated or implied   _____
   - Units used correctly   _____
   - Used all data available   _____

7. Forms a conclusion from   NR   0   1   2   3   4   5 NA
   the experiment
   - Consistent with scientific principle   _____
   - Sources of error   _____
   - Consistent with data   _____
   - Relationship among variables stated   _____
   - Variables stated in conclusion   _____

Angle of Insolation

This task was created within the two-part format of the UB/NORC project described briefly for the previous task, "Water Holding Capacity." The problem here is a bit more authentic, as most adolescents would be interested in suntans or sunburns. The concepts involved with the task are key to understanding what causes the temperature variation in our seasons and how the tilt of the Earth's axis explains the occurrence of seasons.

This task is more structured than the previous task and includes detailed procedures, a diagram for the equipment, and a table for collected data. Any or all of these could be deleted, creating a less-structured task (when your students are ready for less structure). The same scoring system used with "Water Holding Capacity" can be used here.

Angle of Insolation
Student Task Sheet

Part A

Introduction:

This laboratory test presents a problem and lists materials available to you. Your task is to design a strategy for solving the problem. Please record all your work. You will have 30 minutes to plan and design an experiment to solve the problem. You will collect data in a later part.

Problem:

The angle of insolation is the angle at which the sun's radiation strikes the Earth. After school's out in June, you and your family, who live in New York State, take a trip south to Florida. Your parents tell you to stay out of the sun between 11 am and 1 pm because, just as the sun is "colder" at the North Pole, the sun is "hotter" here than at home. Using your knowledge of the relationship of the Earth to the Sun's rays during the summer solstice, prove or disprove their statement.

a) Under the heading PROCEDURE, list in order the steps of the procedure you will use to solve the problem. You may include a diagram to help illustrate your plans for the experiment. Include all safety procedures.

b) Construct a DATA TABLE, or indicate any other method that you could use to record the observations and results that will be obtained.

c) At the end of 30 minutes, your answers for Part A will be collected.

Note: In Part A, you are NOT to proceed with any part of the actual experiment. You are just to plan and organize a way to investigate the problem.

Materials:
*   3 right triangular wooden blocks (30°, 60°, & 90°)
*   a watch or clock
*   3 thermometers
*   a high wattage lamp
*   masking tape
*   metric ruler

Part B

Introduction:

You have 50 minutes to complete this part. You are provided with a detailed procedure, which you are to follow. Record your work for Part B, and use appropriate headings.

Problem:

The angle of insolation is the angle at which the sun's radiation strikes the Earth. After school's out in June, you and your family, who live in New York State, take a trip to Florida. Your parents tell you to stay out of the sun between 11 am and 1 pm because, just as the sun is "colder" at the North Pole, the sun is "hotter" here than at home. Using your knowledge of the relationship of the Earth to the Sun's rays during the summer solstice, prove or disprove their statement.

a) Perform the experiment by following the steps outlined in the procedure.
b) Under the heading RESULTS/OBSERVATIONS, record the data collected in the experiment. Use statements, descriptive paragraphs, and tables of data where appropriate.
c) Under the heading CALCULATIONS, show all equations and calculations used.
d) Construct a GRAPH that shows the relationship between the variables measured.
e) Under the heading CONCLUSION, give an interpretation of your results.
f) At the end of the 50 minutes, your answers will be collected.

Materials:

- 3 right triangular wooden blocks (30°, 60°, & 90°)
- a watch or clock
- 3 thermometers
- a high wattage lamp
- masking tape
- metric ruler

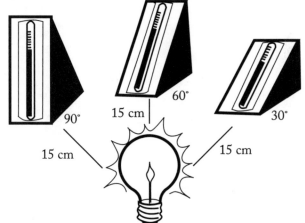

Complete the Procedure as given. Record your data in the table.

Procedure:

1) Tape one thermometer to the 30° angle of one block of wood. Tape the second thermometer to the 60° angle of the second block of wood. Tape the third thermometer to the 90° angle of the third block of wood.
2) Set up the light source.
3) Arrange the three blocks of wood so that each is 15 cm from the light source.
4) Record the temperature in °C of each block at time zero in the data table.
5) Turn on the light and record the temperature of each block every minute for 15 minutes.

Weathering

This investigation task is designed to be completed in one class period (approximately 45 minutes). It involves a key process to weathering—the effect of water on soluble rock material. The rock "model" for this assessment is a common effervescent antacid tablet, which allows students to observe the phenomena in a much shorter time period.

The focus of this assessment task is on students designing and carrying out an experiment. As the materials provided could influence student plans, a teacher could include more materials, such as marbles, aquarium gravel, etc., or allow students to determine an appropriate "model." This activity has been done with single students and with pairs of students, with pairs performing better (Chan 1997). Students may be interested in using different brands of tablets or tablets that had been sitting in the air for some time.

Weathering
Task Information

Time: 45 minutes

Materials:

Teacher:
- distribution method for hot H_2O
- cooler for ice
- hot water supply

Per student:
- 3 clear plastic cups (100 ml line marked)
- 2 Styrofoam or insulated cups (approximately 250 ml each for transfer of hot and cold H_2O)
- 1 thermometer
- 1 timer
- 4 effervescent antacid tablets
- waste bucket
- paper towels
- hot water (45°–50°C)
- ice water
- room temperature water

Preparation:
- Temperatures above 50°C tend to cause the tablet to dissolve so violently that the beaker will overflow. Also, such temperatures are unlikely to occur in nature.
- Students should be encouraged to use 1–3 tablets.
- The <u>time</u> when the tablets dissolve should be carefully observed.
- Teacher needs to mark a 100 ml line on the clear plastic cups.

Safety:
- Students should be <u>cautioned</u> to be careful using the hot plate and the hot water. Water should not exceed 50°C.
- Students <u>must not</u> sample the antacid tablets before dissolving them or the solutions that result after the tablets dissolve.

Extensions/Modifications:

Try experiment with different sized pieces of tablet. They could vary in rates of weathering.

Weathering
Student Task Sheet

Task: You will be observing a model of weathering processes.

Materials:

- 3 clear plastic cups (100 ml line marked)
- 2 Styrofoam or insulated cups (approximately 250 ml each for transfer of hot and cold H_2O)
- 4 effervescent antacid tablets
- paper towels

- 1 thermometer
- 1 timer
- waste bucket
- hot water (45°–50°C)
- room temperature water
- ice water

Background:

What effect does water temperature have on the rate of a chemical reaction similar to the interaction of a weak acid and carbonate rock such as limestone or marble? To examine this question, you will observe a model that simulates the interaction of water and limestone. The "limestone" in your model will be an effervescent antacid tablet. This tablet will dissolve in water much more quickly than the limestone in nature, making it possible for you to collect data during this task.

Procedure:

1. Put 100 ml room temperature water into the marked, clear cup. Construct a data table, and record its temperature.
2. Set your timer to zero or watch the wall clock. Place one tablet into the cup of water. Measure the time it takes for the tablet to dissolve completely, and record this time on your data table.
3. Using only the materials listed above, design a controlled experiment to determine the effect of temperature on the rate of weathering.
4. Write out the steps you will follow in performing a controlled experiment. Be specific enough so that another student could follow your directions and successfully complete the experiment.
5. Conduct your experiment. Do NOT use water with a temperature above 50°C. Summarize all data in your data table.
6. Use the data from your table to construct a graph. Graph your data using temperature and time as your variables. Label both axes.
7. If this experiment was repeated with the antacid tablets ground into a fine powder, what do you think the result would be? Draw a dashed line on the graph that you think would show the result. Use complete sentences to explain why you placed the line where you did.
8. If this activity were an accurate model of the actual weathering of rock material on the Earth, how would temperatures affect the rate of weathering of rock surfaces? Answer in a complete sentence.
9. Describe how you would design an experiment to explore the effects that variations in the strength of weak acid solutions would have on the rate of weathering. Include at least 4 variables that you would consider.

Weathering
Scoring Rubric

Tasks 1–3: Procedures   No Credit

Task 4: Design   5 points total
Standard: Students design an experiment to show effect of temperature on chemical weathering.
Criteria:
Allow 1 point for each of the following:
* the use of two or more water temperatures
* a controlled amount of water used for each test
* the same number of tablets used for each test
* some form of timing of the reactions at the different temperatures
* laboratory safety is reflected in the procedure

Task 5a: Experiment   No Credit

Task 5b: Recording of Data   3 points total
Standard: Students record data that were collected.
Criteria:
Allow 1 point for each of the following:
* recording initial time/temperature data
* recording each experimental value (up to 2 points)
    2 points if all data are accurately recorded
    1 point if some data are inaccurate or missing

Task 6: Graph   4 points total
Standard: Students graph data that were collected.
Criteria:
Allow 1 point for each of the following:
* both axes are labeled properly
* both axes have proper units
* two or more correctly plotted points on the graph
* properly drawn line connecting data points

Task 7: Prediction   3 points total
Standard: The student shows an appropriate line on the graph.
Criteria:
* Allow 1 point for a line drawn that shows a faster dissolving rate (either above or below the line, but with a steeper slope)
* Allow 2 points for an answer that reflects a faster dissolving rate, using complete sentences
* Allow 1 point for a correct answer that is not in a complete sentence
* Allow 0 points for incorrect answer

Task 8: Relating Information   2 points total
Standard: Students relate data from the model to natural materials on Earth.
Criteria:
* Allow 2 points for an answer that reflects that warmer climates increase the rate of weathering and that uses complete sentences
* Allow 1 point for a correct answer that is not in a complete sentence
* Allow 0 points for incorrect answer

Task 9: Generalizing/Inferring   4 points total
Standard: Students describe an appropriate experiment.
Criteria:
* The experimental design should receive 1 point for each appropriate variable (up to a total of 4 points)—temperature, tablet amounts, liquid volumes, and solution type (i.e., weak acid).

Maximum score – 21 points

Earth Science Extended Investigation Task

Most extended investigation assessments are outgrowths of successful instructional activities. The teacher can supplement or adapt some "chunk" of instruction with scoring rubrics—so student performance can be reviewed with a slightly different perspective. At least three ways of scoring are possible, each requiring a separate rubric. The first method is to use rubrics on student work at particular points or lessons (i.e., planning an experiment or graphing results). This has been called "snapshot assessment," as it is composed of separate probes of student skills. A second way is to rate the product of student work (e.g., written reports, an object or model, an oral presentation). Each of these modes needs a separate rubric. A third way of assessing student work on an extended investigation is with a follow-up test that assesses students' ability to apply or transfer the concepts and skills learned to a new situation or context. This technique has been used with much success (Baron 1991). When writing your own tasks attempting to assess transfer, refer to the Novelty section in Chapter 2, page 26. For a discussion of the use of extended investigations, see Chapter 3, page 32.

Earth Science Extended Investigation Task	
Skills Categories	Soiled Again (page 200)
Planning	✔
Performing	✔
Analyzing	✔
Applying	✔

Soiled Again

Lomask, Baron, and Greig (1995) developed the following classroom-embedded assessment to be used as part of statewide assessments in Connecticut. They called the tasks "problem-solving tasks" and evolved a common format or structured shell. This shell became a very concrete beginning for other teacher teams. In the task, "students have to identify their own research questions, design relevant experiments, collect data, and present valid explanations for peer reviews."

The format of the tasks is as follows:

Introduction to the Task

- Short description of task
- Procedures for task administration
- Safety considerations
- Main criteria to evaluate quality of performance

Individual Initial Reflection

- Retrieval of task-related knowledge
- Exploration of possible solution paths
- Design of preliminary investigation

Group Investigation

- Articulation of specific problem to investigate
- Design and performance of investigation
- Creation of final product (i.e., lab report, magazine article, computer simulation)

Classroom Presentation

- Description of study
- Discussion of findings and interpretations
- Use of visual aids

Individual Written Assignment

- Assessment of concepts of understanding
- Critique of task-related research report

Present the top half of page 201 (Soiled Again: Group Investigation) to students. This provides background about the problem and a list of the steps to follow. The steps include interactions with partners, the teacher, and the class as students write and discuss the draft designs and conduct experiments and record data. The amount of class time needed for this activity will vary with the class' experiences with this kind of work.

After the presentation to the class of each group's report, the follow-up test is administered. The test, which consists of five open-ended questions that students complete individually, is a good measure of what students learned in the activity and their skill in planning and conducting investigations. Student response to the open-ended questions can be scored holistically on a 4-point scale (0–3 points).

Soiled Again
Group Investigation

You will be investigating a problem related to acid rain. During this activity, you will work with a partner (or possibly two partners). However, you should keep your own individual lab notes because after you finish you will work independently to write a report about your investigation.

Problem:

Acid rain refers to rain, snow, or other precipitation with a pH below 5.6. In extreme cases, acid rain can have a pH as low as 2.0! Many lakes in the Northeastern United States, although often appearing crystal clear, have had significant decreases in their number of fish and other life forms as a result of increasing acidity. You and your partner will design and conduct experiments to determine which earth material (sand, potting soil, or limestone) or combination of earth materials best reduces the acidity of "acid rain." You will use a vinegar-and-water solution as a substitute for acid rain. You will investigate the problem by studying the percolation rate (the rate at which water seeps through material) and neutralizing ability (the ability of a material to reduce the acidity of acids) of various earth materials.

Procedure:

1. In your own words, write down the problem you are going to investigate.

2. Design one or more experiments to solve the problem. Write down your experimental designs. Show your designs to your teacher; work with your partner to carry out your experiments. (Your teacher's approval does not necessarily mean that your teacher thinks your experiments are well designed. It simply means that in your teacher's judgment your experiments are neither dangerous nor likely to cause an unnecessary mess.)

4. Use the vinegar solution as a substitute for acid rain. Use a pH test strip to determine the acidity of the solution.

5. While conducting your experiments, take notes on your progress and record all observations and measurement data.

Soiled Again
Follow-up Test

The results of one group's experiment are shown in the following table.

Earth materials	pH of "acid rain" before percolation	Amount of "acid rain" percolated in 3 minutes	pH of percolated "acid rain"
sand	3.0	30 ml	3.5
potting soil	3.0	20 ml	3.5
crushed limestone	3.0	90 ml	5.0
all three earth materials	3.0	50 ml	5.5

1. What is one problem that this group is investigating? State the problem in your own words.

2. What are the variables that need to be controlled in this experiment? Explain why it is important to control them.

3. Do you have enough information to replicate this group's experiment? If you think you do, tell what information you have. If you think you do not, tell what other information you need.

4. The group concluded that sand and potting soil have the same ability to neutralize acidity because in each case the pH went form 3.0 to 3.5. Based on this group's experiment and results, do you think the group's conclusion is valid? Explain why or why not.

5. Plan an experiment to investigate the variation of acidity of a nearby river, lake, or pond across the entire school year. Be sure to include enough detail so that a fellow student could use your plan to conduct the investigation.

Works Cited

Baron, J. 1991. Performance Assessment—Blurring the Edge of Assessment, Curriculum, and Instruction. In *Science Assessment in the Service of Reform*, Kulm, G., and Malcolm, S., eds. Washington, DC: American Association for the Advancement of Science.

Chan, A. 1997. Comparison of Individual versus Pair Performance on Laboratory Skills Assessment. Buffalo: University at Buffalo.

Doran, R., Boorman, J., Chan, A., and Hejaily, N. 1993. *High School Laboratory Performance Tasks*. Buffalo: University at Buffalo.

Lomask, M., Baron, J., and Greig, J. 1995. Large-Scale Performance Assessment in Connecticut. Paper presented at the annual meeting of the American Educational Research Association, San Francisco.

New York State Education Department (NYSED). 1991. *Earth Science Performance Exam*. Albany: NYSED.

———. 1996. *Alternative Assessment in Science Task Collections*. Albany: NYSED.

Reynolds, D., Doran, R., Allers, R., and Agruso, S. 1996. *Alternative Assessment in Science: A Teachers Guide*. Buffalo: University at Buffalo.

CHAPTER 8

Illustrative Assessment Tasks for Physics

This chapter is organized in three parts: skills tasks, investigations, and extended investigations. All three parts contain models or templates of physics assessment tasks, many of which are "complete." These models may be used as is, incorpo- rated into existing assessment programs, adapted and modified to address addi- tional educational objectives, or completely redesigned to form entirely new and inno- vative assessments.

Physics Skills Tasks						
Skills Categories	Fill in the Box (page 206)	Height of Bounce (page 208)	Experimenting with a Ball and Ramp (page 211)	What's in the Box? (page 216)	Objects and Images (page 218)	Density of a Sinker (page 221)
Planning			✔	✔		
Performing	✔	✔	✔	✔	✔	✔
Analyzing	✔	✔	✔	✔	✔	✔
Applying						✔

Physics Skills Tasks (continued)			
Skills Categories	Soaps and Water (page 223)	Mystery Card (page 227)	Unknown Liquids (page 233)
Planning			✔
Performing	✔	✔	✔
Analyzing	✔	✔	✔
Applying	✔		

Physics Skills Tasks

The chart on page 204 shows the skills tasks in this chapter and the skills they assess. The skills tasks usually focus on one skill or on a small set of skills assessing a single event or experience. Most skills tasks assessments include student directions, answer sheets, material preparation guidelines, and scoring rubrics. Possible revisions are included with many tasks, so they can be used for other assessments.

A similar chart precedes each of the other two sections of this chapter, Physics Investigation Tasks and Physics Extended Investigation Tasks. The four skills categories—planning performing, analyzing, and applying—are illustrated in Figures 4.5 and 4.6 (pages 62 and 63). Note that the "applying" category here means more than numerically solving an equation with collected data. It includes skills such as relating or integrating results to underlying themes or models, proposing additional investigations/hypotheses, and suggesting applications beyond the context of the specific investigation.

Fill in the Box

This task was used in a trial project by the National Assessment of Educational Progress (National Assessment Governing Board 1996; O'Sullivan, et al. 1996) to determine the practicality of using performance assessment tasks in large-scale assessment programs. In the project, the researchers used performance tasks with students in grade 3, grade 7, and/or grade 11. This task is included because it uses materials and equipment commonly found in mathematics and science classrooms. The student task sheet is unstructured, leaving students to determine which measurements and calculations to make. While several strategies are possible to determine the correct answer (heaviest–A, lightest–C), the rubric might be used by a science teaching team evaluating student responses to this task.

Fill in the Box
Student Task Sheet

Background:

Students are given a sample of three different materials and an open box. The samples differ in size, shape, and weight. The students are asked to determine whether the box would weigh the most (or the least) if it were completely filled with material A, B, or C. The focus is on which of a variety of possible approaches the student uses to solve the problem. For example, some students might recognize that the solution involves the computation of the densities of the materials. Others may use the weights and volumes of both the materials and the box, or just use the weights of the materials followed by estimations of amounts needed to fill the box.

Materials:

- 3 different size blocks (labeled A, B, and C) of different shapes made of materials of different densities (e.g., a rectangular solid, a cube, and a triangular block that is half of a rectangular solid)
- a large open box (e.g. shoe box)
- a balance
- a metric ruler
- a hand calculator

Directions:

1. Would the box weigh most if it were completely filled with material A, or with B, or with C? With which would it weigh the least? You can use all the things on the table to help you find the answers. Keep any notes on what you do and what you find out.
2. Complete the sentences below.
   - The box would be heaviest filled with material _____.
   - The box would be lightest filled with material _____.

Fill in the Box
Scoring Rubric

1. Correct materials   **2 points total**
- heaviest – A   1 point
- lightest – C   1 point

2a. Procedure for determining density of blocks   **6 points total**
Mass
- measures mass accurately   2 points
- measures mass with minor errors   1 point

Volume
- calculates volume accurately   2 points
- calculates volume accurately with minor errors   1 point

Density
- calculates density accurately   2 points
- calculates density accurately with minor errors   1 point

<u>or</u>

2b. Procedure for determining mass and volume of blocks   **6 points total**
Mass
- measures mass of block accurately   2 points
- measures mass of blocks accurately with
  minor errors   1 point

Volume of Blocks
- determines volume of blocks accurately   2 points
- determines volume of blocks accurately with
  minor errors   1 point

Volume of Box
- determines volume of box accurately   2 points
- determines volume of the box accurately
  with minor errors   1 point

3. Use density <u>or</u> mass of blocks to fill the box   **2 points total**
- accurately   2 points
- with minor errors   1 point
- another appropriate procedure should also receive points

Maximum score – 16 points

Height of Bounce

We are all familiar with bouncing balls from our experiences with sports and other activities. But most people probably have not stopped to scientifically analyze how high a ball will bounce without help. The materials for this task, which is from the New York Alternative Assessment in Science Project, *Grade 8 Task Collection* (NYSED 1996), are a Ping-Pong ball, a copying-paper box top (or similar piece of cardboard), and a meter stick. Students bounce the ball off a desk- or tabletop or the floor in their classroom, measure the height of the first bounce, graph the results, and answer some extension questions. There are many modifications that can evolve into additional instruction or assessment activities, such as using different balls and different surfaces. You can use different kinds of surfaces, such as tiles, linoleum, or carpeting, as well as different kinds of balls, such as tennis or squash balls. Also, instead of height of bounce, students can investigate number of bounces.

Height of Bounce
Task Information

Time: 15–20 minutes

Materials:

Per Student:
- Ping-Pong ball
- box top fitted with a metric scale (0–50 cm)
- masking or duct tape
- 3 books or blocks
- calculator

Preparation:
- The metric scale is attached to the outside of a large box top. A copying-paper box top works very well.
- Use adhesive metric tape or a tape measure for the scale.
- The box top must be anchored to the work space (table, desk, or floor) with books, blocks, or tape before the students begin the task.
- An acceptable range of answers for height of bounce needs to be established by the teacher before student testing. To establish ranges for the scoring rubric, testing should be done on the same surface and with the same equipment that the students will be using.
- See the scoring rubric for further clarification on scoring student responses.

Safety:
- The Ping-Pong balls will occasionally roll off of the work space. Instruct the students to retrieve them, but <u>not</u> to run or disturb others around them.
- Remind students <u>not</u> to throw Ping-Pong balls.

Extensions/Modifications:
- Instead of the box setup, a metric ruler may be taped to a vertical surface.
- Use different kinds of surfaces.
- Use different kinds of balls.
- Vary the task's structure by reducing the directions, labels for data tables, and graphs.

Height of Bounce
Student Task Sheet

Task: You will be measuring the effect of height on the bounce of a Ping-Pong ball.

Materials:

- Ping-Pong ball
- box top fitted with a metric scale (taped down or balanced with books or blocks)
- calculator

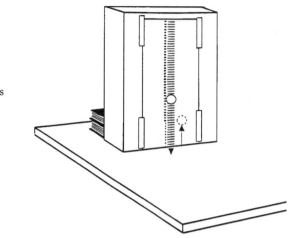

Directions:

1. Check to see that your materials are set up as shown in the diagram above.

2. Before you begin your task, practice bouncing the ball and noting how high it bounces. For <u>practice</u>, release the ball from any point on the scale and note the height to which it bounces. The "height of bounce" is the distance from the table top to the <u>bottom</u> of the ball on the first bounce. Practice a few times to make accurate observations.

3. Your task: Hold the ball near the scale on the box so that the <u>bottom</u> of the ball is level with the 10 cm mark. Release the ball and observe how high it bounces.

4. Record the height that the ball bounced in trial 1 on a data table. Round your answer to the nearest whole number of centimeters. Do two more bounces at this height to be sure your answer is accurate.

5. Repeat steps 3 and 4 for release heights of 20 cm, 30 cm, and 40 cm. Calculate to determine the answers for each height, and record them on your data table.

6. Use the average data from your experiment to construct a graph. Connect the points to make a line graph.

7. Based on your observations, write a generalized statement describing the relationship between the height of release and the height of bounce of a Ping-Pong ball.

8. If you were to bounce this ball from a height of 60 cm, predict how high (in centimeters) that the ball would bounce. Explain how you used your data to make this prediction.

Height of Bounce
Scoring Rubric

4–5: Height of bounce data table   **3 points total**

Height of Release	Height of Bounce
10 cm	3–6 cm
20 cm	10–18 cm
30 cm	15–25 cm
40 cm	20–30 cm

Criteria:
- Allow 1 point for accurately averaging and rounding at least 3 of the 4 heights.
- Allow 1 point for data collection taken three times (3 trials).
- Allow 1 point for data showing height of bounce within the acceptable range (as determined by teacher data) in at least 3 of 4 releases.

NOTE: The ranges in the table above are examples. Teachers should determine their own acceptable range for height of bounce before students do their testing. To establish ranges, testing should be done on the same surface and with the same equipment that the students will be using.

6: Graph of data   **5 points total**
Criteria:
- Allow 1 point for each data point plotted to an accuracy of +/− 2 cm "height of release," and +/− 2 cm "height of bounce" based on student's data.
- Allow 1 point for plotted points connected properly.

7: Relationship between bounce and release heights   **2 points total**
Criteria:
- Allow two points if students state a directly proportional relationship between the height of bounce and the height of release.

Possible answers:
  – As the height of release increases, the height of bounce increases
  – The higher I release the ball, the higher the height of bounce
  – The lower the height of release, the lower the height of bounce
  – The height of bounce is approximately 1/2 to 3/4 that of the height of release
  – The height of the release was higher than the height of bounce
  – The height of the release is larger than the bounce
  – The higher you drop the ball the further away the bounce was from the height you dropped it from
- Allow one point (partial credit) if the student states the relationship only in terms of his or her own data.

Possible answers:
  – A ball dropped from 40 cm bounces higher than a ball dropped from 10 cm
  – A ball dropped from 40 cm bounces up to 30 cm high (or student's own data)

8: Predict and explain the bounce height for release at 60 cm   **3 points total**
Criteria:
- Allow 1 point if students successfully predict a bounce height between 30–45 cm (This range is an example; your teacher should also establish an acceptable range for this height of bounce.)
  – Accept a student's prediction if consistent with his or her data
- Allow 2 points if students explain prediction using data collected.
  – I extended the line on my graph and observed where it crossed over the 60 cm release point
  – Since the heights of bounce were approximately 1/2 to 3/4 the height of release, a ball dropped from 60 cm would bounce 30–40 cm
- Allow 1 point if the student implies or states that he or she tested a ball drop from 60 cm

Maximum score – 13 points

Experimenting with a Ball and Ramp

This task is from the set of tasks prepared to illustrate the nature and format of assessments that would be part of a new (May 2001) statewide testing at the intermediate level (grades 5–8) in New York State (NYSED 1999). (The other two tasks in this sampler, "Cell Size" and "Soaps and Water," are also included in this volume.) All the material cited here (and more) is available electronically on the NYSED website (*www.emsc.nysed.gov/ciai/mst/sci.html*). You may wish to examine the entire website and use that resource in addition to what is included here.

This task is located in the physics chapter because the title and context are related to common physics activities and concepts: acceleration, force, motion, potential and kinetic energy, and so forth. However, the skills being assessed are generic: measuring length, recording data, recognizing experimental errors, formulat-

ing a hypothesis, and identifying control variables. These skills are fundamental to science as inquiry, yet they are not routinely part of many performance assessments.

The materials used in this task are easy to obtain and can be easily modified to create a new assessment task. Also, a host of different questions can be developed for use with these materials. As with all tasks, you can vary the amount of structure (direction, scaffolding) provided to students. As teachers, we seek to prepare students to inquire more and more on their own, so we can gradually reduce the structure provided in structured activities as well as in assessment tasks. Our job as teachers is to prepare students for this transition with the skills and confidence to use these skills. Despite this preparation, students are commonly resistant to even the slightest change, so teachers need to be "ready for some whining" and be supportive as students move on to more authentic—that is, more independent and unstructured—inquiries.

Experimenting with a Ball and Ramp
Task Information

Materials:

- ruler with groove
- support block(s)
- golf ball in a plastic bag
- duct tape or carpet tape
- 1 pint, round, transparent plastic container with hole (about 15 g in mass)

- place mat with 30 cm measuring strip
- masking tape
- 5 g mass or 25 cent coin

Background Information: Detailed preparation instructions (not included here because of space) are available on the NYSED website (*www.emsc.nysed.gov/cia/mst/sci.html*). The detailed instructions explain, for instance, that the hole in the container is about 6 cm x 6 cm—enough room for the golf ball to roll inside. The ramp (ruler) needs to be taped securely to the support block and the place mat so students can use it easily and consistently. The place mat has a diagram of where the cup should be in the "starting circle" and a 30 cm measuring tape. We recommend laminating the place mat so it will be durable. The 5 g mass is available to add to the cup to allow sliding distances within the 30 cm range on the place mat. The height of the block can also be varied to achieve this. The teachers who devised the task used a block of about 6 cm in height. Depending on the equipment available, you will need to "tinker" a bit to create a good system for students. At some stage, students could be involved with designing the parameters of the materials for this task. However, most middle-level students need to have experiences with materials that are ready-to-use.

The task was designed for students' "time on task" to be 15 minutes. Extensive pilot testing was conducted to produce a task with enough, but not too many, questions and activities for this time period. Students with high levels of skills will not need all 15 minutes; they can use the extra time to check their work. Students with more modest skills may struggle to complete the task within the 15-minute constraint, and many will not be able to finish in one hour (as the creators of the task learned through pilot testing and chats with students and teachers). In the case of formal, statewide testing, some students will have Individualized Education Plans (IEPs), which may specify that a student receive longer time for testing or other special arrangements.

When observing students doing performance tasks, you can very easily tell which students are "without a clue," as they fiddle with equipment, randomly roll the ball into the cup, and raise their hands to get help. Because this task is a model of statewide assessments, the test administrator is directed to answer students' questions with "Do your best" and "Re-read the directions." In large-scale testing, even acknowledging that a procedure is not correct is inappropriate as the validity and reliability of the assessment would be compromised. The only exceptions to this rule are obvious safety issues, which are not major concerns here but may be in some tasks.

A station diagram is provided below for suggested use with this task. It helps the teacher to assemble the equipment and materials and shows students where to return materials after they have completed the task. The teacher/test administrator still needs to monitor the station, but the diagram reduces confusion. Station diagrams are part of the "official" New York statewide test for which this test sampler was the introduction.

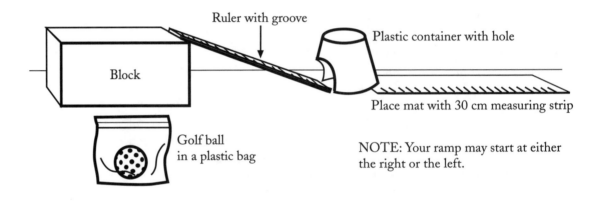

Experimenting with a Ball and Ramp
Student Task Sheet

Task:

You will observe a ball rolling down a ramp and moving a plastic cup. You will then identify some variables that would affect how far the cup moves. Finally, you will design an experiment and formulate a hypothesis.

Directions:

1. Be sure the cup is on the Starting Circle, with the opening in the cup facing the end of the ruler, at the start of each trial.

2. Take the golf ball out of the bag.

3. Place the ball on the ramp (ruler) so the middle of the ball is at the 15.0 cm mark on the ruler. Without pushing the ball, carefully release it so the ball goes into the cup. Note the distance the cup moves.

4. On data table 1 below, record the distance the cup moves when the ball is released from the 15.0 cm mark. Record the distance to the nearest 0.1 cm.

Data Table 1

Ball's Release Point (cm)	Mass of Cup (g)	Distance Cup Moved (cm)
15.0	16.0	
20.0	16.0	
25.0	16.0	
25.0	16.0	
25.0	16.0	

5. With the cup returned to the Starting Circle, release the golf ball from the 20.0 cm mark on the ruler. Record the distance the cup moves to the nearest 0.1 cm in data table 1.

6. With the cup returned to the Starting Circle, release the golf ball from the 25.0 cm mark on the ruler. Record the distance the cup moves to the nearest 0.1 cm in data table 1.

7. With the cup returned to the Starting Circle each time, release the golf ball two more times from the 25.0 cm mark on the ruler. Each time, record the distance the cup moves to the nearest 0.1 cm in data table 1.

8. You probably found that the cup traveled slightly different distances when you released the ball three times from the 25.0 cm mark. Give two reasons that might explain why the cup did *not* stop at the *exact* same spot each time.

First Reason: _____

Second Reason: _____

9. Think about how you might design a new experiment. In this experiment you want to study how changing the mass of the cup will change the distance it is moved by the golf ball. Assume that the equipment setup for this new experiment will be the same as it is now at your station. The data table for this new experiment is shown below. (**Do not actually fill in data table 2.**)

Data Table 2

Ball's Release Point (cm)	Mass of Cup (g)	Distance Cup Moved (cm)
	20.0	
	40.0	
	60.0	
	80.0	

10. What would you recommend about the release point of the golf ball each time a new cup is tested?

11. Write a hypothesis about the distance the cups of different masses will be moved by the golf ball.

12. Return all materials to their positions as shown on the station diagram.

Experimenting with a Ball and Ramp
Scoring Rubric

Directions 3-7: Gathering and recording data   **6 points**
- Allow 1 point if the student's data table contains a distance recorded in each of the five designated cells.
- Allow 1 point if all values are recorded to the nearest 0.1 cm.

The distances recorded in the table should show a general pattern of increase over the first three trials (from 15 to 25 cm release points):
- Allow 2 points for an increasing pattern in all three values.
- Allow 1 point for an increasing pattern in two of the three slides.
- Allow 0 points for no pattern or a decreasing pattern.
- Allow 1 point if two (or three) of the three 25 cm trials recorded on the data table are different.
- Allow 1 point if the range of the three 25 cm trials is not more than 4 cm.

Direction 8: Explanation for differences in 25 cm trials   **2 points**
For each point, the student must provide a different scientifically accurate explanation for why the cup does not stop at the exact same point each time it is released from the 25 cm mark on the ruler. (The student should not lose points for incorrect grammar, spelling, capitalization, or punctuation.) (1 point each)

Note:
- a. If more than two explanations are given, score only the first two.
- b. As the place mat is used a number of times, the surface may become smoother, so the cup's sliding distance may increase over time.

Sample 1-point responses:
"I released it from slightly different points each time."
"The table might have shook when the ball was dropped."
"The cup may not have been at exactly the same place each time."
"The speed of the ball was different at some times."
"There might have been a slight push when I released the ball."
"The ball may not have been exactly at the 25 cm mark every time."
"It might have happened because of inaccurate measuring with the ruler."
" I think the mat becomes smoother each time."

Sample incorrect responses:
"The golf ball weighed less."
"The ball was held longer sometimes."

Other incorrect responses would be those related to controlled variables—slope of the ramp, mass of the cup, numbers on the ruler or placemat.

Direction 10: Recommendation for release point and explanation   **1 point**
The student should state or imply that the release point should be the same for all of the cups. (The student should not lose a point for incorrect grammar, spelling, capitalization, or punctuation.) (1 point)

Sample 1-point responses:
"I would recommend a release point of 17 cm for all four cups so that the mass of the cup is the only variable."
"I think that the release point should be at least 15 cm for each cup."
"I would start at the same distance on the ruler each time. This way you can get an exact measurement."

Sample <u>incorrect</u> responses:

"I would recommend the release point to be sturdy because it could bend more one time than another."

" I recommend that the release point should be higher for the cups that weigh more."

"I would recommend that the distance be doubled each time a new cup is added, to keep it proportional to the original test."

Direction 11: Hypothesis   **1 point**

The student's hypothesis must relate the variable (weight/mass) of the cup and the distance moved. (The student should not lose a point for incorrect grammar, spelling, capitalization, or punctuation.) (1 point)

Sample 1-point responses:

"If the ball is released from the same point each time, the cup with the least mass will travel the farthest and the cup with the greatest mass will travel the least."

"The golf ball will move the lighter cups a longer distance than the heavier cups."

"The smaller the mass the cup has, the farther it will go."

"Cups of different masses will move different distances."

"The lighter cups will move farther than the heavier ones."

Sample <u>incorrect</u> responses:

"The bigger the slope, the more the cup moves. If the ball starts at a higher centimeter, it will move a cup more."

"The higher the mass, the harder it will be for the golf ball to move."

Maximum score — 10

What's in the Box?

Many people view most of nature as a "black box" that scientists try to describe and explain. Many black box activities have evolved for use in science classes at all levels. Some of these use sound, shape, smell, or electrical conductivity as properties to observe and use to infer the contents of the black box. This activity (from Doran, et al. 1993) is a magnetic black box. Students are given some common lab materials (iron filings, compass, magnet, and a mystery box) and asked to determine the number, kind, and location of the magnets. In this case a transparency master box is suggested, but many gift boxes (relatively thin) will work fine. The number and kind of magnets used should depend on the academic level of sophistication of students. This task includes two relatively large bar magnets located parallel to one another and with parallel polarity (i.e., with north and south poles in the same direction). This task is recommended for middle-level physical science students.

To score student work, it is recommended that teachers follow the sections of the task: Procedure, Data Table, Observations/Data, and Conclusions.

What's in the Box?
Task Information

Time: 30 minutes

Materials:

- container of iron filings
- compass
- 2 bar magnets
- white paper
- mystery box
- masking tape or glue

Make the mystery box from some small thin box (transparency master box works well). Glue or tape two bar magnets on the bottom of the box and seal the box securely with tape, according to the following diagram.

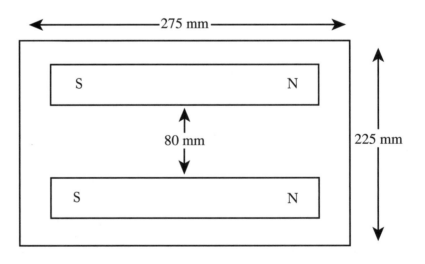

What's in the Box?
Student Task Sheet

Introduction:

This laboratory task presents a problem and lists materials available for your use. Your task is to design and carry out a plan for solving the problem. Please record all your answers on these sheets. You will have 25 minutes to plan and conduct an experiment to solve the problem.

Problem:

Determine the

- location
- arrangement
- polarity of the magnet(s) inside a sealed mystery box using the materials and equipment provided

Materials:

- container of iron filings
- white paper
- compass
- mystery box

a) Under the heading PROCEDURE, list in order the steps of the procedure or plan you will use to solve this problem. You may include a diagram to help illustrate your plans for the experiment. Include any safety procedures you would follow. Your procedure should be detailed enough for a friend to follow successfully.

b) Construct a DATA TABLE, or indicate how you will record your observations.

c) Conduct the EXPERIMENT by following the steps outlined in your procedure.

d) Record all OBSERVATIONS from the experiment in the data table you prepared. Use statements, descriptive paragraphs, and tables of data where appropriate.

e) Under the heading CONCLUSION, summarize your findings and the reasons for you conclusions.

f) At the end of the 30 minutes, your answer sheets will be collected.

What's in the Box?
Scoring Rubric

Procedures:

- sufficient details to follow
- will provide observations to solve problem
- appropriate safety considerations
- diagram of equipment/materials

1 point for each element
4 points possible

Data Table:

- consistent with procedures
- labeled appropriately
- spaces for data and observations

1 point for each element
3 points possible

Observations/Data:

- accurate and detailed
- extensive enough to describe context
- differentiates observations and inferences
- reference point for observations

1 point for each element
4 points possible

Conclusions:

- correct number of magnets
- correct placement of magnets
- correct polarity of magnets
- based on observations

1 point for each element
4 points possible

Maximum score — 15

Objects and Images

This task requires students to measure distances in order to determine the focal length of a convex lens. It was one of a set of three tasks in a doctoral dissertation (Ossei-Anto 1995). Students measure the distance of an object and image from a convex lens and use a formula to calculate or graphically determine the focal length based on their measurements. Students are provided with a workable experimental plan or prepared procedure, diagrams from which they measure distances to obtain data, and a data table for recording their measurements. There are three "ray" diagrams based on observations from one lens. However, these diagrams can be modified to represent three different lenses. Students require only a 30 cm ruler and a calculator (preferably with sine func-tions). We suggest a time limit of 30 minutes if the task is for summative purposes. A longer time period would be needed if this were part of an embedded task.

This task focuses on measuring, graphing, performing, calculating, and estimating skills. As with any assessment task, you can modify its structure and cognitive challenge. The task that follows is relatively structured, but if students don't have a prepared procedure, they can design their own and use a convex lens and light source to experimentally determine the object and image distance. Students can also design their own data table for recording their results. Furthermore, students can investigate the use of lenses in industry and medicine, making the task authentic. Such a modification can involve students working in pairs or small groups.

Objects and Images
Student Task Sheet

Introduction:

You will have 30 minutes to complete this part. Record your work on the answer sheet under the appropriate headings. Take 2 minutes to read the entire task <u>before</u> you start.

Problem:

You are to determine the focal length (f) of a convex lens using the lens formula: $1/o + 1/i = 1/f$

where

o = distance from object to the lens

i = distance from image to the lens

f = focal length of the lens

Materials:

- ruler (30 cm)
- graph paper
- calculator
- a sheet of 3 ray diagrams

Ray Diagrams:

Diagram A:

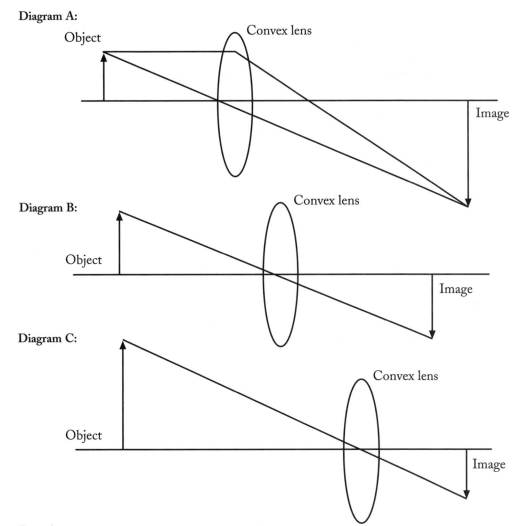

Diagram B:

Diagram C:

Procedure:

a) For each diagram, measure and record the value of the object distance (o) and the corresponding value of the image distance (i). Construct a data table, and record your values.

b) Determine the focal length (f) of the lens from your data. You can use calculations or graphs to do this.

c) Under the heading CONCLUSION report the value you determined for the focal length (f) of the lens.

d) Cite any possible errors that were involved with the procedure.

e) At the end of 30 minutes, your answers will be collected.

Objects and Images
Scoring Rubric

1. Circle the NR code when there is no student response or attempt to answer the question.
2. Circle the number 1 for each element present, and sum up to determine a student's score for each item or skill category.

Measurements/Observations:

• One or two are accurate	NR	0	1
• Additional one/two are accurate (i.e., total 3/4 are accurate overall)	NR	0	1
• Additional one/two are accurate (i.e., total 5/6 are accurate overall)	NR	0	1

Reciprocal Calculations (columns 1/o and 1/i):

(at least three are correct)	NR	0	1

Calculations/Graph:

• Adding reciprocals (1/o + 1/i)	NR	0	1
• Calculating sources of error	NR	0	1
• Measuring distances, calculating mistakes	NR	0	1

Conclusion:

• Value of "f" (between 2.6 and 2.9 cm)	NR	0	1

Sources of Error:

	NR	0	1

Total: NR   0   1   2   3   4   5   6   7   8   9

Density of a Sinker

This task is very similar to density activities in most middle school science programs. In the section on novelty in Chapter 2 (page 26), this task is described as representing "near transfer." The Earth science task "Density of Minerals" (page 179) is even more novel, and the chemistry task "Unknown Liquids" (page 233) is an illustration of "far transfer" from standard school activities on density.

The materials used are standard to any middle school science laboratory, except for the lead sinker. Lead sinkers can be purchased from some hardware stores, most sports/outdoors shops, and science supply companies. Despite the importance of the density concept, it is surprising how few activities students experience on this topic. In addition to the related tasks mentioned above, tasks that focus on relative density of several objects, density of liquids, and density of gases are logical extensions. The scoring rubric for this task is on page 61.

A paper-and-pencil task on density was included in the most recent National Assessment of Educational Progress science survey (NAEP 2000). Students are asked to determine the density of a metal ring and to specify the necessary laboratory equipment. Specifically, the task reads, "Suppose that you have been given a ring and want to determine if it is made of pure gold. Explain the steps you would follow, including the equipment you would use, and how you would use this equipment to determine the ring's density." The students' responses are scored on a four-level scale of *unsatisfactory, partial, essential,* and *complete.*

Density of a Sinker
Task Information

Time: 10–15 minutes

Materials:

- spring scale or balance
- 100 mL beaker with water
- modeling clay
- calculator
- graduated cylinder (at least 50 mL)
- 1 oz or 3/4 oz lead sinker
- string

Preparation:

- Put a small piece of modeling clay in the bottom of the graduated cylinder. This will pad the graduate in case the student drops the sinker into the graduate.
- Tie a string to the lead sinker so that the students can gently lower the sinker into the graduated cylinder. This will also help them to get the sinker out of the graduate.

Safety:

- Caution the students against dropping the sinker into the graduated cylinder.
- If any glassware should break, instruct the students **not** to attempt to clean it up themselves but to inform the instructor immediately.

Other Physics Task:

- Unknown Liquids (page 233).

Density of a Sinker
Student Task Sheet

Task: You will be determining the density of a sinker.

Materials:
- spring scale or balance
- graduated cylinder
- beaker with water
- sinker
- calculator

Directions:

1. Find the mass of the sinker. Include units in your answer.

2. Describe the procedures you will use to find the VOLUME of the sinker.

3. Find the volume of the sinker. Include units in your answer.

4. What is the <u>density</u> of the sinker? Round to the nearest tenth. Include units in your answer. Show your work using the formula:

$$\text{Density} = \frac{\text{mass}}{\text{volume}}$$

5. Suppose you cut the bottom half off the sinker. What would be the density of the upper half of the sinker? Explain your answer.

Soaps and Water

This task is from the test sampler produced by the New York State Education Department (NYSED 1999) to introduce students and teachers to the kinds of skills, equipment, and format to be expected in future statewide tests at the intermediate level (grades 5–8). The task "Cell Size" (on page 87) is also from this test sampler, as is "Experimenting with a Ball and Ramp" (on page 211).

In this task, students are expected to measure three dimensions (length, width, and height) of objects; calculate volume; measure mass (using a triple beam balance); calculate density; and interpret observations and data related to the density concept. Density is one of the most important and widely used scientific concepts, with obvious applications to Earth science, biology, and chemistry, as well as to physics.

There are many tasks that are described as "density tasks." Often, they are restricted in some way—for example, they may call for the use of only metallic cylinders, only wood blocks of the same dimension, and so forth. The task below includes several elements not found in many other density tasks: an object (soap B) whose volume *cannot* be determined by the usual measuring and calculations, and interpretation combining observations and calculation. This is a very busy station in terms of equipment and material. Parts of the task can be used with students in the upper-elementary grades (e.g., grades 5 or 6). The station requires quite a bit of teacher attention—for example, the teacher must make sure that the balances are left in "zero" position, that balls are taken out of the water and dried, and that there is sufficient water in the cup. The directions to students get most of this done, but teachers still need to monitor the activity.

**Soaps and Water
Task Information**

Materials:

- balance (triple beam)
- ruler (metric)
- calculator
- Soap A (any soap with flat sides and square corners—e.g., Neutrogena)
- Soap B (any bar soap, whose density is less than 1—e.g., Ivory)
- masking or duct tape
- Styrofoam ball

- water
- permanent marking pen
- rubber ball that floats
- 3 small, resealable, lightweight plastic bags
- plastic transparent cup (about 9 oz)
- paper towel

Background Information:

This task, like most, begins with simple measurement and recording of data in appropriate spaces or prepared data tables. Toward the end of the task, students are directed to predict where several objects would float in water and explain (using densities) the different positions of two balls in water. Although this task requires considerable time by students to complete (some will use the 15-minute limit), much of the time for those struggling to finish is "dead time" as they wrestle with question 7 (density of Soap B, using its mass and density), *not* by measurement of dimensions and calculation *nor* by water displacement (as it was in a sealed plastic bag). The task is quite structured, as students are provided with formulas for volume and density. As always, you can modify tasks so that they are aligned with your science standards and are cognitively appropriate for your students.

Station Diagram: Soaps and Water

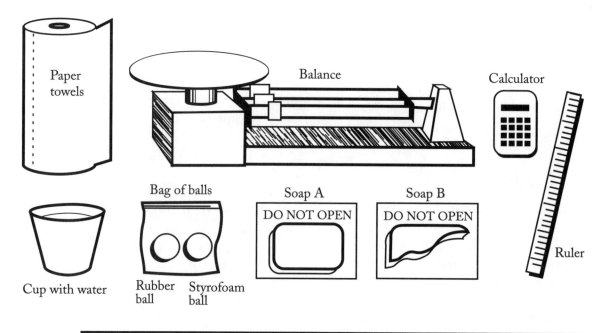

Paper towels

Balance

Calculator

Cup with water

Bag of balls

Rubber ball   Styrofoam ball

Soap A
DO NOT OPEN

Soap B
DO NOT OPEN

Ruler

Soaps and Water
Student Task Sheet

Task:

You will be determining some properties of two soap samples and predict how the samples would behave if they were placed in water. You will then place two objects in water and compare their densities.

Directions:

1. To protect the soap samples, do *not* take them out of the plastic bags and do *not* place the soaps in water. Disregard the effect of the plastic bags for all measurements and calculations.

2. What is the number on the bag for Soap A? _____
   What is the number on the bag for Soap B? _____

3. Use the data table below to record your answers to questions 4–7.

Data Table

Some Properties of Two Soap Samples			
Soap	Mass (g)	Volume (cm³)	Density (g/cm³)
A			
B			0.8

4. Measure the mass of Soap A and measure the mass of Soap B. Record the values to the nearest 0.1 g for each in the data table above. (Note that the unit, g [grams], has been provided.)

5. Measure the length, width, and height of Soap A to the nearest 0.1 cm. Record these dimensions in the work space below. Substitute your values in the formula provided. Then use the calculator to determine the volume of Soap A. Show your work in the space below. Record your value to the nearest 0.1 cm³ in the data table.

Work Space

Length _____ cm   Width _____ cm   Height _____ cm

Volume = Length x Width x Height

6. For Soap A, substitute your values for mass and volume in the formula provided. Then use the calculator to determine the density of Soap A. Show your work in the space below. Record your value to the nearest 0.1 g/ cm³ in the data table.

Work Space

Density = $\dfrac{\text{Mass}}{\text{Volume}}$

7. Notice that the density of Soap B has been provided in the data table (0.8 g/ cm³). For Soap B, substitute your values for mass and density in the formula provided. Then use the calculator to determine the volume of Soap B. Show your work in the space below. Record your value to the nearest 0.1 cm³ in the data table on page 224.

Work Space

Density = $\dfrac{\text{Mass}}{\text{Volume}}$

8. The diagram below represents a glass container with water. Think about what would happen if Soap A and Soap B were removed from the plastic bags and placed in this container. **Remember, do _not_ actually put the soaps in the water.**

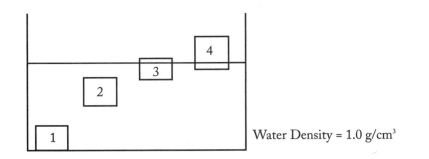

Water Density = 1.0 g/cm³

Base your answers to questions 9 and 10 on the values in your data table on page xxx.

9. Which block in the diagram above shows about where <u>Soap A</u> would be if it were placed in the container of water?

   (Circle one)   Block 1   Block 2   Block 3   Block 4

10. Which block in the diagram above shows about where <u>Soap B</u> would be if it were placed in the container of water?

    (Circle one)   Block 1   Block 2   Block 3   Block 4

11. Take the rubber ball and the Styrofoam ball out of the bag. Place them in the plastic cup with water. Observe the position of the balls in the water. Based on your observations, how does the density of the rubber ball compare with the density of the Styrofoam ball? Explain your answer.

    _____

    _____

12. Remove the balls from the cup, wipe them off, and return them to the bag.

13. Return all materials to their positions as shown on the station diagram.

Note: To score student responses for this task, the teacher must have already measured the dimensions of Soap A (any soap with rectangular dimensions) and the masses of Soaps A and B. This data should be recorded carefully so it can be easily accessed during the scoring process. On this record sheet, the teacher can also include the acceptable range of student data for each of these variables with each object (Soap A and Soap B). This data can be used in subsequent assessments as well. If this assessment data will be used for high-stakes student evaluation, we recommend massing each object with the balance at a specific station. (Balances and soaps are then coded to make that connection easier at the scoring stage.) Feel free to add details to the scoring rubric as you find unique responses or measurements. Any scoring rubric is always a "work in progress.")

This rubric covers questions 9, 10, and 11 only.

9. **Position Soap A would have in water**   1 point

   (*Note:* This prediction will need to be checked against the student's data table. There will be more than one "correct" answer here if earlier errors are carried forward.)

   The student circles the block that correctly reflects the density of Soap A as shown in the student's data table or work space. (1 point)

   If the student-determined density is > 1.0, the student should circle Block 1.

   If the student-determined density is = 1.0, the student should circle Block 2.

   If the student-determined density is < 1.0, the student should circle Block 3 or Block 4.

10. **Position Soap B would have in water**   2 points

    The student circles the block that correctly reflects where Soap B would be if it were placed in the container of water. (*Note:* The density value of 0.8 g/ cm³ was provided in the data table.)

    - Allow 2 points if the student circles Block 3.
    - Allow 1 point if the student circles Block 4 or both Blocks 3 and 4.
    - Allow 0 points if the student circles Block 1 or Block 2.

11. **Compare the density of the rubber and Styrofoam balls**   2 points

    The student must support her or his statement with accurate observations.

    Sample 2-point responses:

    - "The rubber ball must be denser than the Styrofoam ball because it sinks lower in the water."
    - "The density of the rubber ball is more than the Styrofoam ball because the rubber ball is almost completely underwater while the Styrofoam ball is floating on top of the water.

    Sample 1-point responses:

    - "The rubber ball is denser than the Styrofoam ball." (Student does not explain answer.)
    - "The rubber ball is heavier, so it sinks more. The Styrofoam ball was so light that it floated on the top." (Student explains answer, but addresses weight rather than density.)

    Sample incorrect responses:

    - "Because the rubber ball is heavier."
    - "The Styrofoam ball stays on the top and the rubber ball is in the water half and half."

Mystery Card

This task on electrical circuits is designed for middle-level students. It is from the Collection of Alternative Assessment Tasks in Science (Reynolds, et al. 1996) developed in New York State as part of a National Science Foundation (NSF) grant (MDR 9154506). The version presented here is quite structured, with detailed directions and labeled data tables. It can be "de-structured" by removing some of these aids, if students are comfortable with fewer directions.

The task begins with very simple observations of the bulb lighting (or not) for all the pairs of contacts on the first card. From their results with this testing, students are then asked to draw a diagram showing a way the contacts (circles) on that card could be connected. With the second card, data is provided and students are asked to infer a possible circuit that could produce such data (and an explanation). Most students enjoy creating their own mystery cards, which could also be used in such assessments.

Mystery Card
Task Information

Materials:

Teacher

- 4" x 6" index cards
- heavy-duty aluminum foil
- hole punch
- masking tape
- permanent black marker
- heavy-duty, clear packing tape

Per Student

- 1 D cell battery
- 1 battery holder
- 3 6" wires with alligator clips
- 1 flashlight bulb (1 or 1.5 volts)
- 1 bulb holder
- 1 circuit card ("Mystery Card")

Preparation:

- The circuit card (Mystery Card #1) can be made by taping aluminum foil (heavy-duty) between two 4" x 6" or 5" x 8" index cards. You can use old folders or poster board too. It is better to use colored index cards rather than white because they are not as transparent.
- Punch holes for the terminals on one of the index cards and label the holes. A standard size hole punch is large enough.

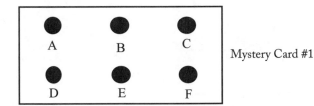 Mystery Card #1

- Cut a piece of aluminum foil large enough to fit over the top of the six terminals. Heavy-duty aluminum foil works the best.
- Cut out the bottom middle of the aluminum foil so that terminal "E" is not connected to the other terminals.
- Tape the foil securely to the index card.
- It is important to put foil over <u>all</u> of the terminals because it is visible in each of the holes.
- Be sure that you do <u>not</u> put tape over the top of the terminals, or the Mystery Card will not work properly.
- Tape the two index cards together on <u>all</u> four sides so that it cannot be taken apart easily. Clear packing tape works well for this.

- Connect wires, bulb, and battery to form an electrical tester. (See diagram on student task sheet.)
- Be sure that all electrical testers and mystery cards are in good working condition before students begin the task. It may be necessary to use two (2) batteries for the light bulbs to light sufficiently.

Extensions and Modifications:

Have students create their own mystery cards.

Mystery Card
Student Task Sheet

Task:

At this station, you will be using an electrical tester to determine where electricity flows between circles on Mystery Card #1.

Materials:

- 1 electrical tester
- 1 Mystery Card

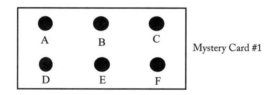

Mystery Card #1

The diagram below represents an electrical tester.

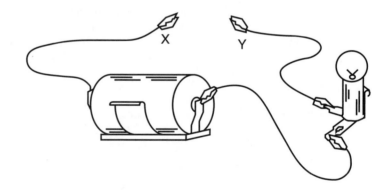

Directions:

1. Look at the electrical tester in front of you and make sure that it looks like the electrical tester shown in the diagram above.

2. Touch the free ends of the wire clips together to see if your bulb will light up. If it doesn't, please raise your hand to let the teacher know right away.

3. Touch circle A on Mystery Card #1 with one wire clip. **At the same time,** touch circle B with the other wire clip. If the bulb lights, put a check in the **yes** column in the Mystery Card Data Table. If the bulb does not light, put a check in the **no** column in the chart.

4. Do the same for all of the other pairs of circles on Mystery Card #1. Be sure to record **all** of your results in the table.

Touching		Bulb Lights	
		YES	NO
A ⟷ B			
A ⟷ C			
A ⟷ D			
A ⟷ E			
A ⟷ F			
B ⟷ C			
B ⟷ D			
B ⟷ E			
B ⟷ F			
C ⟷ D			
C ⟷ E			
C ⟷ F			
D ⟷ E			
D ⟷ F			
E ⟷ F			

5. On the basis of your findings, draw a diagram which shows a possible way the circles on your card could be connected. Use lines to show where the electricity travels.

6. Suppose your data table for a Mystery Card looked like the one below. Use that data to draw a diagram on Mystery Card #2 showing the possible ways the circles could be connected.

Touching		YES	NO
A ⟷ B			✔
A ⟷ C			✔
A ⟷ D		✔	
A ⟷ E		✔	
A ⟷ F			✔
B ⟷ C		✔	
B ⟷ D			✔
B ⟷ E			✔
B ⟷ F		✔	
C ⟷ D			✔
C ⟷ E			✔
C ⟷ F		✔	
D ⟷ E		✔	
D ⟷ F			✔
E ⟷ F			✔

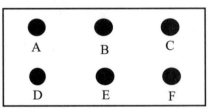

Mystery Card #2

7. Could the following circuit diagram be in Mystery Card #2?

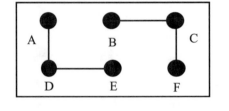

Circle your answer below.

YES   NO

8. Explain how you used the data table to answer questions #6 and #7.

4. Data Table   1 point total

Standard: The student tests the circles on the Mystery Card and correctly indicates which connections made the bulb light or not light.

Criteria:

- 1 point if the whole data table is filled in.
  - *** Credit should be given even if some check marks are incorrect.
  - *** No credit is given if the table is incomplete.

Example of completed data table

Touching			YES	NO
A	⟷	B	✔	
A	⟷	C	✔	
A	⟷	D	✔	
A	⟷	E		✔
A	⟷	F	✔	
B	⟷	C	✔	
B	⟷	D	✔	
B	⟷	E		✔
B	⟷	F	✔	
C	⟷	D	✔	
C	⟷	E		✔
C	⟷	F	✔	
D	⟷	E		✔
D	⟷	F	✔	
E	⟷	F		✔

5. **Diagram**   1 point total

   Standard: The student makes a valid drawing <u>based on his or her data</u> from question #4.

   Criteria:

   •   1 point for a drawing that correlates correctly to the student's data table.

      ***   Students still receive 1 point if their drawings correlate with their data tables even if the data in their tables are incorrect

      ***   Some example drawings are shown below. The rater will have to be sure that the student data table and drawings correlate with one another.

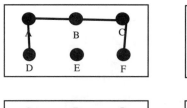 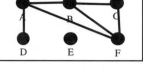 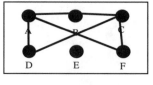

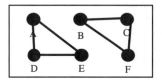 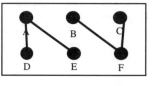 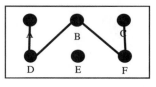

6. **Using given data table to draw a diagram for Mystery Card #2**   1 point total

   Standard: The student makes a valid drawing based on the data in the table for Mystery Card #2.

   Criteria:

   •   1 point for a drawing that correlates correctly with the data in the Sample Mystery Card Data Table.

      ***   Some example drawings are shown below. The rater will have to be sure that the data table and the drawings correlate with one another.

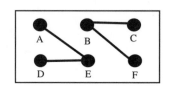

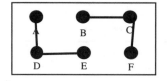

7. **Circuit diagram for Mystery Card #2**   1 point total

   Standard: The student will decide whether or not the given drawing could be possible for Mystery Card #2.

   Criteria:

   •   1 point for a correct answer - **YES**

8. **Explain use of given data table to answer questions # 6 and 7**   1 point total

   Standard: The student explains how the chart helped him or her to make his or her drawing.

   Criteria:

   •   1 point for a reasonable explanation telling that the student looked at the entries in the data table to draw the diagram.

   •   Even if the student's drawing is incorrect, he or she may still be able to explain the use of the data table.

   Maximum Score — 5 points

Unknown Liquids

This task was also included in the New York State Alternative Assessment in Science Project (Reynolds, et al. 1996). It assesses students' understanding (beyond applying formulas) of density and their ability to design an investigation to solve a problem. The most difficult part of this task is not having the equipment to measure volume of the vials. If that equipment were there, students could directly measure mass and volume and calculate density in the usual way. This task has been a challenge for many students—as well as their middle school teachers!

All middle-level and high school science labs will have some kind of balance (double pan or triple beam). Students should use the balance that they are most familiar with from their laboratory experiences. The materials used in this task are very readily available and not expensive.

**Unknown Liquids
Task Information**

Time: 10–15 minutes

Materials:

Teacher
- yellow and blue food coloring
- water
- rubbing alcohol
- salt
- sealant – hot glue/paraffin

Per Student or Station
- 2 screw top bottles (approx. 30 ml) for solutions X and Z
- double pan balance (with no weights)
- eye goggles
- calculator

Preparation:
- The yellow solution (Z) is a saturated salt solution with yellow food coloring.
    - start with one liter (1000 ml) of **warm** water. Add as much salt as will dissolve with constant stirring. Let cool. Filter out any undissolved salt. Add a few drops of yellow food coloring.
- The blue solution (X) is isopropyl (rubbing) alcohol and blue food coloring.
- Bottle – screw cap vials – flint glass, 28 ml.
- Seal the caps on the bottles with glue or liquid paraffin to avoid evaporation and to facilitate reuse.
- Determine the mass of the bottles before student use.
- Pretest the mass difference between X and Z to determine if sufficient for proper grading.

Safety:
- Safety goggles must be worn.
- Check MSDS (Materials Safety Data Sheet) for further precautions.
- Proper lab safety precautions are required.
- Students should be instructed **not** to open the bottles.
- Caution should be exercised to avoid breaking the bottles.

Extensions/Modifications: In a class, have different colors or letters of solutions.

Unknown Liquids
Student Task Sheet

Task: You will be determining which of two solutions is liquid X and which is liquid Z.

Materials:
- bottle containing a blue liquid
- bottle containing a yellow liquid
- double pan balance (with no weights)
- calculator
- eye goggles

Directions:

The labels on the two bottles have fallen off. The labels had read "Liquid X" and "Liquid Z." Your job is to determine which bottle contains liquid X and which contains liquid Z. The real challenge is that you must do this **without opening the bottles**. All the equipment to solve this problem is provided at this station. In addition, all of the information you need to reach your conclusion is as follows:

- The bottles and lids are identical in mass, volume, and shape when empty.
- Both bottles contain the same volume of solution.
- The density of liquid Z is greater than the density of liquid X.

1. List the steps you will follow to determine which bottle contains liquid X and which contains liquid Z.

2. Put on eye goggles. Be careful not to drop either bottle. CARRY OUT YOUR PLAN.

3. Record the results of your experiment. Show all your work.

4. Using the data collected in your experiment, which bottle contains liquid X and which contains liquid Z?

5. Based on the results of your experiment, write a statement explaining the relationship between mass, volume, and density. Writing a formula is <u>not</u> sufficient.

Unknown Liquids
Scoring Rubric

Question 1: Procedure for Identifying Liquids   **3 points total**

Criteria:

- Allow 3 points for a valid, logical procedure that includes <u>comparing</u> the masses of the two liquids. (The specific mass, volume, and density of the bottle is irrelevant to the student's responses for this activity.)
- Acceptable approach includes:
  1. Put one bottle on each pan of balance. (1 point)
  2. Determine which bottle has the greater mass. (1 point)
  3. The bottle with the greater mass has the greater density, as their volumes are identical. (1 point)

Question 3: Results of Experiment   **2 points total**

Criteria:

- Allow 1 point for "Bottle with greater density contains liquid Z."
- Allow 1 point for "Bottle with the yellow liquid is denser than the bottle with the blue liquid."

Question 4: Identification of Liquids   **1 point total**

Criteria:

- Allow 1 point for correctly identifying both liquids.
  - Blue liquid = X
  - Yellow liquid = Z

(Accept any student identification correctly based on his or her data)

Question 5: Density/Mass Relationship   **2 points total**

Criteria:

- Allow 2 points for a generalized statement about the density/mass relationship.
  - if two substances (solutions) have equal volumes, the one with the greater mass will have the greater density
  - the mass of the yellow was greater than the blue; since the volumes were the same, the yellow is more dense
- Allow 1 point if the student does <u>not</u> address a constant volume.
  - the liquid with the greater mass has a greater density

Maximum score – 8 points

Physics Investigation Tasks

For most of these Investigation Tasks, students need to record their answers in either their laboratory logbooks or on two blank sheets of paper. Specific instructions for what students should record, and the labels they should use, are given in each task. Generally, students are asked to record their hypothesis, their procedure (including any diagrams), and their data table (including their observations) on one sheet in a reasonably finished form. The other sheet is to be used as scratch paper.

If the task has a Part B, students will usually need a piece of graph paper and a third sheet for recording their conclusions. You may wish to hand out prepared answer sheets with the headings already in place. See Chapter 2 (page 24) for further information about structure.

The three tasks in this section illustrate some of the variety possible in the design of assessment activities. The chart below identifies the categories of skills assessed by the three physics Investigation Tasks that follow.

Physics Investigation Tasks			
Skills Categories	Stretching Springs (page 237)	Acceleration (page 240)	Bending Light (page 242)
Planning	✔	✔	✔
Performing	✔	✔	✔
Analyzing	✔	✔	✔
Applying			✔

Stretching Springs

In this task, students are asked to test a spring for the spring manufacturer, to be sure it meets a particular specification (stretching 0.3 meters with a force of 15 Newtons). In Part A students are asked to design an experiment to solve this problem, including a data table. After handing in their answers to Part A they receive Part B, in which they are given directions and a data table, so most students will be able to collect meaningful data. They are assessed on how well they are able to record the data, make calculations, construct a graph, and formulate appropriate conclusions.

To modify this task, different students can be given different springs as well as different specifications. Refer to pages 25–26 to see how this task can be modified by altering the sequence of task components, such as using different starting points or altering the task's stages. Further, it can be made less structured by deleting some of the directions, the formula, or the labeled data table. If students are proficient in planning and designing investigations, you can eliminate the Part A–Part B separation and create a "unified" task.

Stretching Springs
Task Information

Materials:

- a set of masses (<u>not</u> more than 1 kg total mass)
- Hooke's Law Apparatus (or ring stand, clamp, and metric ruler)
- graph paper (if grid is not supplied on answer sheet)

- C-clamp
- calculator
- sample Spring A

Preparation:

The objective is to have students determine whether their spring will stretch 0.3m when 15N is attached. They should <u>not</u> have 15N available to make this determination,

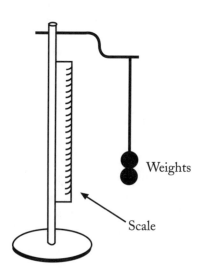

Weights

Scale

Stretching Springs
Student Task Sheet

PART A

This laboratory test presents a problem and a list of materials available to you. Your task is to design a strategy for solving the problem. Please record all your answers on these sheets. You will have 15 minutes to plan and design an experiment to solve the problem.

Problem:

You will remember that Hooke's Law describes the relationship between the force applied to a spring and its elongation (stretch). That is, if a force stretches a spring, the elongation is directly proportional to the force applied.

$$F = kx \qquad \text{Where:} \qquad \begin{aligned} &F = \text{force in Newtons} \\ &k = \text{spring constant in Newtons/meters} \\ &x = \text{elongation in meters} \end{aligned}$$

Imagine that you work for a spring manufacturer and your job is to determine whether Sample Spring A will elongate to exactly 0.3 meters when a force of 15 Newtons is applied. Your job is to conduct an experiment that will determine whether sample Spring A meets this specification, even though you do <u>not</u> have enough mass to test the spring directly.

a) Under the heading PROCEDURE, list in order the steps of the procedure you will use to solve the problem. You may include a diagram to help illustrate your plans for the experiment. Include any safety procedures you would follow. Include enough detail so someone else could follow your procedure easily.

b) Construct a DATA TABLE, or indicate any other method that you can use to record the observations and results that will be obtained.

c) At the end of the 25 minutes, your answers for Part A will be collected.

NOTE: In Part A, you are <u>not</u> expected to proceed with any part of the actual experiment. You are just to plan and organize a way to investigate the problem.

Materials:

- set of masses which totals 1 kg
- Hooke's Law Apparatus
- graph paper
- sample Spring A
- C-clamp
- calculator

PART B

You have 30 minutes to complete this part. You have been provided with a detailed procedure which you are to follow. Record your work under appropriate headings.

Procedure:

a) Perform the experiment by following the steps outlined in the procedure.
b) Under the heading RESULTS/OBSERVATIONS, record the data collected in the experiment. Use statements, descriptive paragraphs, and data tables where appropriate.
c) Under the heading CALCULATIONS, show all your equations and calculations used.
d) Construct a GRAPH, that shows the relationship between variables measured in this experiment.
e) Under the heading CONCLUSION, give an interpretation of your results.
f) At the end of the 45 minutes, your answers will be collected.

Stretching Springs
Answer Sheet

PART B
Procedure:

1. Check the spring apparatus. Be sure it is ready to begin your experiment.

2. Attach increasing amounts of mass. Record both the mass and the elongation of the spring in the data table provided.

3. Plot a graph of force against elongation, where the scale of values for force include 0 to 15 Newtons and values for elongation include 0 - 0.4 meters.

4. Determine whether spring A will stretch exactly 0.3 meters with a force of 15 Newtons applied, by extending the graph to a force = 15 Newtons.

5. Report your analysis of this problem under Conclusions.

Results/Observations:
$g = 9.8 \text{ m/sec}^2$

Trial #	Mass (kg) [1000g = 1 kg]	Force (N) $W = mg$	Elongation with no load (m)	Elongation with load (m)
1			0	
2			0	
3			0	
4			0	
5			0	

Calcuations and Graphs:

Conclusions: Based on a graphical analysis of the data you collected in this experiment, discuss your conclusion as to whether Spring A could stretch to exactly .0.3 meters if a force of 15 Newtons is applied. Be certain to explain how you used your data to arrive at this conclusion.

Acceleration

We experience acceleration whenever our car starts stops or turns a corner, whenever we are in amusement park rides such as roller coasters, giant slides, and Ferris wheels, as well as playgrounds on a swing or a seesaw. Yet few of us know much about acceleration or simple ways to explain it to others. Acceleration is a major concept in motion or kinematics units within physical science and physics courses. This task uses simple equipment (ball and track) and some common measuring equipment (meter stick, stopwatch, calculator). The metal track can be purchased at a hardware or home supply store.

This task could be revised into a two-part task (like "Stretching Springs") if students are relatively unfamiliar with less-structured tasks. Students could do the experiment with different angles, to explain the relationship between acceleration and angle of the track. A 90° angle corresponds to free-fall. While there are considerable errors possible in making time measurements, students could time free-fall of the ball from about 2 m to estimate "g." Students could do some library work to learn more about Galileo and the materials he used for his measurements.

The scoring of student work on this task can be done with the scoring system developed for all the University at Buffalo/ National Opinion Research Center tasks (see Doran, et al. 1993). After using this system for a while, you may wish to adapt it to better fit your program.

Acceleration
Task Information

Materials:

- 1.5 meter metal track
- meter stick
- graph paper
- calculator

- metal ball (approximately 2 cm— needs to fit into track)
- rubber stopper
- stopwatch

To begin the experiment, set the track at approximately a 30° angle.

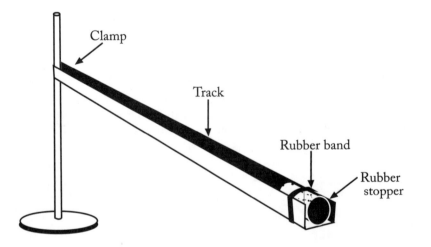

Acceleration
Student Task Sheet

Introduction:

This laboratory task presents a problem and lists materials available to you. Your task is to design a strategy and conduct an experiment for solving the problem.

Problem:

One of Galileo's most significant experiments was his measurement of acceleration. He rolled a brass ball down a wooden ramp and determined its acceleration using his pulse as a timer! Using similar equipment, your task is to conduct an experiment for determining the acceleration of a ball down an inclined plane. You will recall that acceleration is:

$$a = \frac{\Delta v}{\Delta t}$$

where:
$$a = \text{acceleration}$$
$$\Delta v = \text{the change in velocity}$$
$$\Delta t = \text{the change in time}$$

Materials:

- 1.5 meter metal track
- meter stick
- rubber stopper
- stopwatch

- metal ball
- graph paper
- calculator

a) Under the heading PROCEDURE, list in order the steps of the procedure you will use to solve the problem. You may include a diagram to help illustrate your plans for the experiment. Include any safety procedures you would follow. Be detailed enough so someone else could follow your procedure.

b) Construct a DATA TABLE or indicate any other method that you could use to record your observations and results.

c) Perform the experiment by following the steps outlined in your procedure.

d) Under the heading RESULTS/OBSERVATIONS, record your observations collected in the experiment. Use statements, descriptive paragraphs, and record all measurements in the data table you constructed.

e) Under the heading CALCULATIONS, show all the equations and calculations you used.

f) Construct a GRAPH that shows the relationship between the variables measured in this experiment.

g) Under the heading CONCLUSION, give an interpretation of your results. Based on your graphical analysis of the data you collected in this experiment, discuss the acceleration of the steel ball as it rolled down the ramp. Be certain to explain how you used your data to arrive at this conclusion.

h) At the end of 45 minutes, your work will be collected.

Bending Light

This physics task was designed to measure planning, performing, and reasoning skills at the high school level within the context of refraction. During the activity, students are asked to determine the purity of a substance by measuring its index of refraction. The students are provided with a laser pointer that is attached to a movable arm on an optical bench. The laser pointer is turned on and directed toward the center of a semicircular Lucite target. The target is placed at the center of a polar graph paper grid. The students are provided with a data table and are given five angles of incidence (θ_i); they are asked to measure the angles of refraction (θ_r). The students determine the values for $\sin \theta_r$ and then plot $\sin \theta_i$ vs. $\sin \theta_r$; the units and the scale for each axis is given to the students. The students use their data to calculate the index of refraction for this sample; they are asked to state if the material meets the purity standard that is described in the background section of the lab. Students are asked to reflect on ways to improve the precision of their measurement—they predict the effect of using different sizes of targets or laser beams. The students then design a new procedure that can be used to measure the index of refraction of a rectangular sample; the students are required to indicate the materials they will use and the steps that they will follow.

The task can be administered within a 45-minute period. The optical benches make the task easier for students to make measurements; they are not absolutely necessary. Polar graph paper, semicircular targets (liquids in semicircular dishes or solid shapes), and laser pointers are the essential components.

This task was one of three tasks that were developed to evaluate the impact of task organization on student achievement (Zawicki 2002). This task asked the students to make measurements and calculations under one overarching question: "Was the given sample 'pure'?" A second iteration of the task provided students with sets of questions that were not necessarily related—a context akin to the station model of laboratory testing. A third version of the task provided students with a diagram of the data and sample student results. The students were asked to assess the work that the students completed. (The students were required to use the data to calculate the index of refraction based upon the recorded data.)

Bending Light
Task Information

Materials:

- optical bench (as shown in Figure 1)
- Polar graph paper
- Semi-circular Lucite sample (or semi-circular dish)
- Laser pointer
- Calculator or sine table
- Velcro strip

The laser pointer should be rotated so that the Velcro keeps the laser turned on.

The arm should then be aimed so that the beam is visible on the surface of the graph paper both before and after the target. (The adjustment screw on the bottom of the arm can be used to fine-tune the height.)

Safety – Laser pointers are tools; they should be handled with care and caution. Do not look directly into any laser beam; do not direct the laser beam at anyone else. Retinal damage does not occur unless the laser beam is directed toward a fixed location for an extended period of time. It is best, however, to err on the side of caution and to avoid problems.

Bending Light
Student Task Sheet

Background

Light changes direction as it travels through transparent media. The refraction, or bending, of a light ray as it passes from air into a transparent substance may be determined by using the index of refraction:

$$n = \frac{\sin\theta_i}{\sin\theta_r}$$

Where:

n = the index of refraction

$\sin\theta_i$ = the sine of the angle of incidence in air

$\sin\theta_r$ = the sine of the angle of refraction in the material

Indices of refraction have been established for a great number of substances. It is well known that optical properties are affected by the composition of a substance; impurities cause a change in the value of the index of refraction. In fact, the index of refraction is often used to determine the purity of given material. You will be measuring angles that can be used to determine the index of refraction of an unknown substance; the material has been cut into a semicircular shape.

You have been hired as a consultant by the O. P. Tics Optical Supply Company. O. P. Tics is preparing to send a number of plastic blocks to NASA for use in an experiment. The purity of the plastic is critical for the success of the experiment. Your job is to verify that a plastic sample from this project matches the standard of 1.5 (1.2 –1.8).

Procedure and Data Collection:

1. The apparatus consists of a semicircular target placed on a small tray; a laser pointer is attached, with Velcro, to a movable arm. You will need to rotate the laser underneath the Velcro until the tension in the Velcro loop turns the laser on. A circular (polar) graph paper grid has been placed beneath the target.

2. Place the laser so that the laser beam strikes the center of the flat side of the target and the center of the graph paper.

3. The arm was initially positioned so that the laser beam struck the center of the target along the 0° line on the graph paper. In this position, the laser beam exited the plastic target along the 0° line at the top of the diagram. You should turn the laser on and move it to the 0° position to verify this step. Call your instructor if you have a problem.

4. The arm should then be moved so that the angles of incidence are set at various angles at 15° increments. The circular graph paper should be used to determine the angle of refraction of the light beam as it passes through the plastic block. You should estimate the angle to the nearest degree.

5. Record the angle of refraction that you have measured in the data table under the column *Angle* θ_r.

6. Repeat the procedure for the following angles of incidence: 15°, 30°, 45°, and 60°.

7. Use the calculator to determine *Sin* θ for each angle of incidence and refraction. Record your answers in the data table.

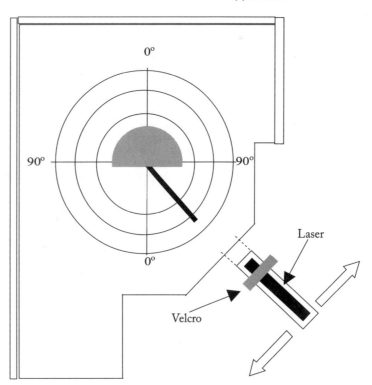

Figure 1. Experimental apparatus.

Data Collecting

Angle θ_I	Sin θ_i	Angle θ_r	Sin θ_r
0°	0.00	0°	0.00
15°	0.26		
30°	0.50		
45°	0.71		
60°	0.87		

Graphing

Construct a graph that shows the relationship between sin θ_i and sin θ_r.

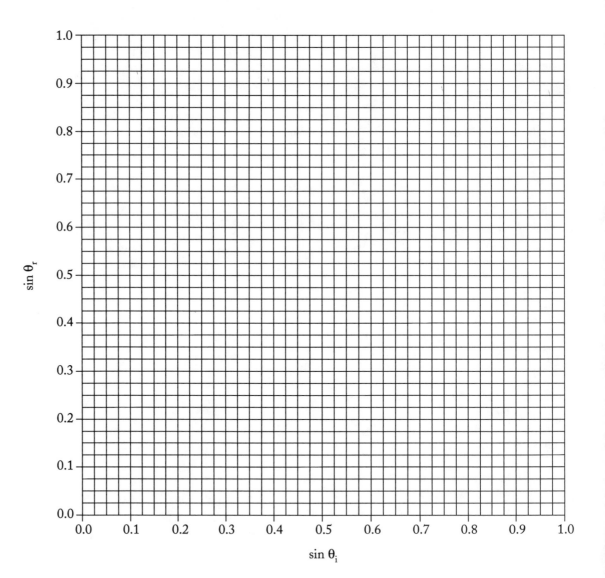

Calculating:

Use your data to calculate the index of refraction for the semicircular sample. Show all of your work, as well as any equations that you use.

Analyzing:

It is now time to report back to the O. P. Tics Optical Supply Company. Your task was to determine whether the plastic sample fit the standard of 1.50 +/- 0.3. Based on *your* data, was the material composed of the correct type of plastic? How did you make this decision?

Predicting:

Errors can be caused by a number of factors. Students have suggested that changing either the size of the plastic target or the width of the laser beam can reduce measurement errors. To improve the quality of your data, how would you change the

- size of the target? (Would you make the target larger or smaller?) Why would this change improve your measurement?
- laser beam? (Would you make it narrower or broader?) Why would this change improve your measurement?

Planning:

How might you redesign the current experiment to test a rectangular sample of similar material? You may include diagrams to help clarify the procedure. You may use any reasonable materials, including items such as regular graph paper or a protractor. Your procedure should be detailed enough to allow a fellow student to perform your activity. Be sure to

- list necessary materials.
- outline a procedure.

Bending Light
Scoring Guide

Data Collecting

Students measure angles of refraction. The data is recorded in the data table. The values for sin θ are recorded correctly.

Angles (4 points)

- all 4 angles of refraction are correctly measured +/- 3°
- the range of acceptable answers includes: 7°-13°, 16°-22°, 25°-31°, 32°-38°

Sines (2 points)

- award 2 points if all 4 values for sin θ are correctly reported +/- 0.01
- award 1 point if 2 or 3 values for sin θ are correctly reported +/- 0.01
- award no points if either 1 or none of the values for sin θ are correctly reported +/- 0.01
- award no points for values of sin θ based upon the angles of refraction recorded in the data table

Graphing

Points are plotted precisely; a line of best fit is drawn.

Plotting Points (4 points)

- all 4 points are plotted correctly (+/- 0.025)

Line of Best Fit (1 point)

- a straight line is drawn
- no credit is awarded if a line is not drawn or if a line is drawn by connecting data points

Calculating

The index of refraction is calculated.

Calculating Index of Refraction (4 points)

- award one point for the equation ($n_1 \sin \theta_1 = n_2 \sin \theta_2$)
- award one point for substitution (with units)
- award one point for a final answer (with units)
- award one point for an answer based upon an average of the four values or the line drawn on the graph

Analyzing

Students correctly identify the type of material based upon their data for the index of refraction

Type of Material (1 point)

- Matches standard (1.5 +/- 0.3)

Predicting

Size of Target (2 points)

- Target should be made larger
- A larger target will be easier to use *or* more accurate *or* …

Size of Laser Beam (2 points)

- Beam should be made narrower
- A narrower beam will be more precise, more accurate, easier to use

Planning

Materials (2 points)

- All necessary materials are listed (2 points)
- Some appropriate materials are listed; one or more items missing (1 point)

Procedure (2 points)

- All steps are listed; the steps are in a correct order (2 points)
- All steps are listed but they are not in the correct order *or* some steps are listed but one or more steps are missing (1 point)

Physics Extended Investigation Task

This assessment format is the most natural and normal to experienced teachers, but is a "late entry" in the recent assessment reforms in science education. Much time has been spent with developing station tasks and investigation tasks (as in the two previous sections of this chapter). Extended investigations are also called curriculum-embedded assessment as the distinction between instruction and assessment continues to blur (Baron 1991).

Various methods are used to assess students while they are completing an extended investigation. One approach is to use certain lessons/activities for assessment, such as measuring temperature or time, graphing data, and citing the limitations and assumptions of an inquiry. This is known as a "snapshot" approach. Another approach is to assess the lab report or the product developed. Still another is to develop a "follow-up" test, to determine if students can apply the skills and concepts to slightly different situations. Many teachers also use the extended investigation to assess group work dynamics and to give students an opportunity to assess themselves and their peers.

Physics Extended Investigation Task	
Skills Categories	Keep It Hot (page 248)
Planning	✔
Performing	✔
Analyzing	✔
Applying	✔

Keep It Hot

This task is part of a Connecticut Academic Performance Test (1996) cumulative assessment covering science content and skills that students should have acquired before grade 11. The assessment plan includes clusters of multiple-choice items (around a particular scenario), open-ended items on conceptual understanding, and open-ended items administered several weeks after this performance task. "Keep It Hot" was designed for one to two class periods, but can easily be extended over a longer time. "Keep It Hot" is an example of an authentic task (keeping drinks hot) and one that uses common, familiar materials. Teachers need to provide students with four lined pages for their reports, as well as a grid for tables, charts, or graphs.

A similar task is being trial tested in New York State for assessing some inquiry and content outcomes as part of *Learning Standards for Mathematics, Science, and Technology* (NYSED 1996). In this task, students must design a container to transport organs. A block of ice is the model of an organ for this simulation activity. A follow-up test (administered 2–3 weeks after the instructional unit) composed of questions on the relevant math, science, and technology concepts and skills is being validated.

Keep It Hot
Student Directions

Introduction:

Have you ever bought a hot drink in a paper cup and found that it was cold before you finished drinking it? Is there anything that can be done to a paper cup to help keep a hot drink warm? Wrapping the cup to insulate it might help, but what should you use to wrap the cup?

Your Task:

You will design and conduct an experiment to explore the insulating abilities of different materials for keeping a liquid in a paper cup warm. During this activity you will work with a lab partner (or possibly two partners). You must keep your own individual lab notes because, after you finish, you will work independently to write a lab report about your experiment. You have been provided with the following materials and equipment. It may not be necessary to use all of the equipment that has been provided. You may use additional materials or equipment if they are available.

Materials:

- 6 paper cups with lids
- 1 sheet of cloth
- 2 sheets of black construction paper
- 2 sheets of white construction paper
- 1 large sheet of aluminum foil
- 1 liter of hot water
- a clock or watch with a second hand
- paper towels for cleanup

- ruler
- 2 large styrofoam cups
- splash proof goggles and aprons
- 2 thermometers
- graduated cylinder
- scissors
- tape

Procedure:

1. In your own words, clearly state the problem you are going to investigate. Include a clear identification of the independent and dependent variables that will be studied.

2. Design an experiment to solve the problem. Your experimental design should match your statement of the problem, should control variables, and should be clearly described so that someone else could easily replicate your experiment. Include a control if appropriate. Write your experimental design on a separate sheet of paper. Show your design to your teacher before you begin your experiment.

NOTE: The hot water used in your experiment should be in the range of 50° to 60°C. The water should <u>not</u> be heated above 60°C for safety reasons.

3. After receiving approval from your teacher, work with your partners to carry out your experiment. Your teacher's approval does not necessarily mean that the teacher thinks the experiment is well designed. It simply means that in your teacher's judgment your experiment is not dangerous or likely to cause an unnecessary mess.

4. While conducting your experiment, carefully label all data and observations. Record the results of your experiment. All data should be organized in tables, charts or graphs, which should be properly labeled. Your notes will <u>not</u> be scored, but they will be helpful to you later as you work independently to write about your experiment and results. You <u>must</u> keep your own notes because you will not work with your partner(s) when you write your lab report.

The next stage of this task is the Laboratory Report. Students work on the report individually, based on the notes they took and the tables, charts, and graphs prepared by the lab group during the experiment.

You can grade these lab reports without a rubric or, from the clear criteria listed in the student directions, develop a reliable scoring rubric. A beginning point might be the scoring rubrics used in the UB/NORC tasks (see Doran, et al. 1993).

As part of the "Keep It Hot" task, four follow-up "experimentation questions" were developed to focus student attention on skills in experimentation. The follow-up questions (page 251) are based on data, questions, and conclusions by "other" students on the same performance task, and were designed to promote assessment of students'

- understanding of what constitutes an appropriate statement of a problem for a scientific investigation;

- understanding of conclusions drawn from scientific investigations and factors that affect their validity;

- ability to draw conclusions from the results of a scientific experiment and discuss their validity; and

- understanding of what constitutes an appropriate experimental design.

Keep It Hot
Student Laboratory Report

Working on your own, summarize your experiment and the results. Use the notes you took while working with your partner(s). You will have approximately 40 minutes to complete your report, which should include the following:

• A clear statement of the problem you investigated. Include a clear identification of the independent and dependent variables that were studied.

• A description of the experiment you carried out. Your description should be clear and complete enough so that someone else could easily replicate your experiment.

• The results of your experiment. All of your data should be organized in tables, charts, or graphs, which should be properly labeled.

• Your conclusions from your experiment. Your conclusions should be fully supported by your data

• Comments about how valid you think your conclusions are. In other words, how much confidence do you have in your results and conclusions? Any factors that contribute to a lack of confidence in the results or conclusions should be discussed. Also, include ways that your experiment could be improved if you were to do it again.

Keep It Hot
Scoring Rubric for Student Laboratory Report

Score 3

The response is an excellent answer to the question. It is correct, complete, and appropriate and contains elaboration, extension, and/or evidence of higher-order thinking and relevant prior knowledge. There is no evidence of misconceptions. Minor errors do not necessarily lower the score.

Score 2

The response is a proficient answer to the question. It is generally correct, complete, and appropriate although minor inaccuracies are present. There may be limited evidence of elaboration, extension, higher-order thinking, and relevant prior knowledge, or there may be significant evidence of these traits, but other flaws (i.e., inaccuracies, omissions, inappropriateness) are evident.

Score 1

The response is a marginal answer to the question. While it may contain some elements of a proficient response, it is inaccurate, incomplete, or inappropriate. There is little if any evidence of elaboration, extension, higher-order thinking, or relevant prior knowledge. There may be evidence of significant misconceptions.

Score 0

The response, although on topic, is an unsatisfactory answer to the question. It fails to address the question, or it may address the question in a very limited way. There is no evidence of elaboration, extension, higher-order thinking, or relevant prior knowledge. There is evidence of serious misconceptions.

Keep It Hot Experimentation Questions

A class of students performed a series of experiments to determine which of several materials would be most effective for insulating a paper cup. One group of lab partners tested four different materials: black paper, white paper, aluminum foil, and cloth. The following tables show their results.

Insulating Materials	Temperature of water in cups at start of the experiment	Temperature after 5 minutes	Temperature after 10 minutes
Black paper	70°C	60°C	52°C
White paper	50°C	45°C	40°C
Aluminum foil	70°C	55°C	45°C
Cloth	60°C	54°C	48°C

1. This group's statement of the problem was: "We wanted to see which of four materials would be good for wrapping around a cup." Is this a clear statement of the problem?

2. The group concluded that the white paper was the most effective insulator because the cup wrapped in white paper showed the smallest drop in temperature. Is this group's conclusion valid? Explain why or why not.

Another group in the class tried to use various materials and combinations of materials. The following table shows their results.

Insulating Materials	Temperature of water in cups at start of the experiment	Temperature after 5 minutes	Temperature after 10 minutes
4 thicknesses of black paper	70°C	64°C	60°C
4 thicknesses of white paper	70°C	65°C	61°C
4 thicknesses of aluminum foil	70°C	62°C	56°C
4 thicknesses of cloth	70°C	63°C	57°C
1 thickness each of black paper, white paper, aluminum foil, & cloth	70°C	68°C	56°C

3. What valid conclusions can you draw from these results? Explain your answer.

4. Do you have enough information to replicate this group's experiment? If you think you do, tell what information you have. If you think you do not, tell what other information you would need to replicate the experiment.

Works Cited

Baron, J. 1991. Performance Assessment—Blurring the Edge of Assessment, Curriculum, and Instruction. In *Science Assessment in the Service of Reform*, Kulm, G., and Malcolm, S., eds. Washington, DC: American Association for the Advancement of Science.

Connecticut Academic Performance Test. 1996. *Released Items and Scored Student Responses*. Hartford: Connecticut Academic Performance Test.

Doran, R., Boorman, J., Chan, A. and Hejaily, N. 1993. *High School Laboratory Performance Tasks*. Buffalo: University at Buffalo.

National Assessment Governing Board. 1996. *Science Assessment Framework for the 1996 National Assessment of Educational Progress (NAEP)*. Washington, DC: National Assessment Governing Board.

National Assessment of Educational Progress (NAEP). 2000. *The Nation's Report Card: Science*. Available at *nces.ed.gov/nationsreportcard/science*

New York State Education Department (NYSED) website: *www.emsc.nyed.gov/ciai/mst/sci.html/*

———. 1996. *Learning Standards for Mathematics, Science, and Technology*. Albany: NYSED.

———. 1999. *Intermediate-Level Test Sampler*. Albany: NYSED.

New York State Alternative Assessment in Science Project. 1996. *Grade 8 Task Collection*. Buffalo: University at Buffalo.

Ossei-Anto, T. 1995. *Performance Assessment Tasks for Optics*. Doctoral diss., University at Buffalo.

O'Sullivan, C., Reese, C., and Mazzeo, J. 1996. *NAEP 1996—Science Report Card for the Nation and the States*. Washington, DC: National Center for Education Statistics.

Reynolds, D., Doran, R., Allers, R., and Agruso, S. 1996. *Alternative Assessment in Science: A Teachers Guide*. Buffalo: University at Buffalo.

Zawicki, J. 2002. *Assessment of Inquiry Skills in High School Optics*. Doctoral diss., University at Buffalo.

Glossary of Assessment Terminology

Alternative assessment: Any assessment that is not of the multiple-choice, matching, or true/false, paper-and-pencil formats. Requires students to complete a task or demonstrate a performance in solving a problem.

Assessment: The collection of information about student achievement and performance.

Assessment task: A goal-directed activity in which students complete a task; includes a format for recording student responses and criteria for scoring student responses.

Authentic assessment: Assessment tasks that use "real-world" and "real-life" contexts and are aligned with the assessment and content standards in use by your school or district. Students are challenged to demonstrate their achievement and skills within these domains of knowledge.

Benchmarks: These are examples of student achievement. Note that benchmarks are not goals or standards of achievement.

Congruence: The process of ensuring that content standards, assessment standards, and the instructional program are aligned with each other.

Content standards: Narrative statements that describe what students should know and be able to do in a domain of knowledge or skills.

Criterion-referenced assessment: The comparison of student knowledge, achievement, or skills to predetermined standards of what students are expected to know and be able to do, rather than against the achievement of other students.

Curriculum-embedded assessment: Part of the ongoing instruction and learning in a classroom. Examples are projects, investigations, and oral presentations.

Diagnostic assessment: A variation of formative assessment, whereby the data is used to identify student strengths, target domains of skills for improvement, and identify gaps in conceptual understanding.

Domain: An area of subject knowledge, such as acids and bases, or a domain of skills, such as forming conclusions. By their nature, performance assessments focus on a narrow domain of content or skills. Multiple-choice formats, by comparison, focus on a wider domain of knowledge.

Embedded assessment: A format of assessment that occurs within the unit or lesson. Usually is not obvious to students. Should not be used for high-stakes assessment.

Equity: Equity in assessment ensures that all groups are treated with fairness and that no students or groups are at a disadvantage in performing to their full potentials. Assessments use examples and content from a variety of sources to illustrate different perspectives and the impact of these perspectives on learning and knowledge construction.

Evaluation: The interpretation of assessment data, based on a set of criteria, to judge student achievement and capabilities.

Formative assessment: The collection of data about student achievement and performance that is part of regular teaching and learning in classrooms. Teachers use this data collaboratively with students to modify instruction in order to promote student learning and conceptual understanding.

Inter-rater reliability: The scoring of assessments by more than one person, usually in pairs, to reduce the influence of human subjectivity. Assessment scores are compared to obtain the degree of agreement between two scorers, and inter-rater reliability is estimated by Cronbach's alpha, a Product-Moment (PM) correlation between pairs of raters, or percent agreement between scores. Reliable scoring procedures should generate inter-rater reliabilities of above 0.75.

Item: A question or simple problem within a test or assessment tasks.

Moderation: A process in which teachers analyze a set of different assessments scored by different people to ensure that the assessments are comparable; includes coming to agreement on the assessment formats and the scoring criteria.

Norm-referenced assessment: The comparison of student achievement or skills to the achievement or skills of a peer group, commonly referred to as the "normed group."

On-demand assessment: Formal test that is scheduled in advance. Usually is a high-stakes test that is part of end of unit, semester, or course evaluations.

Open-ended questions: Items in which a specific answer is not expected; rather, the teacher is looking for a range of possible appropriate, correct responses.

Opportunity to learn: Through planned instructional activities, students are provided with an "opportunity to learn" the concepts and skills of a domain of knowledge. Schools support student learning by providing appropriate instruction through qualified professional teachers and support staff and by providing materials and equipment.

Peer evaluation: When other students or peers score a student's assessment in relation to established criteria for success.

Performance assessment: A style of assessment in which students manipulate equipment or materials as part of the task. Commonly oriented to skills rather than content outcomes.

Performance standards: Illustrate student competencies and achievements in a domain of knowledge or skills. They answer the question "How well is well?"

Portfolio: A collection of student work that can include assignments, projects, laboratory reports, tests, or any other samples of work that illustrate the development of skills and conceptual understanding in a domain of knowledge or skills. Student work samples in a portfolio serve as checkpoints for student learning.

Reliability: The consistency with which assessments produce the same results or scores when the assessment is administered over time. Similar student responses should receive the same scores over time.

Rubric: An established set of criteria for scoring or rating student responses on assessment tasks where the response is more involved than selecting an answer from a prescribed list. Good scoring rubrics minimize the biases inherent in human judgment. *Holistic* rubrics focus on an overall process or product without evaluating component parts. *Analytic* rubrics evaluate each attribute of a task or process on a continuum of poor to excellent work.

Self-evaluation: The process whereby a student judges his or her achievement in relation to personal goals. This personal probe of understanding promotes confidence and self-esteem and, with appropriate support from teachers, can promote student achievement.

Standardized test: An assessment that is administered and scored the same way for all students to enable a comparison of scores.

Standards: Statement of outcomes for instructional programs; the outcomes are broader or more inclusive than individual facts or concepts.

Summative assessment: Assessments given at the end of a unit, semester, or course with the resulting data being used to generate grades and marks; placement and selection decisions certifying student accomplishments are based on summative data.

Test: An assessment task, primarily for measuring student achievement in a domain of knowledge or skills, that is summative in nature.

Validity: The extent that an assessment measures what it sets out to measure. There are many "kinds" of validity, such as construct, content, and consequential validity. An assessment can be reliable but not valid.

National Science Education Standards for Assessment

Assessment Standard A

Assessments must be consistent with the decisions they are designed to inform.

- Assessments are deliberately designed.
- Assessments have explicitly stated purposes.
- The relationship between the decisions and the data is clear.
- Assessment procedures are internally consistent.

Assessment Standard B

Achievement and opportunity to learn science must be assessed.

- Achievement data collected focus on the science content that is most important for students to learn.
- Opportunity-to-learn data collected focus on the most powerful indicators.
- Equal attention must be given to the assessment of opportunity to learn and to the assessment of student achievement.

Assessment Standard C

The technical quality of the data collected is well matched to the decisions and actions taken on the basis of their interpretation.

- The feature that is claimed to be measured is actually measured.
- Assessment tasks are authentic.
- An individual student's performance is similar on two or more tasks that claim to measure the same aspect of student achievement.
- Students have adequate opportunity to measure their achievements.
- Assessment tasks and methods of presenting them provide data that are sufficiently stable to lead to the same decisions if used at different times.

Assessment Standard D:

Assessment practices must be fair.

- Assessment tasks must be reviewed for the use of stereotypes, for assumptions that reflect the perspectives or experiences of a particular group, for language that might be offensive to a particular group, and for other features that might distract students from the intended task.
- Large-scale assessments must use statistical techniques to identify potential bias among subgroups.
- Assessment tasks must be appropriately modified to accommodate the needs of students with physical disabilities, learning disabilities, or limited English proficiency.
- Assessment tasks must be set in a variety of contexts, be engaging to students with different interests and experiences, and must not assume the perspective or experience of a particular gender, racial, or ethnic group.

Assessment Standard E:

The inferences made from assessments about student achievement and opportunity to learn must be sound.

- When making inferences from assessment data about student achievement and opportunity to learn science, explicit reference needs to be made to the assumptions on which the inferences are based.

"Assessment data provide students with feedback on how well they are meeting the expectations of their teachers and parents, teachers with feedback on how well their students are learning, districts with feedback on the effectiveness of their teachers and programs, and policy makers with feedback on how well policies are working."

"[Assessment] feedback leads to changes in the science education system by stimulating changes in policy, guiding teacher professional development, and encouraging students to improve their understanding of science."

"All aspects of science achievement—ability to inquire, scientific understanding of the natural world, understanding of the nature and utility of science—are measured using multiple methods such as performances and portfolios, as well as conventional paper-and-pencil tests."

Source: National Research Council. 1996. *National Science Education Standards*. Washington, DC: National Academy Press, pp. 76, 78, 79, 83, 85, 86.

Complete Bibliography

This bibliography is composed of the Works Cited and Suggested Readings found in Chapters 1–8, as well as additional relevant resources.

American Association for the Advancement of Science (AAAS). 1989. *Project 2061: Science for All Americans*. New York: Oxford University Press.

———. 1993. *Project 2061: Benchmarks for Science Literacy*. New York: Oxford University Press.

American Educational Research Association (AERA), American Psychological Association (APA), and National Council on Measurement and Education (NCME). 1999. *Standards for Educational and Psychological Testing*. Washington, DC: American Educational Research Association.

Assessment of Performance Unit. 1984. The assessment framework of science at age 13 and 15. In *APU Science Report for Teachers, 2*. London (UK): Department of Education and Science.

Baker, D. 1991. A Summary of Research in Science Education–1989. *Science Education* 75(3).

Baron, J. 1991. Performance Assessment—Blurring the Edge of Assessment, Curriculum, and Instruction. In *Science Assessment in the Service of Reform*, Kulm, G., and Malcolm, S., eds. Washington, DC: American Association for the Advancement of Science.

Baxter, G., Shavelson, R., Goldman, S., and Pine, J. 1992. Evaluation of Procedure-based Scoring for Hands-on Science Assessment. *Journal of Educational Measurement* 29(1).

Bell, B. 1995. Interviewing: A Technique for Assessing Science Knowledge. In *Learning Science in the Schools: Research Informing Practice*, Glynn, S. and Duit, R., eds. Mahwah, NJ: Lawrence Erlbaum Associates.

Ben-Zvi, R., Hofstein, A., Samuel, D. and Kempa, R. 1977. Modes of Instruction in High School Chemistry. *Journal of Research in Science Teaching* 14.

Biological Sciences Study Committee. 1962. *Processes of Science Testing*. New York: The Psychological Corporation.

Black, P. 1991. APU Science—The Past and the Future. *School Science Review* 72(258).

Black, P., and Wiliam, D. 1998. Inside the Black Box: Raising Standards through Classroom Assessment. *Phi Delta Kappan* 80 (2): 139–48.

———. 1998. Assessment and Classroom Learning. *Assessment in Education* 5 (1): 7-74.

Bryce, T., and Robertson, I. 1985. What Can They Do? A Review of Practical Assessment in Science. *Studies in Science Education* 12.

Buffalo Public Schools. 1995. *Portfolio for Grade 7 Science*. Buffalo: Buffalo Public Schools.

Bybee, R. 2000. Teaching Science as Inquiry. In *Inquiring into Inquiry Learning and Teaching in Science*, Minstrell, J. and Van Zee, E., eds. Washington, DC: American Association for the Advancement of Science.

Carr, M., Barker, M., Bell, B., Biddulph, F., Jones, A., Kirkwood, V., Pearson, J., and Symington, D. 1994. The Constructivist Paradigm and Some Implications for Science Content and Pedagogy. In *The Content of Science—A Constructivist Approach to Its Teaching and Learning*, Fensham, P., Gunstone, R., and White, R., eds. Bristol, PA: Falmer Press.

Chan, A. 1997. *Comparison of Individual versus Pair Performance on Laboratory Skills Assessment.* Buffalo: University at Buffalo

Chan, A., Doran, R., and Lenhardt, C. 1999. Learning from the TIMSS. *Science Teacher* 66 (1): 18–22.

Collins, A. 1992. Portfolio for Science Education: Issues in Purpose, Structure, and Authenticity. *Science Education* 76(4).

Comber, L., and Keeves, J. 1973. *Science Education in Nineteen Countries.* New York: Wiley.

Connecticut Academic Performance Test. 1996. *Released Items and Scored Student Responses.* Hartford: Connecticut Academic Performance Test.

Doran, R. 1990. What Research Says about Assessment. *Science and Children* 28(8).

Doran, R., and Anderson, T. 1996. Design Task—Unknown Solutions. Unpublished document. Buffalo: University at Buffalo.

Doran, R., Anderson, D., Boorman, J., Chan, F., and Hejaily, N. 1995. *Scoring Manual for Laboratory Assessment in Biology, Chemistry, and Physics.* Buffalo: University at Buffalo.

Doran, R., Boorman, J., Chan, F., and Hejaily, N. 1992. Successful Laboratory Assessment. *The Science Teacher* 59(4).

Doran, R., Boorman, J., Chan, A., and Hejaily, N. 1993. *High School Science Laboratory Performance Tasks.* Buffalo: University at Buffalo.

Doran, R., Reynolds, P., Camplin, J., and Hejaily, N. 1993. Evaluating Elementary Science. *Science and Children* 30(3).

Duit, R., and Treagust, D. 1995. Students' Conceptions and Constructivist Teaching Approaches. In *Improving Science Education,* Fraser, B. and Walberg, H., eds. Chicago: National Society for the Study of Education.

Eglen, J., and Kempa, R. 1978. Assessing Manipulative Skills in Practical Chemistry. *The School Science Review* 56.

Food and Nutrition Board. 2000. *Dietary Reference Intakes for Vitamin C, Vitamin E, Selenium, and Carotenoids.* Panel on Dietary Antioxidants and Related Compounds, Subcommittees on Upper Reference Levels of Nutrients and Interpretation and Uses of DRIs, Standing Committee on the Scientific Evaluation of Dietary Reference Intakes, Food and Nutrition Board. Washington, DC: National Academy Press.

Freidler, Y., Amir, R., and Tamir, P. 1987. High School Students' Difficulties in Understanding Osmosis. *International Journal of Science Education* 9.

Ganiel, U., and Hofstein, A. 1982. Objective and Continuous Assessment of Student Performance in the Physics Laboratory. *Science Education* 66.

Gardner, M. 1990. *Laboratory Assessment Builds Success (LABS).* Berkeley: Lawrence Hall of Science.

Gipps, C. 1995. *Beyond Testing: Toward a Theory of Educational Assessment.* Washington, DC: Falmer Press.

Gitomer, D., and Duschl, R. 1995. Moving Toward a Portfolio Culture in Science Education. In *Learning Science in the Schools: Research Informing Practice,* Glynn, S. and Duit, R., eds. Mahwah, NJ: Lawrence Erlbaum Associates.

Gunstone, R., and White, R. 1986. Assessing Understanding by Means of Venn Diagrams. *Science Education* 70(2).

Gurley-Dilger, L. I. 1982. Use of Gowin's Vee and Concept Mapping Strategies to Teach Responsibility for Learning in High School Biological Sciences. Doctoral diss., Cornell University.

Harlen, W. 1985. Process Skills, Concepts, and National Assessment in Science. *Research in Science Education* 13.

Harmon, M., Smith, T., Martin, M., Kelly, D., Beaton, A., Mullis, I., Gonzalez, E., and Orpwood, G. 1997. *Performance Assessment in IEA's Third International Mathematics and Science Study (TIMSS).*

Chestnut Hill, MA: TIMSS International Study Center.

Helgeson, S., and Kumar, D. 1993. Applications of Technology in Science Assessment. *Cognosos* 2(3).

Hodson, D. 1990. A Critical Look at Practical Work in School Science. *School Science Review* 70(256).

Hofstein, A., and Lunetta, V. 1982. The Role of the Laboratory in Science Teaching: Neglected Aspects of Research. *Review of Educational Research* 52.

Hofstein, A., Lunetta, V., and Giddings, G. 1981. Evaluating Science Lab Activities. *The Science Teacher* 48(1).

Jacob, R. A. 1994 Vitamin C. In *Modern Nutrition in Health and Disease*, 8th ed., Shils, M. E., Olson, J. A., and Shike, M., eds., 432–48. Philadelphia: Lea and Febiger.

Jacobson, W. J., Doran, R. L., Humrich, E., and Keeves, J. 1987. *The Second IEA Science Study—US Second IEA Science Study*. New York: Teachers College, Columbia University

Jeffrey, J. 1967. Evaluation of Science Laboratory Instruction. *Science Education* 51.

Jewett, A., Jones, L., Luneke, S., and Robinson, S. 1971. Educational Change Through a Taxonomy for Writing Physical Education Objectives. *Quest* 15.

Johnson, D., and Johnson, R. 1989. *Cooperation and Competition: Theory and Research*. Edina, MN: Interaction Book Co.

Kanis, I., Doran, R., and Jacobson, W. 1990. *Assessing Science Process Laboratory Skills at the Elementary and Middle/Junior High Levels*. Washington, DC: National Science Teachers Association.

Kelly, P., and Lister, R. 1969. Assessing Practical Ability in Nuffield A Level Biology. In *Studies of Assessment*, Eggleston, J. F. and Kerr, J. F., eds. London (UK): English Universities Press.

Korth, W. 1968. *Life Science Process Test, Form B*. Cleveland: Educational Research Council of America.

Kreitler, H., and Kreitler, S. 1974. The Role of the Experiment in Science Education. *Instructional Science* 3.

Lawrence Hall of Science. 1985. *GEMS Crime Lab Chemistry*. Berkeley, CA: Lawrence Hall of Science.

Lomask, M., Baron, J., and Greig, J. 1995. Large-Scale Performance Assessment in Connecticut. Paper presented at the annual meeting of the American Educational Research Association, San Francisco.

Louks-Horsley, S., Hewson, P. W., Love, N., and Stiles, K. E. 1998. *Designing Professional Development for Teachers of Science and Mathematics*. Thousand Oaks, CA: Corwin Press.

Lunetta, V., and Tamir, P. 1979. Matching Lab Activities with Teaching Goals. *The Science Teacher* 46(5).

Mason, C. 1992. Concept Mapping: A Tool to Develop Reflective Science Instruction. *Science Education* 76(1).

Meng, E., and Doran, R. 1993. *Improving Instruction and Learning Through Evaluation: Elementary School Science*. Columbus, OH: ERIC Clearinghouse for Science, Mathematics, and Environmental Education.

Mirando, Peter A. 1993. *Determination of Validity and Reliability of Four Performance Assessment Instruments Developed For General Chemistry*. Doctoral diss., University at Buffalo.

Mitchell, R. 1992. *Testing for Learning—How New Approaches to Evaluation Can Improve American Schools*. New York: Free Press.

National Assessment of Educational Progress. 1978. *The National Assessment in Sciences: Changes in Achievement, 1969-72*. Denver: Educational Commission of the States.

———. 1986. *Learning By Doing*. Princeton: National Assessment of Educational Progress.

———. 2000. *The Nation's Report Card: Science*. Available at *nces.ed.gov/ nationsreportcard/science*.

National Assessment Governing Board. 1996. *Science Assessment Framework for the 1996 National Assessment of Educational Progress (NAEP)*. Washington, DC: National Assessment Governing Board.

National Center on Education and the Economy, University of Pittsburgh. 1997. *Performance Standards, Volumes I, II, and III*. Washington, DC: National Center on Education and the Economy.

National Education Goals Panel. 1996. *The National Education Goals Report: Executive Summary—Commonly Asked Questions About Standards and Assessment*. Washington, DC: National Education Goals Panel.

National Research Council (NRC). 1996. *National Science Education Standards*. Washington, DC: National Academy Press.

———. 1999. *High Stakes Testing for Tracking, Promotion and Graduation*. Board on Testing and Assessment. Commission on Behavioral and Social Sciences and Education. Washington, DC: National Academy Press.

———. 2000. *Inquiry and the National Science Education Standards: A Guide for Teaching and Learning*. Washington, DC: National Academy Press.

———. 2001. *Classroom Assessment and the National Science Education Standards*. Washington, DC: National Academy Press.

———. 2001. *Knowing What Students Know: The Science and Design of Educational Assessments*. Committee on the Foundations of Assessment. Pellegrino, J., Chudowsky, N., and Glaser, R., eds. Washington, DC: National Academy Press.

National Science Teachers Association (NSTA). 1992. *The Content Core*. Arlington, VA: NSTA.

———. 1992. *Scope, Sequence, and Coordination of Secondary School Science, Volume II: Relevant Research*. Arlington, VA: NSTA.

New Standards Project. 1997. *Performance Standards. Volume 2: Middle School*. Washington, DC: National Center for Education and the Economy. (Tel. 202-783-3668).

———. 1997. *Middle School Science Portfolio*. Washington, DC: National Center for Education and the Economy. (Tel. 202-783-3668).

New York State Alternative Assessment in Science Project. 1996. *Grade 8 Task Collection*. Buffalo: University at Buffalo.

New York State Education Department (NYSED). 1984. *Reflections on Writing in Science*. Albany: NYSED.

———. 1984. *Regents Biology Syllabus*. Albany: NYSED.

———. 1985. *Elementary Science Syllabus*. Albany: NYSED.

———. 1991. *Earth Science Performance Exam*. Albany: NYSED.

———. 1991. *Student Assessment: A Review of Current Practice and Trends in the United States and Selected Countries*. Albany: NYSED.

———. 1992. *Elementary Science Program Evaluation Test (ESPET) Objective Test, Form E*. Albany: NYSED.

———. 1992. *Elementary Science Program Evaluation Test (ESPET) Manipulative Skills Test, Form X*. Albany: NYSED.

———. 1996. *Alternative Assessment in Science Task Collections*. Albany: NYSED.

———. 1996. *Learning Standards for Mathematics, Science, and Technology*. Albany: NYSED.

———. 1999. *Intermediate Level Test Sampler*. Albany: NYSED.

Novak, J. 1980. Learning Theory Applied to the Biology Classroom. *The American Biology Teacher* 42.

———. 1981. Applying Learning Psychology and Philosophy of Science to Biology Teaching. *The American Biology Teacher* 42.

———. 1991. Clarity with Concept Maps. *The Science Teacher* 59(7).

Novak, J., and Gowin, R. 1984. *Learning How to Learn*. New York: Cambridge University Press.

Nussbaum, J. 1979. Israeli Children's Conceptions of Earth as a Cosmic Body: A Cross Age Study. *Science Education* 63(1): 83-93.

O'Sullivan, C., Reese, C., and Mazzeo, J. 1996. *NAEP 1996—Science Report Card for the Nation and the States*. Washington, DC: National Center for Education Statistics.

Ossei-Anto, T. 1996. *Performance Assessment Tasks for Optics*. Buffalo: University at Buffalo.

Parker, J. C., and Rubin, L. J. 1966. *Process as Content: Curriculum Design and the Application of Knowledge*. Chicago: Rand McNally.

Perkins, D., and Salomon, G. 1989. Are Cognitive Skills Context-Bound? *Educational Researcher* 19:16–25.

Pickering, M. 1980. Are Lab Courses a Waste of Time? *Chronicle of Higher Education* 19.

Pittsford Central Schools. 1994. *Problem-solving Standards and Rubrics*. Pittsford, NY: Pittsford Central Schools.

Reynolds, D., Doran, R., Allers, R., and Agruso, S. 1996. *Alternative Assessment in Science: A Teacher's Guide*. Buffalo: University at Buffalo.

Rhode Island Department of Education. 1990-91. *Rhode Island Distinguished Merit Program Handbook*. Providence: Rhode Island Department of Education.

Robinson, J. 1969. Evaluating Laboratory Work in High School Biology. *The American Biology Teacher* 31(3).

Robitaille, D., Schmidt, W., Raizen, S., McKnight, C., Britton, E., and Nichol, C. 1993. *Curriculum Frameworks for Mathematics and Science: Third International Mathematics and Science Study; TIMSS Monograph No. 1*. Vancouver: Pacific Educational Press.

Rosenthal, J. 1996. *Teaching Science to Language Minority Students*. Avon, UK: Multi-Lingual Matters, Ltd.

Roth, W. 1993. The Unfolding Vee. *Science Scope* 16(5).

Roth, W., and Verechaka, G. 1993. Plotting a Course with Vee Maps. *Science and Children* 30(4).

Rubba, P., Miller, E., Schmalz, R., Rosenfeld, L., and Shyamal, K. 1991. Science Education in the United States: Editors Reflections. In *Science Education in the United States: Issues, Crises, and Priorities*. Easton, PA: Pennsylvania Academy of Sciences.

Ruda, P. 1979. *Chemistry Laboratory Practical Examination*. Unpublished. Cheektowaga, NY: Cleveland Hill High School.

Saha, G. 2001. Implementing the Science Assessment Standards: Developing and Validating a Set of Laboratory Assessment Tasks in High School Biology. Doctoral diss., University at Buffalo.

Saha, G., and Chan, A. 1998. Food Nutrient Task. Unpublished document. Buffalo: University at Buffalo.

Second International Science Study. 1987. *General Science Tests for SISS-USA*. New York: Teachers College, Columbia University.

Shavelson, R., and Baxter, G. 1992. What We've Learned About Assessing Hands-on Science. *Educational Leadership* 49(8).

Shepardson, D., and Jackson, V. 1987. Developing Alternative Assessments Using the Benchmarks. *Science and Children* 35(2).

Shulman, L., and Tamir, P. 1973. Research on Teaching in the Natural Sciences. In *Second Handbook of Research on Teaching*, Travers, P. ed. Chicago: Rand McNally.

Silberman, R. G. 1996. *American Chemical Society (ACS) Small-Scale Laboratory Assessment Activities.* Edited by Lucy Eubanks. Clemson, SC: ACS, Division of Chemical Education, Examination Institute.

Slavin, R. 1990. *Cooperative Learning: Theory, Research, and Practice.* Englewood Cliffs, NJ: Prentice Hall.

Stake, R., and Easley, J. 1978. *Case Studies in Science Education.* Urbana-Champaign: University of Illinois, Center for Instructional and Curriculum Evaluation.

Stecher, B., and Klein, S., eds. 1996. *Performance Assessment in Science—Hands-on Task and Scoring Guide.* Santa Monica, CA: RAND.

Stuart, H. 1985. Should Concept Maps Be Scored Numerically? *European Journal of Science Education* 7(1).

Tamir, P. 1972. The Practical Mode—A Distinct Mode of Performance in Biology. *Journal of Biological Education* 6.

———. 1972. The Practical Mode of Performance in Biology: A Distinct Mode. *Journal of Biological Education* 6.

———. 1974. An Inquiry Oriented Laboratory Examination. *Journal of Educational Measurement* 11.

———. 1975. Nurturing the Practical Mode in Schools. *The School Review* 83.

———. 1983. External Examinations as a Means for Teacher Education. In *Preservice and Inservice of Science Teachers*, Tamir, P., Hofstein, A., and Ben-Peretz, M., eds. Rehovot: Balaban Interscience Services.

———. 1990. Evaluation of Student Work and Its Role in Developing Policy. In *The Student Laboratory and the Science Curriculum*, Hegarty-Hazel, E., ed. London (UK): Rutledge.

Tamir, P., and Doran, R. 1992. Conclusions and Discussion of Findings Related to Practical Skills Testing in Science. In *Studies in Educational Evaluation* 18.

Tamir, P., and Glassman, S. 1970. A Practical Examination for BSCS Students. *Journal of Research in Science Teaching* 7.

Tamir, P., and Nussinovitz, R. 1979. *Analysis of Student Answers to Questions in Biology Practical Laboratory Examinations.* Jerusalem: Israel Science Teaching Center, Hebrew University Jerusalem.

Tamir, P., Nussinovitz, R., and Friedler, Y. 1982. The Design and Use of Practical Tests Assessment Inventory. *Journal of Biological Education* 16.

Third International Mathematics and Science Study (TIMSS). Website: *www.csteep.bc.edi/timss* (The TIMSS International Study Center main website). See also the National Center for Education Statistics' TIMSS website: *www.nces.ed.gov/timss*.

Tobin, K., and Gallagher, J. J. 1987. What Happens in High School Science Classrooms? *Journal of Curriculum Studies* 19.

Toronto Board of Education. 1990. *Linking Evaluation with Science.* Toronto: Toronto Board of Education.

Tyler, R. 1942. A Test of Skill in Using a Microscope. *Educational Research Bulletin* 9.

U.S. Department of Education, Office of Civil Rights. 2000. The Use of Tests as Part of High-Stakes Decision-Making for Students: A Resource Guide for Educators and Policy-Makers. Available at *www.ed.gov/offices/OCR*

Wallace, C. 1969. *ERIE Science Process Test.* Syracuse: Eastern Regional Institute for Education.

Wandersee, J. 1990. Mapping and the Cartography of Cognition. *Journal of Research in Science Teaching* 27(10).

White, R. 1988. *Learning Science.* New York: Cambridge University Press.

White, R., and Gunstone, R. 1992. *Probing Understanding*. New York: The Falmer Press.

Woolnough, B. 1991. Practical Science as a Holistic Activity. In *Practical Science*, Woolnough, B., ed. Bristol, PA: Open University Press.

Wright, A. 2002. Development of Performance Tasks—An Alternative Assessment for the New York State Regents Biology Course. Doctoral diss., University at Buffalo.

Yager, R. 1995. Constructivism and the Learning of Science. In *Learning Science in the Schools: Researching Reforming Practice*, Glynn, S., and Duit, R., eds. Mahwah, NJ: Lawrence Erlbaum Associates.

Yeany, K., Larussa, A., and Hale, M. 1989. *A Comparison Of Performance Based Versus Paper-and-Pencil Measures of Science Processes and Reasoning Skills as Influenced By Gender and Reading Ability*. Paper presented at the annual meeting of the National Association of Research in Science Teaching, San Francisco.

Zawicki, J. 2002. *Assessment of Inquiry Skills in High School Optics*. Doctoral diss., University at Buffalo.

Zichitella, G. 2002. *Analysis of the Effect of Structure on Performance Assessment Tasks in High School Chemistry*. Doctoral diss., University at Buffalo.

Index